NATURAL MYSTICISM

TOWARDS A NEW REGGAE AESTHETIC

IN CARIBBEAN WRITING

KWAME DAWES

NATURAL MYSTICISM

TOWARDS A NEW REGGAE AESTHETIC

IN CARIBBEAN WRITING

PEEPAL TREE

First published in Great Britain in 1999
Peepal Tree Press
17 King's Avenue
Leeds LS6 1QS
England

ISBN 1 000715 22 8

CONTENTS

ACKNOWLEDGEMENTS

Thanks to the following for the assistance they gave me during the writing of this book: the Department of English at the University of South Carolina who supported much of my travel to do research and who gave me time and space; Robert Newman, chair of my department, who expressed an early interest and was always encouraging; my various graduate research assistants over the past three years including Valerie Goodwin, Angella Davis, Gary Leising, Ivan Young, Phillip Bramblet and Cile Traywick (may she rest in peace) for their enthusiasm, patience and hard work in supporting my research; the reggae artists who will soon take over the world; Rohan Preston, Geoffrey Philp for good conversations and wonderful insights into the meaning of a reggae aesthetic and for the long distance conversations that helped to firm up this idea. Special thanks to Colin Channer, constant companion on this journey, a remarkable encyclopaedia of reggae trivia, and an intellectual bouncing board for the ideas that have taken shape in this book. Thanks to the encouragement and support of writers such as Linton Kwesi Johnson, Mervyn Morris, Lorna Goodison, Lillian Allen, Afua Cooper, John Agard, Clive Walker, Robert Lee, Kendel Hippolyte, Kamau Brathwaite, and Jean Binta Breeze whose work, ideas and words to me encouraged this effort even more. Thanks to the unlooked for gift of Derek Walcott's celebration of reggae on the BBC. Thanks to Yvonne Brewster for assuring me that this aesthetic is a life force in theatre too. Thanks to Melanie Abrahams, my agent in the UK, whose support of my visits to the UK cannot be overvalued. Thanks to those who have gone before and written about reggae as an aesthetic – critics such as Gordon Rohlehr, Bongo Jerry, Garth White, Pamela Mordecai, and many more who have seen the light of the reggae vibe in literary practice. Thanks to Jeremy Poynting, my editor at Peepal Tree, for his patience and his capacity to re-work some of this book making it something coherent and decent, and thanks also to Hannah Bannister, the able assistant at Peepal Tree, whose constant eye over this book has been invaluable. A special thanks to my family – to Lorna, my wife, Sena, Kekeli and Akua, my children, for reminding me of what is important – family – and to the children especially for assuring me that reggae is a strange genetic aberration that will continue to go through from generation to generation. Thanks to my mother and my siblings, Gwyneth, Kojo, Aba, Adjoa and Kojovi for sending solid and grounding vibes across the seas at all times. My wish is that others will take this as a decent enough beginning and take things beyond this. Thanks, finally, to all the colleges and universities in Canada, Sweden, the USA and the UK that opened their doors to me to give lectures and talks on the reggae aesthetic, and all the students in my Maymester class of 1998 who journeyed with me at 8:00 am each morning on a reggae odyssey called "Towards a Reggae Aesthetic". I will never forget that class and the affirmation it has been. Give thanks. Give thanks.

PREFACE
Natural Mysticism

In London, in November 1997, thawing in the studios of the Caribbean Service arm of the BBC, I listened to Colin Channer being interviewed about his new novel, *Waiting In Vain*[1]. I watched as the engineers in the studio began to look for the track that would take the interview out. What had been selected was, appropriately, 'Natural Mystic' by Bob Marley because Channer's second (unpublished) novel is titled *Natural Mystic* and that novel hints at the notion of Natural Mysticism as an aesthetic framework for a distinctively postcolonial generation of writing from the Caribbean. The engineers were not sure which album the track was on. Someone suggested *Exodus* and I quickly said, yes, that is the one. They began to hustle to cue the CD. There was some panic because the two engineers were not able to hear the song on the monitors even though they had cued it properly. One kept complaining that something was wrong with the console. I could tell what was happening, but I remained quiet, strangely amused by the mysticism of this moment, the slight trickery of it all, which I felt Bob Marley would have appreciated. The interview wound down, and the two engineers were decidedly beside themselves. Just when they were about to put something else on, the cut of the rhythm guitar began to insinuate itself on the ear. Then the lock-step roll of Carlton Barrett, and Bob Marley's faraway, world-weary voice carried across like a balm:

> There's a natural mystic blowing through the air,
> If you listen carefully now you will hear,
> this could be the first trumpet
> Might as well be the last
> Many more will have to suffer
> many more will have to die
> Don't ask me why....

Indeed the mystic was in the air, and the metaphor inherent in the very arrangement of the tune was once again playing its magical self out. Marley constructs the lyric around a musical arrangement that is itself a metaphor. The song begins with a barely perceptible rhythm guitar playing that quintessential reggae chop, a tightly and lightly brushed guitar strum that builds gradually. The mystic is in the distant sound that is only heard and appreciated by those who will listen carefully. In the faint intimations of the melody, in the barely audible guitar, Marley introduces a metaphorical and spiritually powerful articulation of the apocalyptic voice crying in the wilderness: the voice that needs to be heard and heeded. There is nothing declamatory in the rhetoric of the lyric, though the song as a whole is a symbolic 'trumpet', heralding the coming of the new day:

Things are not the way they used to be
One and all got to face reality
No one tries to find the answer
To all the questions they ask
No one knows it's impossible
To go living through the past.
Won't tell no lie

In this seemingly simple lyric, in which Marley brings a spiritual rhetoric of change to bear on political realities, he condenses the meaning and power of reggae and the poetic grounding of his own imagination. The lyric offers us a way of understanding the 'Natural Mysticism' that characterizes all of Marley's work, the work of other reggae artists over the years and the aesthetic which has come to shape the creative context for much of the writing that has emerged out of the Caribbean in the last two decades.

I come to this book as I come to Marley's work: with a combination of personal investment and emotional engagement, and a strong critical and academic consciousness. *Natural Mysticism* will appear to be an eclectic work that shifts in style and intent from moment to moment as I struggle to reconcile these inclinations. I make no apologies for this because I found that my efforts to 'read' reggae and to write about its aesthetic forced me to use a wide range of discursive modes. In some places the writing is driven towards personal, memoir-like narration, while elsewhere it necessarily shifts into more formal language registers as it accounts for the evolution of reggae and the literature I am examining. Yes, this is a memoir of sorts, an intimate journey into the making of my imaginative impulses. I hope this does not sound unwholesomely self-indulgent. If the book manages to celebrate the energy and intellectual power of reggae music this will be my justification.

I suggest that you read this book with a cd or record player at hand. It will all make sense once some reggae is pulsing in the background. To begin, I suggest you slip in Burning Spear's 'Slavery Days'...

INTRODUCTION

NEW SOUNDS

1

He brought the slip of black vinyl,
and let spin the light on black.
Reggae enigmatic engulfed the house,
and in his blue mist of shelter
he tapped his feet to the new sound:
the jazz subtle in the horn section,
calling up the spirit of Don Drummond,
calling up the side-riding of the old jazz folk,
calling up Africa in the dread's journey,
the confirmed journey of the man poet
travelling from first to second to third,
nondescript Trench Town streets, still home
for this pop icon, rude bwoy, skanking dread.
And this is how Thelonious Monk was usurped
from the all wooden, hand-crafted gramophone
cabinet, how the Duke got schooled by a thug,
how a newer path of earth birthing life
suggested itself in our home – this clean tight reggae,
the I-Threes melodious in their response to his call.

from *Shook Foil*.

'New Sounds', the poem that opens this chapter is a true story about my father's gift of 'Natty Dread' to us, and his conversion from being a lover of jazz to an enthusiast for Bob Marley's reggae. It is also about the connection between reggae and Caribbean writing. Sometime in the late 1950s and early 1960s, my father, Neville Dawes, stopped writing poetry. He was in his mid-thirties and had already had some success. His work was being read regularly on the BBC World Service Caribbean Voices programme and he had published a slim volume of verse called *In Sepia*. Then he abandoned poetry. He took up fiction, publishing two deeply political works that offered complex insights into the postcolonial condition from a decidedly Marxist perspective.[1] His poetry, on the other hand, was lyrical, sometimes indulgently introspective, and thoroughly modernist in its subduing of the political 'subtext' in the imagery. I cannot say for certain why he quit poetry: 'I have outgrown verse' was what he said. It may be that he felt his poetry was too derivative and he did not share Derek Walcott's conviction that imitating the Western masters was a necessary act of learning for the colonial poet. Perhaps he simply felt that his talent for verse was less than it ought to have been. I suspect that while he admired Walcott's prodigious talent, and may have been somewhat intimidated by Walcott's unquestioned effectiveness as a 'mimic man', he was also resisting the implications of trying to speak as an anti-colonial in the language of colonialism. In poetry, there is no way of evading the ideological implications of voice and at that time he probably felt that there were no appropriate models to embrace. He would, for instance, have been quite unwilling to return to the linguistic quaintness of the dialect poetry of Claude McKay. He turned to fiction, I think, because he found in it a greater opportunity to develop a nationalistic agenda without the connotations of its form – equally a colonial form – bearing down in such a directly antithetical way on his work. In truth, as I argue later in this book, there are no essential differences between poetry and fiction with regard to finding an autonomous Caribbean voice, but the apparently content-driven nature of the realist novel, and its capacity to grant a nationalistic weight to its treatment of dialogue, character, landscape and history may have made it seem a far less troubling medium for political commentary than the poem. It makes sense to me then that it was in reggae, in the lyrical genius of Bob Marley, that my father felt he had found the answer to his dilemma. Unwilling to assume the role of speaking on behalf of the oppressed, my father chose to look to the oppressed for the poetic breakthrough.

This quest for voice, an attempt to tell stories in a language and idiom that are our own, has been at the heart of the development of Caribbean writing. This quest has been closely connected to political and ideological developments in our region. Central to these developments has been our response to the experience of colonialism and its role as a shaper of the culture of our societies. This response has gone through a number of stages.

My father's quest took him to folk traditions and historical narratives derived from the Caribbean and Africa. Forty years later, I am embarked on the same journey, seeking a grounding in an aesthetic that speaks to my own history. I recognise that in order to do this well, I must explore the journeys taken by earlier generations of West Indian writers. The commonalities that exist between myself and these writers are best understood in the context of understanding the fundamental differences that we have. Reggae's arrival constitutes a pivotal and defining historical moment in the evolution of a West Indian aesthetic, an important stage that stands beside a series of other important stages.

The first stage involved the emergence of ideas, embryonic political movements and, in time, a literary culture which reacted critically to the dominance of metropolitan interests in the Caribbean. These beginnings grew out of the formation of creole societies with an increasing sense of difference from the culture of the state officials who represented the metropolitan powers in the colonies, the strengthening of systems of local government and the growth of Caribbean economic interests which were distinct from metropolitan interests. All these developments began to challenge the notion of the islands as mere colonial satellites. West Indians began to see their societies as distinct ones with national aspirations. This development began as early as the 1830s, though these desires for nationhood did not take a more formal political shape in the British West Indies until after the 1914-18 European war. The earliest generation of Caribbean writers – Claude McKay, Tom Redcam and H.G. De Lisser in Jamaica, A.H. Mendes in Trinidad and A.R.F. Webber in Guyana[2] – can be seen to have grown out of these nationalist stirrings. Their work, mostly set in the Caribbean, sought in the first place to explore its landscapes. Ideologically, much of the writing was critical of colonial dominance but did not explicitly focus on national independence. Their work began to record the sound of Caribbean voices, but within aesthetic frameworks which were still almost wholly metropolitan.

In time, this phase of nationalist stirring moved towards more open confrontation with colonialism and the formation of organisations committed to national independence. What moved it was the emergence of labour movements in the 1930s throughout the Caribbean, and the conviction among the working classes, which they were ready to demonstrate on the streets, that it was the colonial order that blocked their aspirations for the basic decencies of life. Both in literature and in other art forms there was a reflection of these developments. The sculptures of Edna Manley[3], for instance, in the 1930s and 1940s reflected a strong desire to explore the iconography of the Jamaican working class; and, in the poetry of George Campbell[4], images of Jamaican workers and peasants began to define the essence of Jamaican society. In the 1940s, Louise Bennett[5] began to write in the language of the street and to insist on the continuing significance of folk forms in Jamaican society. However, it would be fair to say that despite the efforts of such writers, artists, and cultural and political activists, the dominant cultural force remained British and the education system still privileged the colonial order and the western cultural canon. Though the notion of a national literature was beginning to emerge alongside the formation of political parties committed to national independence in the late 1940s and 1950s, it was a literature which was still hesitant to speak in a Jamaican voice.

What held up this development was the failure of the educated custodians of cultural values, even those with explicit nationalist agendas, to see that the basis for national identity and a specifically Jamaican cultural sensibility was already present within the working class communities. Writers such as Redcam and De Lisser had sought validation as legitimate artists who could stand beside the great British writers *despite* living outside the centre of the western canon. What went largely ignored, except in the mainly ethnographic documenting of 'folk culture' by Jamaicans such as Walter Jekyll in his *Jamaican Song and Story* (1907)[6] and in the work of visiting anthropologists such as Martha Beckwith[7], was that within the working class milieu there were traditions of music, dance, decorative arts, dramatic forms, religious and spiritual belief systems and practices, and above all a language, not only different from, but practised in active resistance to the dominant colonial Euro-centric culture. This Jamaican culture and the cosmologies which sustained it thrived in the world outside the heavily colonised and culturally limited world of the educated elite. The evolution of a Caribbean aesthetics has entailed the recovery and emergence of these elements into the mainstream of Caribbean cultural expression.

At best, though, the writers who emerged in the nationalistic period of the 1950s and 1960s displayed a peculiarly schizophrenic attitude to literary and artistic influences. Without appropriate literary models from the Caribbean, or even from any non-western culture, these writers almost inevitably wrote in dialogue with the standard Western texts that they learnt in school. Some, though, did understand themselves to be working in a state of conflict between their national aspirations and their colonial language and literary heritage. This was what Derek Walcott characterised as being 'divided to the vein' in his poem 'A Far Cry from Africa'[8] or about which Kamau Brathwaite wrote ironically in his early poem 'The Day the First Snow Fell'[9]. Others reflected this conflict in less ironic and self-reflexive ways. There was the lingering taste for classical mythologies and biblical myths incompletely digested in the novels of Roger Mais[10]; there was the highly affected tone of the formalistic poetry of George Campbell and earlier the sonnets of Claude MacKay[11]. The ideological agenda was largely nationalistic and committed to the notion of independence, but the formal practice, the aesthetics, remained uncomfortably defined by western literary models. Much of this was determined by language. How could Caliban 'own' Prospero's language without somehow compromising himself and his quest for cultural and ideological autonomy?[12]

This problem particularly affected literature in comparison to other artistic forms. There were readily available models of the use of non-Western elements in European modernism in the fields of art, dance and music, for instance. Thus, when artists such as Edna Manley and dance innovators such as Rex Nettleford[13] began to find iconographic and aesthetic foundation stones upon which to build an art in the folk and African traditions of the Caribbean, they had the examples of Picasso, Merce Cunningham and others to build on. Apart from the Harlem Movement and jazz[14], there was no parallel tradition within Western literary practice. Thus, while they shared the same nationalist concerns, Edna Manley's work was innovative and located in a working class and largely Afrocentric iconography, but the poetry of George Campbell continued to reflect the formal patterns of western literary practice. This dilemma continued to affect Jamaican and other Caribbean writers throughout the 1950s and 1960s, and it was only through the pioneering work of writers such as Wilson Harris and Kamau Brathwaite in the 1960s[15] that the attempt to establish a Caribbean literary aesthetic began to take shape and is, indeed, still taking form.

The core of my thesis, though, is that even more than through the seminal work of such writers, it was the emergence of reggae in the late 1960s that provided Jamaica (and the Caribbean region) with an artistic form that has a distinctively postcolonial aesthetic. I argue that reggae has provided writers and other artists with an aesthetic model whose impact can already be seen in more recent Caribbean writing. However, reggae, as a Jamaican form, is clearly only one element in the culture of the region as a whole. My book is intended to be seen as part of the construction of an overarching Caribbean aesthetic which includes, for example, the aesthetics which have emerged from calypso and from Indo-Caribbean artistic forms.

The impact of reggae on imaginative writing has been both a necessary and an increasingly fruitful one, particularly since there was, I argue, a period of uncertainty in Caribbean literature after the achievement of independence in the 1960s. Without the anti-colonial animus that gave voice and purpose to much of the earlier nationalist writing, it becomes increasingly difficult to find any major thematic concerns shaping and driving the work of Caribbean writers in the late 1960s and early 1970s.

My own sense of this uncertainty came almost simultaneously with my discovery, as a child and a youth, both of the notion of a West Indian discourse and the existence of Caribbean literary texts. It was a shaping moment for me. On the one hand, I found the Caribbean literature written prior to the late 1960s and 1970s to be genuinely helpful in granting me a sense of belonging and possibility; on the other hand, I experienced a strange disquiet about the relevance and force of this work in the context of the Jamaican society that was flowering around me. What I had no doubts about, though, was the way the reggae music I listened and danced to was defining, shaping and giving expression to this world. It is, then, my aim in this work to argue that any proper understanding of the writing that has emerged in the Caribbean, and particularly in Jamaica, after the 1970s has been directly affected by the emergence of reggae. Unlike the folk forms of an earlier period, this was not an art form to be discovered or recovered from invisibility by the ethnographer from a different class. In the case of reggae, a working class art asserted itself in its own terms and through a language and discourse that would in time shape the way the entire society defined itself and its artistic sensibility.

This is not a history, sociology or discographical guide to reggae music. These aspects of the subject have been ably dealt with by writers such as Sebastian Clarke, Howard MacGowan and Pamela O'Gorman and in Barrow's and Dalton's recent and excellent *Rough Guide to Reggae*.[16] What I am interested in demonstrating is that reggae has a distinctive aesthetic which has a relevance to other art forms. While reggae grew out of an anti-colonial milieu whose cultural and racial dimensions related it to the former colonial power, what distinguishes it is its thoroughly postcolonial Jamaicanness and its unwillingness to be defined by anything other than its own discourse. What gives reggae its fascinating quality for the Caribbean writer is that because of its self-containedness it defies terms such as 'derivative'. It is not that reggae does not represent a hybridisation of other kinds of music, but the resultant entity has shown itself to have a coherent character capable of absorbing other influences without losing that coherence. This is, for me, the definition of a truly national culture. It is in this sense that reggae has been a most significant departure, a clear development in the quest for a Caribbean aesthetic. It is a quality that can be discerned in the work of Caribbean writers over the past twenty years and, as a construct, it provides a complex and cohesive framework for reading what is new and distinctive in that work, and for a creative re-reading of the work of the past.

Fundamentally, I am arguing that any literary analysis that claims to be exploring the postcolonial development of creative writing in the Caribbean that does not recognise the centrality of Bob Marley, Lee 'Scratch' Perry, Don Drummond, Burning Spear and of Rastafarianism has failed to truly grasp the aesthetic developments that have taken place. In the course of this analysis, I hope this book demonstrates my conviction that the work of reggae artists of the 1970s and 1980s represents some of the most innovative and deeply complex work that has emerged in the region. This is not a 'hip' approach to literary analysis, but attempts to be a serious discussion of aesthetics that is best understood in relation to similar efforts by African American critics who have discussed the aesthetics of blues, gospel and jazz as defining impulses in the shaping of a distinctive African American aesthetic.

The book begins with an extended discussion of my own encounter with reggae music – a journey that reflects my quest for an aesthetic grounding for my own writing – and seeks to understand the visceral impact that reggae has had on my sensibility. I then move to an exploration of the relationship between West Indian writing and reggae music. This discussion outlines some of the important parameters of the historical development of Caribbean writing within the context of anti and postcolonialism. In the chapter that follows, I identify the salient characteristics of the reggae aesthetic and the development of my own understanding of its inner dynamic. Then come two chapters which look in greater depth at two aspects of the aesthetic which seem to me to have particular relevance to my own development as a writer and to the work of other writers. The first of these chapters examines the nature of the reggae lyric, the second looks at the erotic dimension in reggae and what it offers as a literary model. This part of the book culminates with a discussion of the relevance of applying an aesthetic derived from one artistic form to others and looks briefly at the impact of reggae on Jamaican writing in the 1970s. In particular I discuss the phenomenon of dub poetry and argue that it represents only a very partial demonstration of the potential for a literature informed by the reggae aesthetic. In the last part of the book, four chapters seek to apply elements of this aesthetic to the reading of the work of several writers, including myself. These chapters trace patterns of meaning that emerge in the work of four important reggae artists: Don Drummond, Burning Spear (Winston Rodney), Bob Marley and Lee 'Scratch' Perry. These four artists I see as essential reggae archetypes. Drummond is a forerunner, pioneer of the Jamaican 'voice' in music and as a model of the complex relationship between the artist and a community not yet ready to hear that voice. Burning Spear is the archetype of the prophetic voice and reggae's concern with history and with Africanness. Bob Marley is the archetypal trickster leader, a Davidian singer of psalms which articulate the indissoluble connections between the *natural* world in all its contemporary political manifestations and the *mystical*. In particular, Marley's work as a lyricist who spoke both in a public, prophetic voice and in a private, self-reflexive individual voice is discussed in relation to the poetry of Dennis Scott, Anthony McNeill and Lorna Goodison. Finally, Lee 'Scratch' Perry is dub organiser, visionary, and trickster-'madman'. I argue that his work – postcolonial and postmodern – offers a potent encouragement to the Caribbean writer towards formal experimentation within wholly accessible forms. I conclude the book by indicating ways in which the issues it raises need to be taken up in expanded and deepened discussion.

The greatest challenge that faces those interested in making sense of the evolution of Caribbean literature is how they tackle its relationship to the seemingly non-literary world of the societies from whence it emerges. Without this kind of examination, analysis is anaemic and frequently misguided. This book attempts to identify what is significant about some of the more recent work from the region, to serve as a kind of manifesto for what has not yet been written, but, ultimately, though, I hope to share something of what reggae has meant for me and what I am certain it will continue to mean.

CHAPTER ONE

BEAUTIFUL REGGAE:
AN EXISTENTIAL APPROACH

SOME TENTATIVE DEFINITIONS I

'Lickle more drums...'

                              Bob Marley

First the snare crack,
a tight-head snare crack like steel,
rattle, then cut, snap,
crack sharp and ring at the tail;
calling in a mellow mood,
with the bass, a looping lanky
dread, sloping like a lean-to,
defying gravity and still limping
to a natural half-beat riddim,
on this rain-slick avenue.

Sounds come in waves
like giddy party types
bringing their own style and fashion,
their own stout and rum,
their own Irish Moss
to this ram jam session.
Everything get like water now
the way steady hands
curve round a sweat-smooth waistline,
guiding the rub, the dub, so ready.
This sound is Rock Steady
syrup slow melancholy,
the way the guitar tickling
a bedrock drum and bass,
shimmering light over miry clay.

from *Shook Foil*

When I hear reggae, my body shifts its rhythms to its syncopations. Reggae is elemental to who I am. Whenever I learn a new song on the guitar, a hymn, a botched jazz number, a church chorus, a rock song, I inevitably recast it in a reggae frame to test it, to delve into its inner dimensions. I can 'reggaefy' anything. These days I have the further pleasure of witnessing my children's indoctrination to the reggae way. Sena, our first child, gestated in her mother to the accompanying, often overloud sounds of Ujamaa[1], a reggae band I played with for several years in Canada. Despite all the nay-saying of my friends, it was undeniable that playing my music on tape was one of the certain ways of making Sena smile before she was a week old. Kekeli, the second, understands the *one-drop* and is becoming a remarkable drummer of reggae rhythms. Akua, who is barely two, mimics with enthusiasm her mother's bad-girl skanks. My crowning moment came when I watched all three children discover the mystery of reggae's off-beat skank! If you ask them anything about Bob Marley, Ziggy Marley, Peter Tosh, Lucky Dube or UB40, they will have amusingly informed (if not quite accurate) things to say. They like reggae and I am elated by this. It may be simply because I am desperate that these children do not become completely assimilated into the homogenizing American culture. It may be because I want them to have some sense of the world that shaped me and Lorna, their mother. I can tell stories of Ghana and Lorna can tell tales about England and ply them with Paddington Bear books, but we both understand that Jamaica is locked into our language, our cooking, our values and our music. Maybe that is all our efforts are about: an overenthusiastic nationalism railing against the rootlessness of migration, but that is more than enough reason to introduce them to the university of youthful meaning, as Lillian Allen,[2] reggae dub poet from Toronto, would say when talking about Bob Marley.

I must begin this book with these confessions for it would be impossible to conceive of it without this obsession, this visceral engagement with reggae. It represents a place of memory and meaning that is sometimes hard to explain. There are reggae songs that evoke places in Jamaica, and no matter how hard I try, I am unable to account for these powerful mental associations. I cannot hear Augustus Pablo's melodica entwined around a very dread reggae bass-line[3] without finding myself in the crowded and steamy tuck shop at my high school, Jamaica College, hustling for empty soda bottles to exchange for a few coins that would add up to my patty money. The music functions as a sound track, an elegant background of meaning that fills my memory and imagination. This makes absolute sense to my poetic sensibilities, but it is only recently that I have had the courage to try to articulate the place of reggae in my sense of aesthetics, my sense of beauty. The journey towards such an articulation takes me both along the memory-salvaging paths of autobiography and verse, and the pursuit of meaning through the construction of theory. This book represents such a fusion; one that I believe is entirely appropriate for talking about reggae, which is, if nothing else, a powerful artistic force that challenges the intellect, the spirit and the emotions of those who take it seriously.

The woman who first brought reggae to our home also brought laughter, the secretive pleasures of teenage sexual discovery, and the gentlest, kindest conspiracy of care that would remain with me forever. It is hard to listen to rock steady tunes such as 'Picture on the Wall'[4] or 'Guava Jelly'[5] without thinking of the day she was buried. I was not allowed to attend Beverly's funeral. I was too young, they said; or perhaps I was too scared. Adjoa, my sister went; she was older by just a year. She stood at the graveside when Beverly was buried. Beverly was young. She could not have been older than twenty-five when she died of stomach cancer. It was my second encounter with intimate death. The first involved Arabna, my six year old playmate in Ghana, who choked to death on fufu. Even as I tried to contend with Beverly's death, the wailing lament that had shaken the small Legon university housing compound sounded in my head. 'Arabna we woo! Arabna we woo!' her mother lamented through the night. Now it was Beverly. Our lament of those days is always recalled in reggae. We played her records and remembered her. This was her legacy – a huge collection of forty-fives that she deposited at our home, as she did most of her other portable possessions.

Beverly had found herself caught up in the government run system for housing delinquent children. My mother, a social worker, was house-mother at one of the largest girls' homes in Jamaica, Glenhope Place of Safety. By the time Beverly had outgrown Glenhope and the government, she was a regular at our home, had adopted my mother and become my big sister. It was her pornographic fiction that I stole to discover the hormone-aggravating world of sexual titillation. It was Beverly who knew the secret terror I used to feel about going to the clinic on Slipe Pen Road to get shots for the chronic infections I suffered, resulting from scratching mosquito bites with filthy fingernails. Beverly would take me on the bus, calming my nerves with stories of her acting career and the drama of her life. At the clinic, she would indulge my fear, turn away while I dropped my pants and took the shot of penicillin in my buttocks howling like an infant, gather me up and lead me out through the dust-bowl of the parking lot into the blazing, chaotic Kingston heat. We would ride the bus to Radio Jamaica (RJR), from where we walked through an avenue of old houses (that used to be middle-class in the 1950s and 1960s) until we came to a tiny, heavily canopied home. In this dark house, we ate stewed salt mackerel and boiled green bananas with an aunt of hers, while we listened to the latest instalment of the British radio soap, 'Thunder in the Straights'. She then took me home, calmly navigating the hazard of mangy dogs that leaped the too low fences of our avenue and came snapping at our heels. Beverly kicked them and sent them yelping for shelter. And every time, every single time she was asked whether I had cried, she would lie; she would casually declare me to be a brave soul who managed to do things she herself could never do. I loved her for it. She kept the secret and preserved my dignity. I regard all of this narrative as part of a memory inextricably tied to the rock steady music that would spin out of the black vinyl forty-fives that Beverly kept in a box beside the old stereo in our home. The songs of Alton Ellis, Ken Boothe, Marcia Griffiths[6] – songs I would later learn were classics of reggae music – all still transport me back to my childhood.

Reggae, then, is part of my conception both of security and grief. There are other touchstones. There is, for instance, the way some reggae songs bring back the peculiar hollow in the stomach that I used to get when I felt that my mother was not happy, that she was homesick for Ghana, that she wanted comfort for herself. Sometimes, she would sing the songs her mother used to sing to us, in the slow, stately manner of a Fanti dirge. But sometimes, she would turn to reggae. In the early 1970s she would sing 'One Life to Live'[7], one of the forty-fives Beverly had left with us. I think she sang it for the four lines: 'I only have one life to live/ and I'm gonna live it/ I only have one life to give/ and I'm gonna give it.' The melancholy of the song, the slow sadness of rock steady was perfectly suited to her pain. The memory is indelible. I accepted reggae as part of the language of emotion in my home.

On the surface, it would seem enough simply to accept this fact and ignore the question of why it should be so. But in trying to establish the way the music insinuates into my sense of memory and self-awareness, I am describing a movement towards an aesthetic. The fact that reggae has come to shape my writing and my theorizing about Caribbean writing makes it important for me to understand why I wept when I heard the strains of Marley's 'Time Will Tell'[8] at the end of a documentary of the same name that was shown on television a few years ago. I was not weeping for Marley, I was weeping in acknowledgment of the sublimation that swept me when images of the landscape, the people and Jamaica's turmoil merged with the mysticism of the lyric. It has long been my hunch that there was a book in all of this, an important book. I took this hunch with me to Canada in 1987, where it blossomed in quite remarkable ways.

I was, during the years I lived in Canada (1987-1992), completely immersed in reggae to the exclusion of other forms of music. This bigotry annoyed disc jockeys at parties when I bullishly bombarded them with demands that they play more reggae, more reggae. I now understand that time to have been a period of deep study in which I was trying to understand the music's internal dynamic and why it was so important to me. This exclusiveness lasted for several years until, much to the relief of countless disc-jockeys, I began listening to and appreciating a wider range of musical forms. The grounding in reggae, though, had been complete, and I came to other music with a certain confidence, an assurance that I truly understood at least one form of music.

I think that when I was in Canada, my obsession with reggae went beyond nationalistic inclination or nostalgia (though it was easier to describe myself as Jamaican than the actual 'I was born in Ghana, grew up in England, and then moved to Jamaica' only to have the follow-up question, 'So why did you leave Guyana?') and was a recognition that my influences as an artist, the ideas that shaped my sensibility, came from the reggae sub-culture that had surrounded me in Jamaica. I had long understood that this music affected my thoughts, my body, my emotions, and my imagination, and I was acutely aware of its political content and the relevance of its lyrics to my sense of history, my sense of race, and my identity. Now I also came to understand the music and its value and appreciate its centrality in my creative psyche. Reggae was becoming an aesthetic for me.

I have, since that time, tried to explore the beauty of reggae in various ways. The most obvious and effective manner was through the writing of poetry and fictional prose that I felt emerged from this immersion in reggae and what I began to call a 'reggae aesthetic'. In this, I was not unique. It was what Perry Henzel was drawing on in the film *The Harder They Come*, a film whose release in 1972 launched reggae internationally and was the first example of the reggae aesthetic permeating other art forms. *The Harder They Come* was a 'reggae film', not simply because of the use of reggae music as part of the soundtrack, but because it constructed a narrative line out of reggae archetypes and motifs: the bad *bwai*, the trickster hero, the culture of violence, sexuality, and political outspokenness; above all the dynamic creative energies which were emerging from the 'grassroots' of urban Jamaican society. What is more, although it had international success, Henzel's film did not attempt to use the language of the international – read British/American – audience/market. Its language was raw Jamaican yard language and demanded subtitles when it was released abroad. In this film, Perry Henzel ensured that reggae was defined by Jamaicans, by those creating that music, with their own principles of beauty and artistic value, and not by a market outside that society. Henzel's vision was fundamentally postcolonial because it was not constructed around the Manichean divide that served primarily to secure the cultural dominance of the colonial Eurocentric world *within* the Jamaican milieu. Previously, regardless of whether Caribbean books sought to demonstrate the evils of colonialism, they had remained trapped in a paradigm that ultimately gave privilege to the centrality of the colonial order, even in the postcolonial Caribbean. Henzel's film shifted the dialogue by demonstrating that a new creative force was operating in the Caribbean, a force that emerged from the working-class milieu with a coherent, dynamic vision centred on the Jamaican imagination. Jamaicans who watched the film were struck by the power of seeing their own day-to-day lives expressed in the cinematic construction of image, song and narrative. Here was a connection between our existence and art. Previously we had come to accept that such works of visual imagination came only from societies outside our own. Now, in the Carib Cinema, we could appreciate the nuances of our language, image, metaphor and icon far more immediately than we had ever before witnessed them in art. Henzel had achieved what Ngugi wa Thiong'o set out to do in 1986 when he decided to write all his novels and as much criticism as possible in Gikuyu, his native language, forcing the rest of the world to translate his work and contend with the internal structures, ideologies and cosmologies of his language.[9] To American and British audiences, Henzel's film was a 'foreign' film, in a 'foreign' language. For this to emerge out of a Jamaican society which was still so touristically defined, and whose elites took pride in its strong Englishness (at least in terms of language) was little short of a miracle. The film forced non-Jamaican audiences to recognise that they did not know Jamaica, that there was a tremendous complexity to its society that was not immediately accessible and which demanded closer scrutiny.

Henzel's film had shifted the balance of power in the areas of aesthetics and socio-political understanding: the metropolitan centres had to work to grasp its meaning, something that significant numbers of Americans and Britons were evidently prepared to do. Sadly, *The Harder They Come* has been a rare moment in Jamaican film-making because no other Jamaican film has matched its artistry, meaning, pathos and sheer cinematic grace.

I was about twelve when *The Harder they Come* was first released in Jamaica. As an 'eighteen and over' rated film it was clear that I would not be able to enter the theatre to see it. My sixteen-year old brother, though, because he had sprouted facial hairs very early in his life, was notorious for getting into adult films. He saw *The Harder They Come*, and as he did with *Blackula*, *Cleopatra Jones*, *Bonnie and Clyde*, *The Godfather I and II*, *Fanny Hill*, *Emanuelle*, *Superfly* and *Shaft*, he related the entire film to me, frame by frame, moment by moment. He was excited by this film that had everything: violence, sex, and great reggae music. But what was most exciting to him was that it was in a language that we all spoke, and for once my brother did not have to assume an American accent to relate the great scenes in the film; it was all done in patois. He kept explaining to me that they were using bad words in the film. I imagined 'fucks' and 'shits', but he explained that they included our very own 'bloodclaat' and 'rassclaat'. This was momentous! We both understood this immediately without being able to articulate its significance. I did not see *The Harder They Come* for myself until I was a student in Canada more than fifteen years later – and I almost did not have to. When I did see it, I had to take my hat off to my brother's demonstration of the power of the oral tradition. I knew the film entirely, I actually knew entire lines of dialogue, and nothing surprised, nothing except the landscape – the very Jamaican landscape that filled me with nostalgia and a powerful sense of connectedness.

The reggae was not simply a backdrop to that film, it was integral to the landscape and the film's inner structure and defined its distinctiveness, as coming from a completely different aesthetic source. I vowed at that time to try to capture the beauty of that cinematic moment in my own work. Henzel offered me a sense of possibility when I began to see that what lay behind his film was an aesthetic model that belonged to Jamaica.

For me, a *vershan* break, a shift to solely drum and bass, is a thing of beauty – it moves me. In the same way, the vacuum left behind by the withdrawal of the drum and bass, leaving the high-ended dance of guitar and keyboard, represents a moment of strange anticipation that affects my whole body. And when the drum and bass enter into that space that has been throbbing with possibility, I am forced to move, to turn, to react. I call this sheer *beauty*. I call the lyrical grace of Marley, his brilliance as a poet and a visionary, a thing of *beauty*. I find the wit, the cussing, the labrish, the slackness, the brilliant turn of phrase, the jazz and improvisation of language in reggae lyrics ranging from Shabba Ranks to Yellowman, to Sister Patra, to Michigan and Smiley, to Ninja Man[10], to be things of *beauty* – of creative genius; and I find the way in which this music captures the cadence of the Jamaican landscape, from the rural lilt of the music of Toots and Maytals, Culture and Stanley and the Turbines[11]; to the urban aggression of Marley, Black Uhuru, and Sly and Robbie[12] to be instances of poetic sublimation that give dimension to the landscape of a country, the pulse of a people. For me these are things of *beauty*, such that my quest to understand how these work, how I have come to be influenced by them in my own writing, and how other writers have been influenced by this *beauty*, amounts to a study in aesthetics.

What I am saying is that contained in reggae music are principles of beauty that can help to define the arts that emerge from the world that has shaped reggae. I am also arguing that the internal musical structures of reggae, the motivations behind reggae composition, and the ethos of reggae production (which are part of and are shaped by the history, culture, and socio-political dynamics operating in Jamaican society) may be read as consistent principles that have come to shape our conception of what is beautiful in the postcolonial arts of Jamaica. The way to engage with this aesthetic must begin with a recognition of the nature of the beauty of the music. I come to reggae moved by its capacity to speak to the human condition in a complex and direct way. I come to reggae moved by its ability to speak to the deeper emotions that I feel. I come to reggae with the awareness that reggae music serves as an entry into my understanding of culture, sexuality and artistic expression. The examination of the aesthetics of reggae is, then, a study in the meaning of beauty in the context of an art that has shaped and moved me. What I am attempting is to uncover 'the principles of beauty' underlying reggae music. If indeed there are coherent principles of beauty underlying reggae, these principles can become the source of *beautiful* expression in other media such as dance, drama, sculpture and painting. However, such a broad study is beyond the scope of this discussion, and I have focused largely on literature, and even then, far more closely on poetry than on the novel. This allows my study to stay within manageable limits, but I hope that the principles of beauty outlined here will lead others to explore how, or indeed whether, a reggae aesthetic is at work in other genres and disciplines.

So far I have relied on a fairly emotive and instinctual definition of aesthetics as that which moves me and which I find to be beautiful from a decidedly subjective perspective. However, I believe that my project has quite honorable precedents in the history of aesthetics, which, whatever the counterclaims of those who have argued 'art for art's sake', has generally been driven by national, regional or class-cultural agendas to find a code of perception that reveals the coherence and deep structures of a particular society or section of society. From this perspective, reggae is conceived first as Jamaican. Jamaicans own reggae and they regard it as part of the culturally defining mechanisms of their society – as Jamaican as Blue Mountain coffee. However, this allegory of commodification is only one part of reggae's nationalist credentials, for even more importantly, reggae has helped to define Jamaica to itself. Reggae is the product of artists working consciously within the historical, social and cultural forces which have shaped Jamaican society. It is the aesthetic form which has brought Jamaicans to see those forces most clearly and which has best expressed their desire to variously change or celebrate aspects of their society. However, while reggae functions as a nationalizing force, it is not one that remains limited to this small island. Indeed, it is reggae's capacity to speak beyond the constraints of nationalism that should convince us of its aesthetic 'readability'.

In many ways, popular culture in North America and England has started to take reggae for granted. This is not a bad thing, for it suggests that reggae's identity has become so inscribed in the minds

of popular artists in many parts of the world that they are now able
to appropriate it whenever they feel the need for a certain emotional
resonance or ethos. In the U.S.A., the Fugees, for instance, have
embarked on an exceptionally successful career that has, with great
political astuteness, applied a reggae sensibility to a hip-hop form.[13]
Any superficial skimming of the video charts in the United States
reveals that reggae inflections and influences are significant in popular
music: the almost *de rigeur* use of dreadlocks among many artists,
for instance. My task is not to trace these influences, but to suggest
that however superficial or 'formal' they are, they point to the fact
that reggae is a scrutable cultural form that is based on a clear aesthetic
which can help to shape and define creative work by artists in other
cultures and working within other forms.

It should be evident from what I have written above that my
exploration of a reggae aesthetic is part of my own attempt to understand
myself as a Caribbean writer. I refer on occasions to something called
a Caribbean aesthetic, though with the awareness that the term is
currently too broad and ill-defined to use as an analytical term in
my study. The problem is that while the notional entity of a Caribbean
aesthetic must by definition embrace the whole range of aesthetic
instincts that operate in the region, we have scarcely begun to examine
the several aesthetic instincts that comprise it, let alone their
relationship to each other. We have to deal with our very real sense
that while there is indeed a regional culture shaped by the common
beginnings of many of our peoples in Africa and by our common
experiences of plantation slavery and colonialism, there is also a
great diversity and distinctiveness from island to island, not least
the presence in the Southern Caribbean of almost two million people
of Indian origin. We have to deal with the fact that there is a great
deal of pressure on those of us who write about this region to speak
in terms which are regionally defined. There is an assumption that
the range of work that would be studied in, for instance, an examination
of Jamaican literature would be necessarily too narrow and parochial
to interest a larger Caribbean reading public, still less the postcolonial
critical industry. This assumption, is, of course, fallacious, for what
reggae reveals is that it is possible for a particular genre of music,
emerging from a small locale, to have an international impact that
is powerful and worthy of study. We should note, too, that American
criticism has no problem with sub-national regionalism in literary
studies. Southern Literature, African American Literature, Western
Literature, and so on, are all elements that feed the larger body of

American literature. The latter is, in truth, a constructed concept that seeks common ground among the various strands of the whole. This principle can apply equally well to Caribbean literature, and it is this conception of diversities giving shape to a larger aesthetic that interests me. I believe that such an approach will generate aesthetic principles that will in fact be far more relevant to understanding creative developments in Caribbean literature than a more generalized approach would afford. Specifically, I think that focusing primarily on the reggae aesthetic in its Jamaican context, and related to the work of Jamaican writers, is a solid basis for contributing to the construction of an overarching Caribbean aesthetic. This is a task which will have to take note of Gordon Rohlehr's work on calypso and literature[14], Kamau Brathwaite's application of the cultural pluralist thesis to imaginative literature in *Contradictory Omens*[15], the beginnings of work on an Indo-Caribbean cultural aesthetic by such critics as Sasenarine Persaud and Jeremy Poynting[16], the work of Denis Williams on the mestiço consciousness[17] and Wilson Harris's on cross-cultural understanding beyond ethnicities and history[18].

It will be apparent that I am at once proposing and describing an aesthetic, but it is certainly not my intention to prescribe the construction of an academy of reggae writing. An exclusive camp of reggae adherents would directly oppose the spirit of reggae. Reggae is not afraid to borrow from other forms, it is not afraid to change and be changed, it is not reluctant to examine itself and try to stretch the limits of its aesthetic. The reason for such flexibility is fairly uncomplicated: reggae is a form which is rooted in the market-led tyranny of popular culture: the creative dynamic which arises from the tension between tradition (or at least the reproduction of commercially successful forms) and the constant quest for new styles, new ways of saying things, new relevancies. As a principle, this cannot be a bad model for literature. The contemporary artist who sees her/himself inscribed in a reggae ethos is compelled to experiment, question, and stretch the range of the aesthetic. In both constructing a manifesto and describing a reality, there should be a tension that will ensure that nothing can be treated as absolute, final and solid. If closure is what occurs after these discussions, then I will have failed, for if nothing else, the reggae aesthetic must be as fluid as reggae itself. Like reggae, the aesthetic should, first and foremost, be characterised by a capacity to reinvent itself again and again. In many ways, this is a Caribbean construct that could also be said to characterise what some would call a calypso aesthetic. I am sure, indeed, that reggae and calypso share a number of qualities that speak to the literatures that have been influenced by these forms. But reggae and calypso are also quite distinct, and my task is to demonstrate that the fluidity of reggae creativity is part of what makes the aesthetic that I am trying to describe so fascinating, complex and accessible.

My attempt to develop a theory of literary practice that draws from artistic influences that extend beyond standard literary sources is not unique. It puts me in the company of such writers as Nicholas Guillen, Albert Murray, W.B. Yeats, Walt Whitman, Langston Hughes, Kalamu ya Salaam, Kamau Brathwaite, Derek Walcott[19] and many others who have sought an aesthetic framework which links their work to wider social and cultural impulses in their societies, or even outside them. I place my work among the writing of such giants not because I think its accomplishments even begin to approach theirs, but to acknowledge a shared anxiety about identity and aesthetics that consumes many writers who are working in the shadow of a larger colonising culture. Nicholas Guillen heard Langston Hughes expound the connections between jazz and blues and the African American writing of the heady days of the Harlem Renaissance, and concluded that there was a similar sense in which the rhythms and ethos of Afro-Cuban music related to the patterns of the writing which were emerging in Cuban society. He went on to formulate a theory of Afro-Cuban writing built around the patterns and aesthetics of the 'son', a folk and oral tradition that Guillen described as the only element in Cuban culture that was still 'ours'.

Like Langston Hughes and Guillen in their respective societies, I am trying to find an aesthetic that both corresponds with my personal instincts and also relates to my sense of the social space I occupy as a writer. Why do I write as I do? What history, what discourse, what experiences have shaped my own sense of poetic and narrative construction? What cosmology has given rise to my cosmology? And what is it that connects me with other artists whose work I sense shares an ideological and formal affinity to my own? I refer in particular to what I regard as the emergence of a distinctive voice in Caribbean writing that is confident in its cultural roots in the region. I am confident that the reggae aesthetic which I am attempting to construct will provide a critical framework which will enhance our understanding of what has been most inventive and original in recent Caribbean writing. This is not an original thesis. Pam Mordecai, for instance, in her introduction to a 1985 anthology of Jamaican poetry, *From*

Our Yard: Jamaican Poetry Since Independence[20], not only notes that many Jamaican writers have been influenced by reggae and Rastafarianism, but argues that this marks a significant development in Jamaican writing. She writes:

> If nothing else does, 'dub' lays to rest the notion that Jamaican poetry is still 'copying' the forms and devices of any other literature (xxiii).

My reservations about the extent to which 'dub' poetry truly explores the full range of literary possibilities which can be drawn from the reggae aesthetic are discussed later in the book, but Mordecai's anthology certainly shows that there was a new voice in Jamaican poetry which was decidedly *not* imitative of the poetry of the metropoles. I believe that some, though not all, of this was defined enough to embrace and transform the reggae influence without losing its distinctiveness as poetry.

For me, the capacity of reggae music to suggest that it contains within it a clear aesthetic is epitomised in such moments as Burning Spear's rendering of a Grateful Dead tune (discussed in greater detail later) or Peter Tosh's 'When the Well Runs Dry',[21] where he transforms a rhythm and blues styling through changes of tempo into what sounds as if it has always been a reggae song, or in the countless reggae covers/transformations of folk songs, mentos, jazz numbers, blues, classical music, western religious music, rock and roll, country and western, rhythm and blues, Indian traditional songs, latino folk melodies, and any number of other forms, including even opera. Reggae artists have never felt intimidated by other musical forms, and have, with varied degrees of success, but consistent audacity, covered songs from all over the world – sometimes with cavalier disregard for questions of copyright! For the writer working within the reggae aesthetic the history of covering 'foreign' songs is a prototype for a dynamic and compelling literature. Purists may complain that this of itself does not appear to be a particularly essentialist concept of an aesthetic – in the national sense at least. My argument is that it is reggae's hybrid but wholly coherent nature – the essentialist bedrock of the reggae off-beat and the bass line (among other reggae 'characteristics') working with or against the inclination to embrace and transform a range of other ideas and styles – that constitutes its fundamental quality and the dynamic core of the reggae aesthetic.

CHAPTER TWO

READING, WRITING AND REGGAE:

FROM ANTI-COLONIALISM

TO POST-COLONIALISM

SOME TENTATIVE DEFINITIONS III

'inna rub-a-dub style...'

In this sound garden,
this constant ground swell
of music relentless as a pulse;
like an engine freshly fired;
or the sweating congo man,
thighs hugging the sides
of a smooth cylinder of sound,
beating, beating a pattern;
waiting on, waiting on,
waiting on the spirit to come,
so that with every repeat,
there is magic found,
a new way of seeing things;
in the monotony, a new way
of understanding sound.

This is the promise reggae
thrives on, the promise
that suddenly so, without rhyme,
without reason, the body
a go merge with the pulse
of a circular bass-line, booming
and the rest will be the magic
of doing impossible things,
never the same again.

Without the blank wall
of sound, there can be no
blue of a harmonica coming
and going like uncertain breath;
no purple guitar song, slipping
like a hypodermic under the skin;
no Hammond drone and then trill
to stir up bumps on the skin.
This way, there is always something
to return to after the hanging
silence of a stripped-down version,
counting out the unspoken pulse,
then wheel and come again.

There is a kind of tune
we must promise our children,
a shape that the quadrant measures,
no North
to turn them
away from the dissonant cities,
the salt songs,
the hunger journeys.

It is time to plant
feet in our earth. The heart's metronome
insists on this arc of islands
as home
          Dennis Scott, 'Homecoming'[1]

When Burning Spear asks 'Do you remember the days of slavery'[2] he is both calling on us to remember and lamenting our condition as people who have forgotten. In my classes on African American literature at the University of South Carolina where I teach, I tend to have a group made up almost evenly of black and white students. I often begin with a lesson of memory that focuses on the phrase 'African American', a phrase that is at once an affirmation of political and cultural affinity with the African past and a tragic (perhaps unintentional) expression of the amnesia wrought by slavery and colonisation. The African American must reduce Africa to a mythological space, a geographic entity void of any real memory, any true remembered sense of home. While white students speak confidently of their Irish, Polish, English, Dutch or German pasts, and while many of them are able to name villages and hamlets associated with their family names, the African American is almost always left stranded on the coast of the Atlantic, helplessly looking across the ocean with no access to a past beyond this New World landscape. The tragedy of this process of forgetting is central to much of the literature that has emerged from Africans in the New World.

Burning Spear's song 'Slavery Days' became for me a haunting reminder of this gulf of history, the strange and disturbing disjunction between the plethora of dates in European history and the absence of such detail in my sense of history as a West Indian. It speaks to the desire in many postcolonials to find a sense of home and rootedness beyond that Atlantic coast. This has become a part of the nationalistic instinct. It also represents a troubling essentialism that is the more disturbing because it is so tempting. At its core this essentialism assumes an Africa that is culturally, politically and philosophically homogenous and at its worst posits a simplistic understanding of Africa that ironically parallels the racist reductionism that characterises so much of the pre-modern literature about Africa. There arises from this reductionism a stark divide between the mythological Africa of the New World Blacks' imagination and the actual African continent.

This disjunction was what led to Derek Walcott's crisis of aesthetics and ideology expressed in his seminal essay 'What the Twilight Says'[3], and to the use he makes of twilight as a metaphor for that middle ground of hybridity in much of his work. For Walcott, the crisis emerged in the discrepancy between the world he saw in his island of St. Lucia – the world of the streets, the world of the fishing community – and the world he was discovering in classical western texts. In his plays he sought to bring those two worlds together, and in his poetry he sought to find voice for a world that he could recognise as his own. This is the same instinct that drove Kamau Brathwaite to try to find the patterns of rhythm and meaning that would give rise to a new and distinct aesthetic – that of 'something torn/ and new'[4]. In many ways, all writers are trying to write themselves into relevance, and most readers are in the business of trying to realise themselves in the narratives created by others.

However, this generalisation should not make us lose sight of the fact that, within the context of Caribbean writing, this desire to find voice for the voiceless, to tell stories not told, to write a culture and a society, formerly marked by the absence of fictional constructions in its own language, is an elemental and defining one. The reason is uncomplicated. As I suggested at the beginning of the chapter, the West Indian individual has very little access to an 'original' self, a kind of 'essential' self located in a communal history that has the stability of age and repetition.

There is a startling amnesia that haunts the descendants of slaves – a rupture of roots that makes the quest for a voice so much more compelling. The absence of a place within which to locate a history, the almost blank slate of memory, is a challenge to Africans (and Indo-Caribbeans) in the Americas to construct ways of coping. These can be either destructive or creative. Much of what is called New World culture or the black culture shaped in the New World can be seen as an edifice built upon the absence of ruins, the absence of memory – or, its remnants, its fickle and sometimes unreliable remnants.[5] That, of course, is the tragic account of the condition. The more hopeful rendering celebrates the creative retrieval and retention of memory, the subterranean and dogged salvaging of Africa in the folk culture, in the traditions of survival. The curse of amnesia when understood as the result of a calculated effort at erasure, of making Africa – and consequently Africans caught in the cauldron of New World society – invisible, is thwarted by the shared sense of suffering and the collective experience of homelessness and namelessness which demands the realisation of a strong Africanness in our collective experience. Ironically, then, white society's efforts to erase or denigrate Africa became a way of foregrounding Africa, of forcing the African exile to look to this Africa as home. What remains, then, is less an absence of memory, than an incomplete memory, a tainted memory that ultimately creates a sense of difference, of otherness which, in many instances becomes a sustaining force. Much of black literature in the New World in the last fifty years has been about salvaging memory and negotiating the complexities of home. Our memory has been sustained in the traditions of drumming and music; in folk-religious beliefs, the rituals of pouring libation, of conjuring up the ancestors, of engaging in a cosmology that has no affinity to Western belief-systems; the proverbs and oral traditions of the people. All these become the links to African memory. But the link is tenuous, for it often lacks those tangibles of history privileged in Western cultures: written texts, ruins, the physical evidence of a past.

In South Carolina where I now live, archeological efforts to recover tangible evidence of the black past have been frustrated by the literal absence of ruins of slave society. Slave quarters were almost always temporary shelters that vanished into the dust with time, while the mansions of slave owners remained intact, visible reminders of their presence. Ironically, the permanent artifacts of the enslaved which remain are things that Blacks built for the consumption of Whites – the exquisite wrought iron gates of Charleston, the furniture in the great houses in Columbia, South Carolina, and the paraphernalia of enslavement (the chains, the shackles, the leg-irons and the tools of torture). In Beaufort, South Carolina, the Penn Center Museum is a humble series of rooms filled with the details of domesticity – fishing nets, eating utensils, clothes irons, worn-out shoes – all placed on display as a dogged and necessary reminder that these people, these Africans, did live in that time, did exist and were not simply apparitions, the constructions of memory.

Our historians and archaeologists will continue the search for the fragments of our past, but it is our writers, our novelists, poets and dramatists, who through the power of their imaginations can create an art which defies the tyranny of amnesia. This is one of the things I look for in our writing, and which as a writer I have sought to do. For whatever the impression I might have given in the first chapter, I am a writer and not a reggae musician manqué, though as I indicate in Chapter Four, my experiences as a reggae musician shaped my knowledge of the form and gave me the confidence to know I was dealing with a distinctive aesthetic. I have written all my life, and seriously in my own voice since the early 1980s. I am committed to writing; it is what I am driven to do, and I start from the position that there are things that writing can do which reggae cannot, just as there are things that reggae does that writing can only imitate in the palest ways. I start too with the acknowledgment that just as being a listener, player and dancer to reggae music has shaped my life and my way of seeing the world, so too have my experiences as a reader of Caribbean writing.

I can look back and see that for the past seventy years, West Indians have been publishing poems, novels, and plays about the West Indies, creating an impressive body of work. The fact that my father, Neville Dawes, was a novelist and poet exploring his Caribbean world is immensely important to me. As I describe below, it was the work of an earlier generation of Caribbean writers who helped me acquire a sense of self, a recognition of the world I lived in.

Yet I reached a point in my writing where I knew that it was reggae which provided me with an ethos and aesthetic framework unavailable in the writing of that earlier generation. Colin Channer, in his unpublished novel, *Natural Mystic*, has his protagonist Colin Robinson as a child growing up in the 1970s, put this view very forcefully. While his argument is perhaps more one-sided than I would hold to, it is nevertheless a perception I understand:

If public impact is the standard for measuring a novelist's importance, there were no important novelists in Jamaica when I was growing up –

no Baldwin, no Gordimer, no Mahfouz. They couldn't make a living at it. So for practical reasons, Jamaican novelists have historically lived abroad.

In any event, I really didn't dig their work. It was largely a generational issue – most of them were middle-aged, and unlike the musicians, none of them was hip. Their writing style to me, was artless, and their focus consistently trailed the zeitgeist which was hurtling along at a frantic pace – Manley was Joshua with the rod of correction, Marley was touring Babylon by bus, dreadlocks were sprouting like wild bloom, and the country was hemorrhaging from an undeclared civil war. But you wouldn't know that from reading the fiction.

So it came to be then, that artistically speaking, reggae, and not writing defines that period to me. I still harbor a deep resentment for Jamaican literature because of this. It failed me when I needed it most, when I needed to understand why girls made me weak, when I needed to understand Rasta, when I needed to understand why men firebombed the old ladies home in Kingston and singed our grandmother's wrinkles to a pork-rind crisp.[6]

We need to remember that this lament relates to a time when high schools taught West Indian History and West Indian novels were on the examination lists, when the University of the West Indies was offering courses in West Indian Literature. Channer's Colin Robinson had Roger Mais, Vic Reid, Neville Dawes, John Hearne, Sylvia Wynter and Orlando Patterson to read[7]. But it was also a time of a new cultural ferment, of socio-political turmoil that represented a celebration of a national character, a national culture, a national sensibility. There was the construction of an evolving Nation language; the growth of a certain international sensibility – a relationship with Africa and things African, and a new place in the world order. While the work of the writers listed above contributed invaluably to the creation of our national literature and our sense of ourselves, at this particular point in our history, it was what this writing did not do which seemed most salient. It was, in the main, writing about the past. What Channer's Colin Robinson was looking for was writing which dealt with our turbulent present in a manner which spoke of that turbulence. The fact was, though, that it was reggae which touched on all these themes and tried to answer the questions that Channer's character had about them. As one reads the passage above, a wash of songs emerges: Marley singing: 'Baby, you so nice,/I'd like to do the same thing twice'[8], or Culture chanting: 'I and I want to see Jah Rastafari/ To look upon Jah pretty-pretty face'[9], or Max Romeo singing: 'War inna Babylon!/ Tribal war inna Babylon!/ It sipple out dere…'[10] Channer's character, like Channer himself, grew up at the height of reggae's ascension into an international force, when Rastafarianism was altering the way society saw itself. Robinson (and, presumably, Channer) saw none of these things reflected in the literature he came across. Reggae made it all too clear that the literature of the past, even the immediate past, did not speak in an aesthetic that derived from within our society, and though this view perhaps reflects more what was being taught, the way it was taught and the limited distribution of the new writing of the 1970s, than what was actually being written, the assertion that the writers lagged behind reggae musicians in expressing this movement, this shift in the culture, is to a large extent true.

What I am asserting, then, was that there was a paradigm shift which occurred throughout the Caribbean in the late 1960s and early 1970s. Politically it was expressed in, for example, the New Jewel Movement in Grenada, the 1970 Black Power uprising in Trinidad, and the Rodney affair in Jamaica when youthful, radical, African-centred movements turned on an older generation of nationalist politicians who had come to be seen as bulwarks of neo-colonialism. It was a paradigm shift from anti- to postcolonialism whose impact, over the years, one can see much more clearly in the cultural sphere than in the political or the socio-economic. Reggae gave expression to this paradigm shift in a way that the imaginative literature of the same period failed to do, and much of the critical discussion of Jamaican writing both fails to recognise that such a qualitative break took place and, where it recognises the emergence of writers with something different to say, fails to see just how important reggae has been in influencing that difference.

For example, in her introduction to Dennis Scott's *Uncle Time*[11] Edna Manley notes the differences between the contexts of the earlier days of Jamaican writing in the 1940s and 1950s and of the early 1970s, when Scott's work first appeared. The earlier period, she felt, was characterised by a spirit of nationalism and anti-colonial activism, with writers regarding their work as being directly related to the political upheavals of the time. She describes these as heady days of discovery and self-awareness, but also days in which the prime movers became aware of how little they knew of their society. What she does not say, but what a reading of the Jamaican writing of that period reveals, is that there is a sharp discrepancy between its revolutionary rhetoric and nationalist commitments and its aesthetic conservatism, not to say subordination to colonial literary models. Edna Manley points to the period of Scott's emergence as a time of 'greater freedom', seeing in his work a willingness to be self-reflexive, to engage in dialogue with himself. There is an implication here that writers such as Scott have been able to build on the earlier period of literary nationalism.

Barbara Lalla is saying something similar when she argues that because the rhetoric of anti-colonialism has become such an accepted part of the contemporary Caribbean landscape, writers have been forced to treat the concept in more complex ways if it was not to become stale.[12] History can no longer be seen in the simple Manichean terms of coloniser and colonised, but within the more complex vision expressed in Kamau Brathwaite's description of Caribbean culture as something 'torn and new' or in Trinidadian novelist Lawrence Scott's characterisation of history as a kind of untrustworthy muse.[13] Similarly, it is possible to see contemporary writers dealing with the theme of identity in more complex ways than in the past. The contemporary Caribbean writer no longer asks with anguish, 'What is a West Indian identity?', but can simply assume it. There is then a generation of writers confident in who they are, drawing on influences outside the Caribbean literary canon, operating without anxiety that they will be subsumed by the force of other cultures. The reason for this confidence is not so much changes in the political and economic context (which might, indeed, instill the reverse), nor, I believe, the pioneering work of the earlier literary nationalists, but the emergence of reggae in the later 1960s and 1970s. This is why it is possible to see in the work of our writers based outside the Caribbean, whatever the American, Canadian or British concerns embedded in their work, voices which are still very clearly Caribbean. This is not, as in the past, to do with a continuing involvement in an exiled Caribbean *political* identity, but in their relationship to the emergence of reggae as a self-created, autonomous Caribbean cultural aesthetic, an aesthetic which, nevertheless, has been genuinely international in its capacity to communicate.

The significance of reggae as a major influence on Jamaican and Caribbean writing, pushing contemporary Caribbean writers towards a genuinely postcolonial voice, is made clear by comparing what has happened in the Caribbean with other paradigms for the emergence of a postcolonial literature. For instance, Stephen Gray summarises the paradigm as it applies to South African writing as follows:

In the first phase, the colony offers what Richard Rive has called a 'Scenic Special': the exotic appeal of a distant place. Its landscape is presented to readers in the centers of power as *different*, a novel entertainment for the armchair traveller back 'home.' It offers a kind of verbal safari, entirely Eurocentric in its assumptions...

The second phase is more distinctly and assertively 'colonial' and emerges with such exceptional figures as Olive Schreiner... 'Phase two' literature reacts to the cultural tourism of the first phase by asserting an inescapable rootedness in the landscape and emotional horizon of the colony...

In the third phase South African writing becomes much less vulnerable to such Eurocentric misreading, since it is associated not only with a full-fledged sense of national identity, but with the emergence of a cultural nexus that supports a national literature: a publishing industry, a community of local readers and critics, and a self-referring use of language, norms, and values.[14]

That cultural nexus – a Caribbean-based publishing industry and a community of local readers and critics – has still to emerge, and it remains the case that literature written by Caribbean authors is still, in the main, consumed by an audience outside the Caribbean. In the past, one can see quite clearly a writing which was trying to achieve a balance between Caribbean concerns and the demands of the metropolitan publishing industry. It took the arrival of the local recording industry (to which there has still been no publishing equivalent) to establish the paradigm identified in 'phase three'. Now it is possible for the emerging writer to participate in the sense of home and local relevance which reggae artists have created, though still having to develop marketability abroad.

At the same time, I do not wish to underestimate the impact that the existence of a Caribbean literary tradition had on my emergence as a writer. I cannot escape the fact that my discovery of Caribbean writing significantly transformed my perception of myself and my relationship to the world around me. It introduced to me an understanding of the politics of representation. Voice and its attendant political and ideological significance became issues for me, for the discovery of a West Indian voice released me from the alienation that I felt as a black boy trying to identify with the landscape and ideologies of people living in a white world. I was able to discover on my father's shelves a world that suddenly had far more impact and meaning than the regular dosage of *The Bobbsey Twins* and the fictions of Enid Blyton that had filled my mind as a child. The pioneers of a West Indian voice were naming, making my world authentic in a format that the education system had given privilege to as the vehicle of all that was true and important in the colonial world: books.

It was a dramatic moment for me when I discovered the Sprat Morrison adventures[15] and the stories of Andrew Salkey[16]. Sprat was the plump young hero of a children's series written by a Jamaican, Jean D'Costa. In Shortwood Practising, a dusty primary school in Kingston's suburbs, I discovered in the cool dark library, with a roof that ticked constantly with falling mango leaves and twigs, something that made absolute sense to me. I say 'discovered', because the discovery was accidental (I have learnt this habit from our great 'discoverer' Christopher Columbus). I was searching for another of Enid Blyton's books (which I was devouring with ferocious intensity) when I came across the tales of Sprat Morrison, a young Jamaican boy of my age who relished crisply fried fish, called sprats, as I did; went to primary school in an area called Papine, which I knew of; and took the same buses – the jolly buses, crammed to the brim and teeming with smells and voices, that I understood to be mine. He played cricket in dust yards – bowl for bat – the chaotic game in which fifty or so boys would flood a field and wrestle, brawl and wage veritable war to get a cheap cork and tar ball which they would then pelt at the upturned desk, the 'wicket', which in turn was being guarded by a proud, foolhardy youth armed only with a piece of wood. This was the cricket we knew, and Sprat played that kind of cricket. Sprat spoke a language that I (as a child who had grown up in Ghana) was trying to learn.

The Sprat Morrison narratives became a critical part of the shaping of my relationship to literature. Sprat Morrison was fiction, but fiction that I knew and understood. Familiarity, for me, dissolved the author as creator of a fiction, a manipulator of narrative, and instead fostered in me a voracious appetite for more of the world in which I could conceive my existence. The problem with *The Famous Five*, *The Secret Seven*, *The Bobbsey Twins*, *Nancy Drew*, *The Hardy Boys* and the rest of the crew, was that these people were white. I sought to replicate their instinct for adventure and coveted their life of comfortable consistency. But the landscape was too different, and their economic circumstances differed too much from mine. They ate different food, and they spoke a different language. Above all, they were white. The realisation of their whiteness was a gradual process for me. Perhaps not all children do this when they read, but I did. I would try to live out my adventures vicariously through them. But every time I pictured myself among this group of lily-white, blond-haired children, who apparently had never heard of black people, I felt a twinge of envy, a sense of indefinable unease.

The significance of this realisation may be better understood through a brief account of my own childhood. I have five brothers and sisters, four of whom I grew up with in Ghana. Somehow, we defied the general trend of childhood fantasy by sharing, collectively, the same imaginary friends. We wrote about these friends, argued about them, and related extensive and involved narratives about each of them as we grew up. This fictional family was called The Rabbit Tails. Each child in the Rabbit Tail family had a name. I can remember only one of the names – the lovely blond-haired daughter, Susan. The Rabbit Tails were white, and we simply accepted this reality. It seemed reasonable to create an imaginary world of people through whom we could vicariously experience adventure and exotic travel. It seemed equally reasonable, practical, and understandable that they be white. In retrospect, I have concluded that our actions were inevitable in light of the literary heritage that we had. The children's fiction available to us – *Tintin*, American classic comics, *The Arabian Nights*, *The Tales of Beatrice Potter*, as well as the titles referred to above – was almost entirely about white children. Our reading of these books was complicated by the fact that the few white people that we knew seemed to have an incredible amount of freedom as children and owned an enviable quantity of toys.

We soon abandoned the Rabbit Tails with more than a smattering of embarrassment. But the inclination to write down our fantasies in piles and piles of exercise books remained with us. We thought of ourselves as writers. And we continued to struggle with the ironies of our fantasies. My sisters' imaginary romance novels, for instance, were peopled with tall, dark, handsome, and white Spanish and Italian men, in keeping with the tradition of their Mills and Boon heroes. And while I was eventually able to find a few black narratives that dealt with sexuality (which was my favourite topic for years), my sisters found no black women authors or romance writers who sought to counteract the pervasive 'whiteness' of the 'pop-novel'. Our fantasies and fictions simply reflected a relationship to literature that was all too often alienating in its content and form. It is not that we had no other cultural narratives to work with. We did. We heard Anancy stories, Brer Rabbit tales; we sang highlife and folk songs; we heard tales about Jamaica, and we recited H.D. Carberry's 'Nature', and

Evan Jones' 'Song of the Banana Man'[17] with great fervour and relish. But we had no sense of how to translate these features of our life into literature. There were few models for this.

My movement away from the white protagonists in the European world took place when I began to read more Caribbean and black literature. It also took place when I began to write erotic letters and short stories to the girls whom I sought to seduce with the dubious device of words. Forced, as I was, to position myself – somewhat overweight, black, with a bulbous nose and squinting eye, living on Carlisle Avenue, somewhere off Red Hills Road, in Kingston, Jamaica – at the centre of these narratives, and to place these girls of similar circumstance in the middle of these tales, I had to develop an appreciation for the 'poetic familiar'. To write in a manner that conveyed the sincerity of my lust, I had to construct fictions that transcended the white-oriented world of *Penthouse Forum* and Mills and Boon, and included, in a viable and attractive way, people like myself and these girls. While my motives for making this political shift were no doubt questionable, the effect was significant and, arguably, quite redemptive. This journey, I suspect, was patterned on that of the early West Indian writers, and my discovery of their work provided me with at least an awareness that such writing was possible.

I did not stop reading the adventures of these white child-heroes (for it was expected of us to do so at school), nor did I stop reading about people who lived elsewhere; but they belonged to a world that was their own, not mine. This ability to understand difference emerged because I now had access to a tradition of fiction that seemed to relate to who I was and to what I looked like.

My accidental discovery of an important text on a library shelf, while searching for something else, was repeated some years later. It is this second accident that began my more advanced encounter with West Indian literature. As a teenager, I roamed my father's shelves to find salacious passages to enhance my emerging sexual fantasies. I searched through ancient Chinese texts, Russian literature in translation, writers such as James Joyce and William Golding, trying to dig up some dirt. My efforts, instead, gave me access to a world that immediately fascinated me. And I did find dirt. But it was not quite what I was looking for, because to discover it required reading entire narratives. I found it in ancient Chinese erotic texts, complete with diagrams; I found it in James Joyce's *Ulysses*; I found it in some African literature; and I found it in copious measure in

Edgar Mittelholzer[18]. And, perhaps for the same reason that Sprat Morrison meant a great deal to me, Mittelholzer became the writer whose work I pored over with the most devotion. I read everything by him that I could find. Realising that he was a West Indian author, a man whose days in school were spent like mine, chasing a red ball to the boundary, I decided to seek out other writers with similar connections to the Caribbean.

This is how I discovered the fiction of V.S. Naipaul, George Lamming, John Hearne, Andrew Salkey, Samuel Selvon, and Neville Dawes. I was about twelve when I began to read West Indian writers. There was nobody spurring me to look at such material; instead my urge to read grew out of a deeper instinct, perhaps not dissimilar to that which was moving many West Indians to write. So, when the Institute of Jamaica published biographies of Herb McKenley (a living Olympic legend) and George Headley (the remarkable cricketer whom we used to visit in Havendale on Sundays to listen to him laugh about the old days), I devoured the books with profound delight.[19]

Later, when I discovered V.S. Naipaul's *Miguel Street*[20] I knew what I cared most about as a reader; I knew what I wanted to read and what I needed to read. I found this outside the classroom, without the prodding of grades and teachers. Naipaul's *Miguel Street* made me laugh and laugh and laugh. And my path of discovery had no end. There were, for example, Victor Reid's Maroon narratives[21], which vividly brought back to me my childhood visit to Accompong Town, where I watched with fear and trembling the explosion of sprayed libation, the sacrifice of a chicken, and heard the blast of an ancient musket and the drumming (primal and yet so rooting) that reminded me of Ghana. As a child, these writers succeeded in grounding me in my own sense of identity and personhood. They did so because their narratives fortified my conviction that they were trying to put into words our experience as West Indians living in the West Indies. Exile may have been an issue for them as writers; but for me, a reading child, these works were about home – discovering home, and giving voice in that home. Naming.

The discovery of West Indian literature was a very private one for me. This fascination with West Indian stories was not shared by my friends or by the curriculum of the school I attended. While we were well-versed in the details of West Indian history and while we experienced the fantastic awakening of consciousness when we studied slavery and emancipation and rebellion in class[22] (and visited old plantation sites and Maroon Town), such revelations – such dramatic epiphanies did not take place in the study of literature. There was no equivalent, for instance, to the tense silent anger and deep resentment that many black boys in class felt after learning about the amputation of the feet of slaves when they tried to escape. I still remember the discomfort of the fair-skinned boys in the class. I recall the accusatory stares, the growing unease, and a peculiar realization that vengeance was a sweet and compelling instinct that cut across time and generations.

In this classroom of boys of so many hues, boys whose history was coloured by mixing, they showed us skeletons of blacks found on old plantations, feet chopped at the ankle, hands chopped off at the wrists, the missing members lost forever, tossed to some stray mongrel who could gnaw bone into manure. And there in the room were two very white boys. They sat still listening. Maybe they felt the same sense of outrage that we did, but I recall the way in which many of the black boys began to look at these two white friends, boys with whom we had played cricket and with whom we had lied about our sexual exploits. And now, suddenly they were being transformed into the enemy. We wanted to take revenge. We wanted to finish the fight that Juan de Bolas had lost, that Cudjoe had lost, that Tacky had lost. Someone shouted out, 'It's all you people' pointing to the white boys, and no one laughed. The teacher sensed the tension. He tried to continue. We were not listening. Maybe five minutes passed in silence. We were all waiting. The white boys wanted to go; we sensed that – but they did not know where to go. Then someone laughed. 'Jesus, Macky, you look frighten nuh hell!' And somehow we all could laugh at that. And we laughed and laughed and laughed until the period was over and then we all went out and played cricket together as if nothing had happened. But somewhere deep in there we knew that something painful had happened. We had encountered history and found we could not change it. We had met the past and discovered that the present had made its easy moral demarcation far more complex. And yet we could not simply accept history as something to get over. This history meant something about the way we lived now. From then on we all said together that Columbus was discovered here. We also said that we would watch and pray that nobody ever again did the evil that was done to us.

For our O-Level exams we were asked to study V.S. Naipaul's *A House for Mister Biswas*. It was taught as just another book. Much can be said for the unwillingness of the teachers to make anything of the novel's Caribbeanness. By not drawing attention to its Otherness, we were forced to accept it as a valid literary expression, as valid as Golding's *Lord of the Flies*. But we were also deprived of the realisation that the existence of *Biswas* was testimony to something significant in our lives. Few students actually read the entire text; it was possible to pass the exam without having done so. In a society that had mastered the art of the oral transmission of narratives, it was possible and common for one student, who had gone through the throes of reading the book, to relate the narrative to the rest of the students a few days before the exam. *Biswas* could have been fascinating to us in its ability to present with humour a landscape with which we were acquainted, and characters whom we recognised. As we prepared for the O-Levels, none of these fundamental issues were explored. The novel was taught with the distance and academic aloofness applied to any literary work.

Thus, while we were trying to discover and appreciate our artistic cultural heritage, the teaching mechanisms and the rigour of Cambridge examinations undermined any genuine connection with the literature. So, it was not surprising that when, during this period, a far more compelling encounter with the culture of the Caribbean took place, it was outside both formal education and books. Here was a phenomenon that had the same kind of impact on my psyche as had my earliest encounters with West Indian literature. It was a new development in Jamaican culture that seemed to parallel, with incredible force, the passion and drama of the history classes. It was a movement that brought great pride and a sense of identity to many boys in school. It was reggae music. It was through my 'discovery' of reggae music that I began to move my ideological (and still embryonic and unarticulated) quest for a cultural state of belonging from the literary – the private and esoteric, if you will – to the more fundamental realm of everyday existence. Where, before, I had been unable to discuss my excitement about Caribbean literature with my classmates (they had not read the books), now, with reggae, I was able to speak of a Jamaicanness that we could all identify with and be proud of.

My older brother was a music buff. He would set up elaborate home-made speaker systems all over his room, gaudily decorated with gallons of coloured marker ink. His sound system was a shrine that remained his domain and his alone. During the summers of my fourth and fifth-form years, he had the misfortune of having to work full-time during the days. This left the shrine unguarded, and I would raid the room, and desecrate it by taking up residence there for the entire day. At about five fifteen in the afternoon, I would attempt to put back every record, every piece of paper, every wrinkle and ruffle in his bedsheets exactly as he had left them. It was in that room that I really discovered Bob Marley and The Wailers.

Marley's album *Kaya* (1978) completely convinced me something significant was evolving in my relationship to art and culture through music. *Kaya* was the music that gave me context. I did not have to sing it with a black American accent. *Kaya* contains a range of lyrics that move from the strident political advocacy of earlier albums such as *Natty Dread, Rastaman Vibration*, and *Burning*, to very reflective, but equally compelling songs of inner debate. The complexity of the multiple guitar lines, and the sheer mystery and density of the lyrics fascinated me. I wanted to decipher, to find meaning in each lyric, each metaphor, each enigmatic proverb:

> Misty morning
> don't see no sun
> I know you're out there somewhere
> having fun
> there is one mystery yes
> Just can't express
> Why you take the more
> To receive the less
> The power of philosophy yeah
> Flows through my head
> Light as a feather
> Heavy as lead
> Light like a feather
> Heavy as lead
> I want you to straighten out my tomorrow...[23]

I was moved from seeing the lyrics as the contorted and illogical ravings of a Rastaman, to experiencing epiphanies as I was drawn into these compositions. It was a practical criticism lesson, all devised and inspired by popular music.

I listened to *Kaya* every day for months. No other artist or writer had so drawn me into a view of the world around me as had Bob Marley. At school, I became impatient with fellow students who found beauty and passion in Earth Wind and Fire or Doctor Hook. There was something shallow in these pleasures that I found impossible to explain. But in Bob Marley, Burning Spear, Peter Tosh, and Third World (the early Third World), I had something that many of the writers of the 1940s, 1950s and 1960s did not have in Jamaica. In these artists was a sensibility that was at once complex and compelling.

Marley was a Rastaman who spoke of Africa as a kind of paradise. But he also articulated in song the passion that many of us had felt sitting in history classes in high school where we learnt about the slave trade and the callous abuse experienced by Africans in Jamaica:

> Slave driver,
> the table is turned
> catch a fire
> You gonna get burnt
>
> Every time I hear the crack of the whip
> My blood runs cold
> I remember on the slave ship
> How they brutalized our very souls.[24]

Here, available to us in a form that was sweetly our own and in a man whom the world was beginning to call its own, was the poetic narrative of our history. That, coupled with the awakening of anti-imperialism and socialism in the 1970s, made it clear that I was emerging into a world very different from that of my father and those before him. In Marley, I was discovering context and tradition.

The dynamic relationship between popular culture and literature has evolved significantly in West Indian literature over the past thirty or so years. There are, however, regional differences. Trinidadians, perhaps, always understood that relationship because of the long and powerful tradition of calypso music, which has expressed, captured and shaped the psyche of the Trinidadian people in remarkable ways.

In the nationalist period (c1920–c1965) of Jamaican literature, there existed no such common feature of popular culture that could shape the structure and tone of the literary work. There was mento, but it was only one folk song form among many and never achieved the national status of calypso or later reggae. Roger Mais, in *The Hills Were Joyful Together*, makes use of folk forms such as the storytelling style of the rural oral tradition, and Kamau Brathwaite has explored Mais's use of call and response patterns in the grouping of characters in the narrative (relating them to jazz, though they could have been related to the dynamics of the revivalist churches[25]). However, it is evident that while Mais is attempting to present these features of folk culture as elemental qualities of the community he is describing, his literary style and tone are not shaped by this culture and he remains distant from it, a writer outside looking in. The same can be said for the work of writers such as Victor Reid, Andrew Salkey,

Neville Dawes, and John Hearne, who are all positioned outside the worlds they are describing, who fail to realise in the form and structure of their work an aesthetic that relates to these worlds.

It is significant, then, that when reggae emerged as the foremost element of the popular culture of Jamaican society, it began to have a similar effect on Jamaican writing as had calypso on Trinidadian writing. However, the two styles of music are very different and have a very different ethos. While reggae, like calypso, evolved as an expression of socio-political angst and as an expression of the folk's ability to create its own sense of self, reggae is distinguished by its close relationship with Rastafarianism, a religious and political movement that has transformed significantly the language and culture of Jamaican society. The kind of self that reggae has enabled the people to establish has been very different from the *picong* self-irony of calypso, though the soca-calypso of singers of the 1980s, such as David Rudder, is somewhat closer to the ethos of roots reggae. Critical to the evolution of reggae has been the violence and suffering of 'inner city' existence and the pertinacious belief that better must come. Unlike calypso, reggae went international and managed to do so on its own terms largely because of the 'universalist' spiritual sentiments that came into reggae from Rastafarianism. Sparrow may well have been no less a brilliant lyricist than Marley, but one suspects that much of the wit of his calypsos failed to travel outside a Trinidadian frame of reference, whereas Marley's rise to world (superstar) status, his appeal to a white Rock audience in Europe and North America, was based on symbols of rebellion and counter-cultural resistance which were readily grasped (if not always accurately) by that audience. Marley's emergence as an international 'star' was a triumph for reggae and Jamaica in that it broke from the typical mould of Third World music in which established stars from the USA and the UK took the music and made it popular on their own, frequently diluted, terms (the Andrews Sisters with calypso, for instance). Reggae established a new standard by which Third World music could enter the mainstream. Marley became reggae's ambassador, and his producer, Chris Blackwell, effectively sold the world the idea that reggae was best understood and performed by Jamaicans. It is an attitude that Jamaicans gladly sought to perpetuate, as it fitted perfectly into their conception of self.

Popular American and British culture saw in reggae something more than the straw-hatted exotica of Caribbean society. There was something compelling in the reggae of Bob Marley and Peter Tosh

– something aggressive, revolutionary and relevant to political developments in the world. When Peter Tosh performed on *Saturday Night Live* (a popular American comedy programme) in the early 1980s, he was accompanied by the Rolling Stones' Keith Richards. A few months later, *Saturday Night Live* comic, Eddie Murphy did a satirical sketch of Tosh. Rigged up in false dreadlocks and a scowl (typical of the clichéd image of Jamaican reggae stars), he chanted 'Kill de white man, kill de white man!' to the strains of a laconic and contagious reggae beat. The crowd watching the performance, all white, were chanting 'Yes! Yes!' to this radical admonition. *Saturday Night Live* understood the irony of reggae music, an irony that Bob Marley lived by. He titled his tour of the USA 'Babylon by Bus', a kind of self-deprecating attack on a society that he was both criticising and using to make his fortune. The Jamaican was no longer a harmless exotic. She/he was a political entity who had the capacity to challenge the arrogance and power of larger states like the USA. This was the new popular conception of the Jamaican – an aggressive figure who took no crap from anybody anywhere.

The Jamaican now has an image and identity that has been forged through popular culture. While reggae cannot be credited with providing Jamaicans their sense of self – a quality that has remained a fundamental part of the Jamaican personality for several hundred years – there is little doubt that it has shaped the perception of Jamaicanness over the past twenty years. There is little doubt also that the combination of reggae and the extensive migration of Jamaicans has given both Jamaica and Jamaicans a profile in the world that previously did not exist. I understand the image and I find myself drawn to it, not because I like it (in many ways it is negative and filled with its own reductionist stereotypes and misconceptions), but because it distinguishes me: it removes me from the status of the invisible to that of the highly visible. (Just show your Jamaican passport at a US, Canadian or British customs office and watch the reaction.) In Africa, reggae did for the West Indies what no politician, or writer was able to do. It offered a connection between the West Indian and the African that moved away from the sometimes strained relationship that existed between the two peoples. Bob Marley is as popular in Nigeria as Fela Kuti[26] and seen throughout Africa as representing the collective reality of all Africans across the world. Marley's embrace of African culture, a connection that had been eroded in the Caribbean by colonialism, was recognised by the new leaders of Zimbabwe who invited him to join them in heralding in the arrival of the new independent state. There was something deeply significant about this. Reggae artists now exist all over Africa. Majek Fashek is an outstanding reggae voice in Nigeria, while, from the Ivory Coast, Alpha Blondy has led a dynamic French-flavoured reggae movement throughout Europe and North America. In South Africa, Lucky Dube, with his raw, Peter Tosh-inspired reggae, is an icon of prophecy and possibility. All of these artists have established themselves as international stars who have brought their musical heritages to bear on reggae music[27]. As I will argue later in this book, the ability of artists outside Jamaica to become legitimate reggae voices speaks to the potency of the reggae aesthetic.

For me as a writer, these indices of identity derived from the international status of reggae served as a forceful source of grounding and consciousness that were only partially fulfilled during my encounter with the literature of the region. It was only too easy to see the earlier generations of Caribbean writing as belonging in a 'branch-plant' way to the English literary tradition, albeit with a different accent. Reggae belonged to nobody but us. But it was not just what reggae achieved for our international position which was important to me, it was also how reggae addressed one of the central issues in Jamaican society: race. In reggae I discovered a willingness amongst Jamaicans to recognise the dignity and strength of African society and culture, a quality that seemed absent when I arrived on the island from Ghana in the very early 1970s. As I explore in greater detail later in the book, the truth is that there long existed in Jamaica – though submerged, embattled and voiceless in the wider society – a strong Pan-Africanist vision, expressed most clearly in the life and work of Marcus Garvey. (Such sensibilities were also apparent in my own family, in the work of my grandfather, Augustus Dawes, who spent many years as a missionary teacher in Nigeria.) But while the instinct was strong, even in the case of Garvey, whose symbols and aesthetic values were curiously Eurocentric,[28] there was not really a corresponding embrace of an African derived aesthetic as it had survived in transmuted form in Jamaica. The Rastafarians and cultural activists of the 1970s changed all this, and reggae played a crucial role in this development. This change is illustrated by the way Marley's 'Redemption Song'[29] became an anthem of West Indian society because of its candid examination of our cultural roots as people of the African diaspora. It enters the historical and then uses the revelations of history to interpret current realities. I had found nothing which matched it in the Jamaican literature I had read. There is a recognition of Africa in Jamaica in such novels as Salkey's *A Quality of Violence* (1959) or Sylvia Wynter's *The Hills of Hebron* (1962), but it is still one associated with otherness, with a difference which is problematic. In his four-minute song, Marley condenses spirituality and politics, history and the present in a way which closes up the gulf left by the middle passage and the four hundred years since the first slaves were imported from Africa to the New World:

> Old Pirates, yes they rob I
> Sold I to the merchant ships
> Minutes after they took I
> From the bottomless pit
> But my hand was made strong
> By the hand of the Almighty
> We'll forward in this generation, triumphantly.

The past is regarded as a tool with which to identify the conditions of the present. The pirates are presented as the devils of the biblical Hades – 'the bottomless pit', literally the dungeons in the slave factories on the coast of West Africa, and more metaphorically, the vastness of the unknown that lies beyond the open seas – the devouring horizon that kept taking the Africans away from their homeland. In the triumphant coming out of 'this generation', Marley condenses the pain of the past, the calling of the world to account for past wrongs, and the new self-confidence of a prophetically inspired destiny. To reinforce the relevance of this song to the present, the second verse presents a series of moral exhortations which give the piece a universal relevance.

> Emancipate yourself from mental slavery,
> None but ourselves can free our minds
> Have no fear from atomic energy
> For none a dem can stop the time
> How long shall they kill our prophets
> While we stand aside and look?
> Some say it's just a part of it;
> We've got to fulfil the book.

Marley's genius is to shift from the historical to the present recognition that there is an equally debilitating form of slavery that has taken hold of black people. This 'mental slavery' is represented by inertia, fear, and the lack of perspective about where true power comes from.

The suggestion that the destruction of black people is simply a product of fate in the lines, 'Some say it's just a part of it/ we've got to fulfil the book', is quickly dispelled by the chorus: 'Won't you help to sing/ These songs of freedom/ Cause all I ever had/ Redemption songs'. The line 'We've got to fulfil the book' is thus transformed into a positive statement of prophecy that the reawakening of black people is part of an inevitable reality that will soon overtake society.

For me, Marley's song assumed a heritage that was confident and proud. There is no apology for singing in his own language, no attempt to win the approval of white culture by fulfilling a certain stereotyped image of the Jamaican. This capacity to assume a self-confident cultural history represents, for many Caribbean people, progress beyond the tentative, even if admirable, pioneering work of many earlier writers.

Perhaps growing up in a home with a father who bought Bob Marley's single, 'Natty Dread', and played it over and over and over again, even more than he played his beloved Thelonious Monk, ensured that the richness of Caribbean culture, and reggae music in particular, was firmly ingrained in my way of thinking. The point is that I, like many emerging writers, grew up in an environment in which I could become engrossed in reading and listening to art generated by the culture with which I was most familiar, without at any point feeling as if I would run out of things to discover. For me, then, it would have been difficult to accept Naipaul's assertion that nothing was created in the West Indies. My objection to what he wrote did not stem from anger or political angst, but from a simple inability to reconcile it with my own experience. After all, Naipaul himself had played a great part in convincing me of the fallacy of that statement. But if the nationalist phase of Caribbean writing was concerned with the act of naming, acknowledging, and clarifying a sense of self, I knew that the new literature had both to find the language and forms with which to contend with current realities; had to possess a reflexivity that allowed for irony, for satire; had to find a poetic and aesthetic articulation that emerged not merely from a progression of the literary tradition but represented a qualitative shift from an anti-colonial literature which in its aesthetics still privileged colonial forms, to a post-colonial writing which was rooted in our own way of seeing and speaking. The task was no longer to create a literature from the West Indies, but to allow the voice of that region to reflect on the world that it met. From here, it is not difficult to begin to talk about a reggae aesthetic, for I am convinced that my grounding as a writer is inextricably linked to the shape and ethos of reggae music.

CHAPTER THREE

THE REGGAE AESTHETIC
AND LITERARY FORMS

SOME TENTATIVE DEFINITIONS XI

'Every time I hear the sound of the whip...'

For every chekeh of the guitar,
a whip cracks,
how can you hear the sound
and not weep?

Follow the pattern with me,
always on the off.
We are forever searching for spaces
to fill with us.

If you walk straight down on the one
you will stumble
cause the reggae walk is a bop
to the off beat.

We are always finding spaces
in the old scores
to build our homes, temples and dreams
and we call it back-o-wall.

For every wooku of the Hammond B
a body hums.
How can you smell the sound
and still sleep?

Sooner or later those who are truly interested in the promotion of black consciousness or of a black dimension in American literature are likely to discover that 'black aesthetics', as the saying goes, is not as some agitprop rhetoricians seem to think, simply a matter of a group of spokesmen getting together and *deciding* and then prescribing how black experience is to be translated into poetry, drama, fiction and painting, but rather of *realizing what any raw material of any experience must undergo in order to become art*. How do you give aesthetic articulation to the everyday facts of life? The problem of every writer is how to make his personal sense of experience part of the artistic tradition of mankind at large

Albert Murray [1]

In the same way that poets such as Linton Kwesi Johnson and Jean Binta Breeze have found the rhythms of reggae inspiring, a number of Caribbean poets have found carnival, steel pan and calypso inspiring as well. One thinks of Trinidadian poet Abdul Malik's 'Pan Run', Guyanese writer John Agard's 'Man to Pan' in which he celebrates the steel pan; and in the works of other poets like Derek Walcott, Amryl Johnson, Victor Questel, James Berry, John Lyons... I myself have grown up with words and tunes and rhythms of calypso constantly in my head – sweet calypso with its wit, wordplay, bravado and gusto. It is the music of my childhood through which we got the news and scandals of the day; love and celebration, crime and tragedy, fantasy, politics, philosophy; in fact all of human experience and all in the people's language no matter how 'high sounding'.

Grace Nichols [2]

In the previous chapters I set out to establish that reggae has created a rich and complex body of work from which a distinctive postcolonial Caribbean aesthetic can be drawn. The focus of this chapter is to advance my argument that this aesthetic can be related rewardingly to other creative forms, specifically imaginative writing. I locate my argument within the theoretical context of other attempts to derive more general aesthetic frameworks from particular forms, in this instance from African American blues, from jazz and from calypso. I argue that there are already a number of significant Caribbean writers who are consciously working within a reggae aesthetic, whose work needs to be read with an awareness of this; I suggest, too, that there are other writers not obviously connected to reggae whose work can be read rewardingly from this perspective. I look briefly at some of the pioneering attempts in 1970's Jamaica to create work in artistic forms which draw on reggae's example. In particular I discuss the emergence of dub poetry and argue that a good deal of what has been written within this form, and its critical reception, draws on too narrow a conception of the reggae aesthetic.

In the late 1960s, Kamau Brathwaite, searching for an aesthetic framework within which to approach Caribbean literature and for his own Caribbean-centred writing, settled on jazz. Brathwaite saw in the creation of jazz out of the diversity of its sources something that suggested a fantastic hybridity of hope and possibility, something that was rich and complex made from very disparate and sometimes quite 'artless' and unspectacular parts – Delta blues, gospel, Negro spirituals, French folk tunes, the classical music of Western Europe, Southern and Western folk songs, Irish popular tunes, bar songs, hymns and so on. Brathwaite saw this as a perfect metaphor for Caribbean society – a society made up of people of various cultures trying to make a life for themselves out of a complex mix of creativity and violence. In focusing on jazz, Brathwaite knew that he was borrowing, but he felt that he had to borrow.[3] In the first place, when Brathwaite began developing this aesthetic, reggae was only just coming into existence, and he has admitted that he grew up with less knowledge of Caribbean folk culture and the African elements in that experience than he would have wished. He found a living and meaningful connection with jazz at an early age, and it is this connection that fuelled his creative impulses during that period. In looking to an African American music with its own aesthetic form, quite distinct from European musical forms, as something that would connect him with the landscape and culture of his own Black people, Brathwaite was borrowing from the practitioners of the Harlem Renaissance and the Beat Generation among others. His evolution as a writer has been a telling one, one which entailed a shift from a very Eurocentric education, through a period of Afro-centric focus, to the embracing of a diversity of cultural and literary sources which are made native through Brathwaite's creative processes. Jazz played a part in that movement but the movement back to the Caribbean,

the movement charted in the poem 'Islands' amounts to a reclamation
of an aesthetic other than jazz, an aesthetic that begins to embrace
folk and popular culture in Caribbean society[4]. What he evolved
was quintessentially Caribbean in that it moved beyond the focus
on an African American jazz sensibility (his Jazz suite of tributes
published in *Other Exiles*[5] indicate that jazz continues to be a major
love), to become a more universalistic valuation of the role of musical
structures in the understanding of literary works. He wanted something
that spoke to the African element of the Caribbean psyche, something
that reflected the hybridity of Caribbean cultures, and something
that contained both ideological and structural connections with the
literary work that emerged. These expectations offer us a way to
approach the question of aesthetics in Caribbean literary practice
today.

In 'Jazz and the West Indian Novel', Brathwaite articulates an
approach to jazz that is echoed later by Kalamu ya Salaam when
he writes about the blues. It is an approach that I echo in my examination
of the reggae aesthetic. The point, repeated in various ways by each
of us, is that these musical forms contain within them the substance
for an aesthetic, where an aesthetic is defined as a cultural, ideological,
and formal framework that is identifiable within an artistic form to
which it gives coherence, and this aesthetic can be related fruitfully
to other forms:

Within that context it is obvious that what we are dealing with is
more than solely a music form or aesthetic, although it is mainly in the
musical form that the blues aesthetic has most often been recognized
by non-blues people. The comparative uniqueness of this music is
impossible to confuse or mis-classify, especially when heard in juxtaposition
to any euro-centric music. However, the mere thought that the blues is
mainly music is a grossly euro-centric misconception. This misconception
is based partially on an inability to perceive African Americans as having
a self-defined total culture that includes abstract aesthetical considerations,
mundane manifestations in everyday life, and classical manifestations
in archetypal artistic creations. [6]

Kalamu ya Salaam, in his brief, but profound essay on the blues
aesthetic, offers us a model for constructing an aesthetic as a way
to understand a culture and as a way to speak about the artistic
and cultural forms produced within a society. He locates the meaning
of the blues in a socio-historical examination of the form which he
argues is inextricably connected to the history of racism and survival

among African Americans. He makes the point of distinguishing these experiences from any other kind of black experience elsewhere in the world. It is an important part of Kalamu ya Salaam's thesis that the blues did not originate in other black communities in the western hemisphere, even those that had also been slave communities. Again, while acknowledging African elements, he is quite specific about the blues not originating in Africa. Their genesis, for him, is purely African American and they speak to a specific moment of socio-political reality. I am drawn to this idea, not particularly because I seek to claim any exclusive ownership of reggae for Jamaica (although Lucky Dube's intentionally vague sense of history does smart a bit: 'Some say it came from Africa/ Some say it came from England,/ Some say it came from Jamaica,/ Some say it came from "I don't know where" '[7]), but because Kalamu ya Salaam presents us with a fleshing out of Brathwaite's desire to find an aesthetic framework for artistic expression that is indigenous to the society within which he writes. My own argument is similarly based on the very specific origins of reggae in Jamaican culture at a particular point in time and on reggae's very specific form and aesthetic, and this focus on specifics is, as I will show, wholly compatible with recognising the permeability of Jamaican culture and the interconnections between reggae and other black musics of the New World.

There are, for instance, interesting ways in which the blues intersect with reggae, and one can see in the basic structures of the blues that Kalamu ya Salaam presents to us, a number of similar qualities in reggae. From such a perspective, it may seem difficult to see what is so distinct about either and why they cannot be regarded as belonging to single aesthetic with variations. Reggae is influenced by the blues, and much of Marley's music, for instance, is decidedly blues-oriented – a certain kind of lament, a certain kind of wit, a certain view of the world. Both represent a reaction to white oppression by Blacks who belong to the lineage of the enslaved, and both represent a realisation of a distinctly black voice that uses black idioms and presents a world view that is unabashedly black. But then there are distinctions. The blues is founded upon a spirit of survival, the capacity to creatively translate the master-language/text of oppression into a resolute call for persistence in the face of tragic abuse. The politics of the blues is contained in the profoundly important assumption by the blues artist (and her/his community) of a world in which the Black is at the centre, whether she/he is speaking of shoes, sex, lost love or the pains of hard labour. This perspective, this voice, is a realisation of something that many slave societies sought to demolish: the conception of an individualised black voice within a community with its own culture and social norms. The result is a discourse that is carried on within the circle of black experience, sometimes to the exclusion of white experience. But what is also implicit is that all this takes place within a white world which has to be resisted, which can at best be ignored (for it exists only across the other side of the tracks), but which will never go away and whose position as the racial majority cannot be abolished. In this sense, the blues can be said to have made boldly explicit what the gospel songs of the black churches sought to practice in clandestine ways during slavery and afterwards. There is, too, within all black American music an almost inevitable ambivalence with regard to its position within American society: the competing desires to turn its back on the white world or demand admittance on equal terms. Reggae, on the other hand, emerged in a society which was 90% black, whose postcolonial political elite is (belatedly) black, as is its police force and, in the main, its judiciary. Yet it is also a society whose past was dominated by white colonialism and further back by the white slavemaster, and this past remains reflected in an socio-economic structure in which light-skinned and brown Jamaicans dominate the upper and middle-classes and oppression and poverty still go hand in hand with blackness. But while such contradictions remain, 'the Man', in the main, had gone. The internal class struggle was with a powerful but relatively small social elite and, as a consequence, in comparison to the blues, reggae's rhetoric of revolution was not allegorical or metaphorical but strikingly literal. Even more importantly, as I indicate in a later chapter, the emergence of reggae coincided with the permeation of Rastafarian influence from the ghettoes to the wider society. In one stroke, Rastafarianism abolished the white world, or at least cast it into the outer darkness, and provided reggae with a cosmology and iconography which make it very distinct from the blues and other black musics. Again, while the blues was conceived and birthed in a pre-electric world which retained some connection to a more African-centred folk past, its electric, urban forms evolved in an increasingly industrialised, 'modern' world in which the sound of African folk forms grew fainter and fainter. By contrast, reggae emerged in a postcolonial and increasingly postmodern environment in which, in its beginnings, ska and rock steady could be seen as the confident musics of national independence, and where, alongside the digital recording studios of the late 1980s, African-centred folk-cultural forms (hear Steely and Cleevie's *More Poco*, or Digital B's *Digital B Presents Kette Drum* [8]) continue to have a real existence. While, therefore, there is much that is shared, reggae's close connections with Rastafarianism and with the politics of Pan-Africanism distinguish it from the largely secularised and elementally American world of the blues. Thus while in 'universal' terms, these two forms are related, in the particular, and, more significantly, as they express a definable and relevant aesthetic that grows from national history or culture, they remain quite distinct.

In a sense, these distinctions are seen even more clearly with regard to those African American musics which fed more directly into reggae and its precursors. What is significant about the connection between the rhythm and blues of the fifties and early sixties and ska is that there came a point when the Jamaicanisation of R & B (hear for instance a compilation such as *Ska Boogie – Jamaican R & B, The Dawn of Ska*) evolved into something wholly different (hear for instance any of the Studio One Skatalites recordings, particularly those composed by Don Drummond[9]). Similarly, while there are significant influences from African American soul groups (such as the Impressions and later from Philadelphia soul) on vocal harmony reggae groups from the Heptones through to the Mighty Diamonds[10] what is significant about all such borrowings are their profound transformations within a reggae aesthetic – which is both rhythmically and lyrically distinct. There are parallels: the political consciousness of an artist such as Marvin Gaye, for instance, shares an affinity with reggae artists in many ways. But what continued to make reggae a species-defining genetic mutation that never quite took root in the African American pop world in the 1970s was its revolutionary rhetoric, its strong religious overtones and its involvement with Rastafarianism. The few instances in which reggae caught the attention of popular African American artists indicate that reggae had to discard its edge, its political and religious underpinnings if it was to be popular. Johnny Nash's work with Bob Marley was noticeable for the emphasis on love ballads, well-wrought but highly benign pop songs that seemed to compromise Marley's spiritual and ideological vocation[11]. It took the parallel emergence of ragga and hip hop and their shared sexual explicitness, shared celebration or denunciation of a gun culture and shared basis in the technologies of digital sampling for a crossover process to begin in earnest. Whether this will be equally true of the current generation of conscious singers and deejays, with their return to Rastafarianism and cultural concerns (artists such as the post *Voice of Jamaica* Buju Banton, recent Capleton, Sizzla and Anthony B[12]), time will tell; for in general, reggae's ethos, its aesthetic foregrounding of Jamaicanness and Africa, has not been especially popular in Black American society. Finally, where rhythm and blues, soul and funk were largely co-opted into mainstream corporate American pop-machinery, reggae has largely remained a radicalised form of music, walking on the fringes and maintaining its working-class character. This *otherness* continues to define the aesthetic.

Thus though Marley, for instance, embraced the idea of the blues and often sang the blues,[13] it is not simply in the manner in which he takes the form and departs from it that we encounter the workings of the reggae aesthetic, but the fact that so many archetypal reggae songs such as 'Get Up Stand Up' (Bob Marley)[14], or 'Equal Rights' (Peter Tosh)[15], or 'Revolution' (Bob Marley)[16], or 'This Time' (Culture)[17], or 'War Ina Babylon' (Max Romeo) cannot be said to be blues in any sense. These are warrior songs of political and spiritual anger and revolutionary activism that cannot be said to have any real equivalents in African-American music:

> Get up stand up
> Stand up for your rights
> Get up stand up
> Don't give up the fight
>
> Preacher man don't tell me
> Heaven is over the earth
> I know you don't know
> What life is really worth,
> They say all that glitters is gold
> Half that story has never been told
> And now you see the light
> What you gonna do?
> Stand up for your rights

Of course, this revolutionary voice is certainly not the only one present in reggae. There are reggae songs of conciliation, that call for and celebrate peace ('What we need is peace, love, and harmony', Culture [18]), but in the turmoil of the political warfare in Jamaica in the 1980s, it is almost always from the perspective of the warrior, the combatant calling for a dignified end to the hostilities.

While, as I have argued above, reggae has remained a largely localised form in its production (even the reggae distributed by multinational record companies has almost always been recorded in Jamaica with Jamaican producers) and has as a result kept its radical edge, it is a music that has had international status and was for a period happily co-opted by the western apparatus for mass commercialism. Nevertheless, as I have argued, there is a certain dialectic that has characterized the evolution of reggae. At one level it represents an indigenous development that speaks in a language and code that is specific to the working class subculture of Jamaican life (a language that is sometimes quite exclusive); at another level, particularly in the case of Marley, it has achieved a substantial international appeal. This capacity to be at once radical, highly localised, and internationally accessible (and commercially viable) is clearly something that is highly pertinent as a model for Caribbean literary forms.

Thus, though reggae is related to other New World African musical forms, I hope that my argument above (and my more detailed description of its aesthetic in the following chapter) shows clearly that reggae is a distinctive form with its own aesthetic base. What then is the legitimacy of drawing connections between reggae and other artistic forms, particularly imaginative literature? In the first place my concern with an aesthetics derived from reggae is not simply an attempt to trace the appearance of Bob Marley lyrics in the poetry or fiction of Caribbean writers or the mention of the word 'reggae' in a few pieces, but a recognition of something far more consuming and embracing than that: aesthetics in the broadest sense of the term. Nor am I arguing a simple causal model for the relationship between reggae and other forms. What I am arguing is that in Jamaica in the late 1960s and 1970s there was a major shift in the political and cultural sensibility of its people. This was the product of, among other things, the rapid urbanisation of the society, the expectations raised by political independence, and the ensuing social unrest engendered by the frustration of those expectations. The manifestations of this shift in sensibility included the attraction of socialist ideas and black working-class hostility to the privileged white and brown middle class, an Afro-centric foregrounding of issues of race and culture within the context of the historical legacies of slavery and the spread of Rastafarianism among the black urban poor. This was, of course, the social context out of which ska, rock steady and reggae came, the issues which these musical forms articulated and amplified in a manner unmatched in other artistic forms, and the raw material out of which artists, sound engineers and producers created a confident and coherent aesthetic.

Clearly, artists working in other forms responded to this social ferment in their own ways, not necessarily influenced by what was going on in reggae. I have already indicated that, for instance, Jamaica has had a tradition in the visual arts which since the 1930s has been rooted in folk, neo-African and Jamaican iconography. Similarly, the National Dance Theatre company has been evolving a Jamaican language of dance since its formation in 1962, exploring, for instance, the attraction and relevance of Rastafarian ideas in its *Two Drums for Babylon*, performed in 1964.[19] Equally, my argument for the potentiality of the reggae aesthetic for other forms does not depend on there being, for instance, an existing body of imaginative literature which displays an aesthetic connection to reggae. In reality, as I discuss in later chapters of the book, such a body of imaginative work does indeed exist. Even here, though, my argument does not depend on trying to prove that writers have derived their literary style from listening to and seeking to pattern their work on reggae music. There are two basic ways in which the aesthetic works. On the one hand, the aesthetic may serve as a self-consciously applied frame, guiding and shaping the work being produced, where the artist is looking to reggae for a model of creative expression. On the other hand, reggae music epitomizes an aesthetic development within an artistic community as a whole or within a society at large. Consequently, grasping the principles of reggae's aesthetic will, at the very least, provide a framework with which to analyse art produced in other forms around this period and even outside it. Two examples, one from the blues, the other from calypso, will illustrate the point I am trying to make. A reading of Langston Hughes's blues poems foregrounds, of necessity, the direct influence of blues music in shaping his poetic expression. Here our critical practice discovers how Hughes uses the structures, tropes, and language register of blues in his poetry. By contrast, a critical discussion of Toni Morrison's *Song of Solomon*[20] as a manifestation of the blues aesthetic operates in a more metaphorical way. Here, the principles of beauty derived from a study of the blues can be applied to Morrison's narrative technique to reveal that, as an aesthetic, the blues offers a legitimate and appropriate frame within which to read her work. One might start from the assumption that Morrison may have subconsciously imbibed the blues and been influenced by its aesthetic principles; but it would not be necessary to invoke this as a literal and historical connection. As Albert Murray argues in his work on Faulkner,[21] the blues is a quintessentially American aesthetic that has become a part of literary and cultural practice for most artists. A 'readerly' analysis of writing using the blues as a point of reference is thus a legitimate way of understanding the work – as legitimate as applying the Aristotelian principles of tragedy to modern dramatic literature.

A similar distinction can be made in exploring the ways in which a good deal of Trinidadian writing relates to the calypso. Social commentary is not all that calypso has engaged in over the years. It also celebrates an attitude to life, a self-deprecating wit and irony that has provided Trinidadians with a sense of identity through popular culture that had no real parallel in Jamaica before the advent of reggae. The work of a critic such as Gordon Rohlehr has shown that Trinidadian writers of the 1950s and 1960s were deeply influenced by the structure, cadence and attitude of calypso[22]. It is impossible to read Naipaul's early novels without an appreciation of the calypso as a literary form. Sheer delight in storytelling, irony and humour form an elemental part in his writing. The connection is made even stronger in a novel such as *Miguel Street*[23] where Naipaul constantly quotes from calypso songs. This is no exotic decoration on Naipaul's part; on the contrary, it is a fundamental attempt to enter the psyche of his society, something that only makes sense with an understanding of calypso. A look at the work of other prominent Trinidadian writers of that generation and beyond shows a similar relationship. Sam Selvon's short stories and novels have a loose balladic, episodic form, whose coherence comes from patterns of contrast or parallelism rather than from their linear structures, which is akin to the patterning of the calypso stanza. Similarly, Earl Lovelace situates his novels in a world that is marked by a combination of suffering and resilience, themes that characterise much of calypso music, and his most recent novel, *Salt*,[24] is a study in what can be termed a calypso aesthetic. Carnival and calypso are not simply aesthetic framings for the work, but are the substance of the narrative, organising metaphors, and implicated in the very texture of the writing. The same pattern can be found in other Trinidadian writers, in Lawrence Scott's brilliant *tour de force*, *Witchbroom*[25], which uses calypso and the carnival to construct a thematic and narrative climax for the work and in marina ama omowale maxwell's *Chopstix in Mauby*[26] where pan, kaiso and carnival express the people's collective psyche and the connection of their energies to the forces of history. Derek Walcott, a St. Lucian who lived for many years in Trinidad, found in calypso music a form and structure that could be applied to his poetic sensibility. There is no other way to read 'Spoiler's Return'[27] or the entire *Star Apple Kingdom* without a fairly solid understanding of the dynamics of calypso. At the same time, most of Walcott's plays, including *The Odyssey*, *The Last Carnival*, *Pantomime*, *No Meat No Chicken*, *Remembrance*, and *Dream on Monkey Mountain* rely heavily on calypso as an operating principle – as an aesthetic grounding for the writing. One can make the critical distinction that Lovelace's work can be examined quite explicitly for its *use* of the calypso or carnival aesthetic. Reading Sam Selvon's *Lonely Londoners*[28] in this manner undoubtedly makes sense, but one would need to take into account the fact that Selvon rarely, if ever, spoke of any use of a calypso aesthetic in his work[29]. Here one would be making use of a calypso aesthetic as an heuristic device, as a way of entering the novel – and undoubtedly discovering ways in which the ethos and form of the calypso ballad define and shape it. The distinctions I am making might appear slight, but I present them here because I think it is important to recognise that even those writers who may not admit to working within a reggae aesthetic framework, or who may indeed reject the idea out of hand, can be read rewardingly from this perspective. Thus to read John Hearne's *A Sure Salvation*[30] in this way could offer intriguing insights into a work that is not a 'reggae' novel in the way that Michael Thelwell's *The Harder They Come*[31] undoubtedly is. In the main, though, I will rely on the analysis of the works of artists who have encountered reggae and have, in some way, sought to engage with the music and its aesthetic. Many of these are, needless to say, the 'children' of the 1960s and 1970s, and it is my argument that an examination of the way in which Marley and the other reggae artists of the period gave shape to a new aesthetic is integral to an understanding of the way in which writers of the current period have begun to break decisively from the concerns and aesthetics of the Caribbean writers from the 1940s to the 1960s.

It is possible to distinguish four kinds of relationship between Jamaican writers and reggae and its aesthetic. First, there have been those for whom reggae was a crude ghetto music whose language, political concerns and sexual explicitness were anathema to the concerns of literary culture.[32] Secondly, there have been those such as Kamau Brathwaite, Dennis Scott, Anthony McNeill and Lorna Goodison whose writing careers either began before or were co-terminous with the beginnings of reggae, who, starting from the basis of established literary forms, found in reggae a bridge to the wider Jamaican society. Third, there are those who have been directly influenced by reggae to the extent that, as in the case of the dub poets, they have seen their work as a subset of the forms of reggae developed by reggae deejays[33]. Fourth, there are writers who grew up in Jamaica (and other parts of the Caribbean) in the 1970s and 1980s, whose formative aesthetic influence has been reggae and whose approach to literary forms has been through the medium of the reggae aesthetic. I include myself in this group. There are also those such as Linton Kwesi Johnson and Jean Binta Breeze whose recent work displays a movement towards more literary forms without losing its connection to the performance orientation of dub poetry. These are, of course, oversimplifications of the actual positions adopted by individual writers, and these categories must be seen as having highly permeable boundaries.

However, all discussion of the relationship between imaginative writing and reggae needs to be put into the context of their relative outputs. There is a fundamental and instructive comparison to be made in terms of both impact and sheer volume. The recently published *Rough Guide to Reggae* (1997) presents a selective guide to what is, in the main, currently available in reissued CD or vinyl LP formats. For the 1970-80 period this amounts to over 600 albums. There are probably at least as many CDs again not listed in the *Guide*. This in turn represents only a fraction of what was actually released in the period, mostly in the form of 7 inch 45s in Jamaica. The *Rough Guide* estimates that over 100,000 individual records were released between 1965 and 1990, and the 1970s to 1980s period was a particularly productive one.

By contrast, Kamau Brathwaite's exhaustive *Jamaica Poetry: A Check List* (1979) lists only 70 collections of poetry written by Jamaicans in the same period. Of these only 31 were published in Jamaica, though some of those published outside Jamaica (mainly Toronto and London) were by writers still working in Jamaica. Many of the collections were small, self-published works of no particular poetic quality. Of those published in this period, only 14 writers appeared in Pam Mordecai's fairly inclusive anthology *From Our Yard: Jamaican Poetry Since Independence* (1987). The number of collections that were truly significant is small enough to be listed: Lorna Goodison's *Tamarind Season* (1980), Linton Kwesi Johnson's *Voices of the Living and the Dead*, (1974), *Dread Beat and Blood* (1975) and *Inglan Is a Bitch* (1980), Anthony McNeill's *Hello UnGod* (1971), *Reel from 'The Life-Movie'* (1975) and *Credences at the Altar of Cloud* (1979), Mervyn Morris's *The Pond* (1973), *On Holy Week* (1976) and *Shadow*

Boxing (1979), Mutabaruka's *Outcry* (1973) and *First Poems 1970-79* (1980), Oku Onuora's *Echo* (1977), Andrew Salkey's *Jamaica* (1973) *In the Hills Where Her Dreams Live* (1979), *Land* (1979) and *Away* (1980) and Dennis Scott's *Uncle Time* (1973). There was also, of course, Barbadian Kamau Brathwaite's work of the 1970s, some of which, such as *Black + Blues* (1976) and *Days and Nights* (1975), reflected his time in Jamaica. Mikey Smith's *It a Come* (which belongs to this period) was not published until 1986, three years after his death and Jean Binta Breeze's *Riddym Ravings* not until 1988[34].

There were also a number of publications by Rastafarian writers during this period which, while not of the quality of say Mutabaruka's or Onuora's work, are nevertheless significant documents of the period. These include Ras Dizzy's work (for instance, *The Human Guide Line: Poems and Inspirations by Ras Dizzy, the Poet*, 1969, and *Rastafarian Society Watchman*, c. 1971); *One Love* (1971), edited by Audvil King, which included King's poems and prose pieces by Althea Helps, Pam Wint and Frank Hasfal, and Rod Taylor's *Ras Fari* (1976)[35].

Between 1969 and 1982, the flow of adult fiction by Jamaicans about Jamaica was decidedly a trickle – fifteen publications in all. Again there are few enough to list them: Erna Brodber's *Jane and Louisa Will Soon Come Home* (1980); Hazel Campbell's *The Rag Doll & Other Stories* (1978); James Carnegie's *Wages Paid* (1976); Neville Dawes' *Interim* (1978); Hall Anthony Ellis's *The Silence of Barabomo* (1979); Neville Farki's *Countryman Karl Black* (1981); John Hearne's *The Sure Salvation* (1981); Perry Henzell's *Power Game* (1982); John Morris's [pseudonym of John Hearne and Morris Cargill] *Fever Grass* (1969) and *The Candywine Development* (1970); Ivor Osbourne's *The Mango Season* (1979); Orlando Patterson's *Die The Long Day* (1972); Victor Reid's *The Jamaicans* (1976); Andrew Salkey's *Anancy's Score* (1973) and Michael Thelwell's *The Harder They Come* (1980). There was also N.D. Williams's (Guyanese by birth) *Ikael Torass* (1976) which is set in Jamaica and deals with the Mona campus upheavals of the early 1970s.[36]

There has been a degree of resonance between some of this trickle of fiction and the deluge of reggae recordings. The connections, though, indicate that while there have been a number of more recent works of fiction (such as Erna Brodber's *Myal* (1988)[37], Geoffrey Philp's *Uncle Obadiah and the Alien* (1996)[38]; and N.D. Williams's novella 'My Planet of Ras' (in *Prash and Ras*, 1997)[39]) that reveal an absorption of the reggae aesthetic into their formal and stylistic structures, the process of absorption has been much slower than is the case for other literary forms. Thus the resonances in the fictional works of the 1970s-1980s are chiefly those of content.

One can note in Carnegie's *Wages Paid*, Hearne's *The Sure Salvation*, and Patterson's *Die the Long Day* a focus on the slave past which has clear parallels with the concerns of reggae, though of these only Carnegie's novel displays a style and formal structuring which reveal it to have been part of the artistic ferment of 1970's Jamaica. One has to wait until 1992 for Hazel Campbell's novella 'Jacob Bubbles' (in *Singerman*)[40], for a treatment that achieves the kind of interplay between past and present that has been a signal element of the reggae lyric.

Other novels, such as Henzell's *Power Game*, Osbourne's *The Mango Season*, and Clyde Knight's *We Shall Not Die* (1983) focus on contemporary Jamaica's violent social upheavals in a style which is consciously 'popular' and 'rootsy' but which is in truth social realist in an old-fashioned kind of way. Similarly, N.D. Williams's *Ikael Torass* is conventional in style and structure, though its content is far more alive to the seismological shifts in the consciousness of Jamaican society. Michael Thelwell's novelisation of the film *The Harder They Come* goes deeper in its understanding of the popular energies and creativity which went into the flowering of reggae, and in its formal structure (its 'version' structure of passages told through the perspective of a multiplicity of characters) it creates a fictional analogy to the structure of dub in its mixing of elements. One may note, too, Salkey's reworkings of the folk tale in a contemporary, politicised setting in his *Anancy's Score*[41], where he can be seen to be doing something akin to what Marley does with the duppy story in a song such as 'Mr. Brown' [42].

It is possible that in comparison to poetry (particularly dub poetry) and drama, it was harder for writers of fiction to work out a way of adapting the novel form to deal with the shift in ideologies and aesthetics that was taking place in Jamaican society. Outside Jamaica too, with the exception of the work of Wilson Harris and to a lesser extent George Lamming, there was not a great deal in the tradition of the Caribbean novel (up to the mid 1970s at least) which challenged the dominance of conventional Eurocentric forms. It can also be argued that during this period the novel may well have been seen as an elite, Eurocentric and private form and for this reason received less attention than other forms. By contrast, performance-based activities corresponded perfectly with the grassroots populist/socialist tendencies that gave priority to didactic contact with the community over the tenets of art for art's sake. The phrase 'reaching the masses' was at its most popular during this period and it is possible that this did not make for a particularly welcoming climate for the novel. What makes this argument hypothetical was that the very small local publishing industry did not really have the resources to take on the publication of fiction. Of the novels listed above, only five were published in Jamaica and most of these were, except for two books published by the Institute of Jamaica, slim volumes. The publishers abroad sold primarily either to their domestic market or to the secondary schools examination market and this tended to preclude more experimental fiction.

Some of the most engaged work of this time, (apart from the reggae lyric and dub poetry) came from dramatists such as Trevor Rhone and Dennis Scott and theatre directors such as Carroll Dawes and Honor Ford Smith (with *Lionheart Gal*[43], artists who have continued to be largely ignored in discussions of Caribbean writing. Plays which deal with contemporary issues in experimental forms that reflect the influence of folk and popular culture included Rhone's *Old Time Story*, *Smile Orange*, the screenplay for *The Harder They Come*,[44] and Dennis Scott's brilliant plays (*An Echo in the Bone*, *Live and Direct from Babylon*, and *Dog*[45]) in all of which one can see the presence of a reggae aesthetic.

Much more needs to be written about the Jamaican theatre of the 1960s and 1970s, and beyond; to explore, for instance, the extent to which its inherited context as a pastime of Jamaica's elite gave way to the 1970's pressure for immediacy and social relevance, the extent to which popular cultural elements, including reggae, shaped the nature of dramatic structure as well as the more obvious elements of language use. However, in the absence of documentation, we know even less about the actual impact of theatre in the period.

It is unlikely, though, that apart from the yearly pantomime, much of this work reached young men like Colin Channer's fictional creation Colin Robinson. Nick Carter pulp fiction was much more readily available. Not until the emergence of yard theatre in the 1980s was there a theatre which could be regarded as accessible to a working class populace. But any evaluation at this point is bound to be incomplete because there is much in this period that has never been documented: the impact on the evolution of a Jamaican aesthetic sensibility of the national festivals, work in schools, the collaborations with African and Cuban artists and the several Carifestas held during that decade.

The work in theatre was paralleled by developments in dance. Led by the pioneering work of the National Dance Theatre Company (NDTC), a new aesthetic space was being constructed around the invocation of African sensibilities and forms contained in traditional religious beliefs such as myal, obeah and revival; as well as in folk dances such as dinkimmini, john canoe, (johnkuna) and maypole dances. The NDTC also choreographed dance dramas to reggae songs that reflected both the condition and sensibility of Jamaican society.[46]

In the visual arts, painters such as Osmond Watson, Karl Craig and Ras Daniel Heartman, Kapo, Everald Brown, Milton George and Karl and Seya Parboosingh continued the development of the language of Jamaican art into the new politics of artistic expression.[47]

The statistical comparison between the outputs of reggae and imaginative writing in Jamaica in the 1970s is, though, not limited to the numbers of individual titles produced, but also to the relative volumes of circulation and their social impact. Much local book production was either self-financed or the product of the pioneering and heroic efforts of individuals (such as Kamau and Doris Brathwaite as the core of Savacou Publications) and in most cases circulation was numbered in hundreds. Where metropolitan publishers were concerned, book sales of Jamaican authors in Jamaica were rarely higher. Best selling reggae records regularly sold between 20,000 to 30,000 copies, this in a country with a population of around two million. Thus, though *Savacou* played an absolutely invaluable role in the creation of a postcolonial Jamaican and Caribbean literature, publishing fifteen issues of its journal (some double issues) and some fifteen other publications (poetry, fiction and criticism) between 1968-1986, it must be acknowledged that much of its impact was limited to the university community, though it made determined efforts to carry its influence wider.

Beyond the issues of scale, there is a contrast of confidence. Reggae existed in multifarious forms, giving expression to the rude bwoy[48] and the Rastafarian elder[49]; the complexities of Lee 'Scratch' Perry's multilayered vision[50] and the powerful simplicities of religious faith in the songs of Prince Allah[51]; the Nyabingi sounds of Ras Michael and the Sons of Negus[52] and the rock-infused sounds of Marley and Tosh; the uptown, carefully constructed reggae of Third World[53] and the back o' wall rawness of countless groups: heaviness and lightness, dreadness and slackness, the erotic and revolutionary existed side by side and influenced one another. Again, though there remained persistent attempts to restrict reggae's access to the airwaves and to censor it, reggae swept aside all such restrictions by possessing its own means of production and distribution and had a total lack of interest in what the old cultural elite thought of it.

By contrast, literary culture found itself immersed in an aesthetic war which was fought with considerable bitterness. From the perspective of the present, it is important to acknowledge that those writers and artists of the 1970s who were beginning to engage with reggae music and the Rastafarian-steeped subculture had to struggle for artistic credibility. Reggae was an outlaw culture that did not have the respect of the Jamaican middle class. Kamau Brathwaite, in his forthcoming *Love Axe:/l*, documents the acerbic struggles between those writers whom he dubs the 'Gorillas' and the cultural establishment, particularly as these exploded at the 1971 ACLALS Conference at the University[54]. As in most wars, people were driven to taking up extreme positions, or at least found their positions characterised in extreme, monolithic ways. Among writers and intellectuals there was a debate about ideologies of race and identity and their place in forging an aesthetic. In retrospect, the strong divides seem rather contrived, but at the time appeared earnestly constructed and sustained. There was, indeed, a real conflict which reflected differences of attitude towards language, the role of literature, the relationship between literary nationalism and the literary heritage derived from colonialism and the centrality or irrelevance of issues of race. The positions taken tended to reflect differences in the age, class and racial origins of the participants. Thus, whereas reggae swept aside all opposition in the wider society, the literary and cultural elite were nothing like as ready to concede to the radicalisation of literary culture. In truth, participation in Jamaican literary culture, even in the 1990s, still displays very noticeable divisions of race and class.

With the luxury of hindsight, this polarisation can be seen to have had both positive and negative results. It undoubtedly energised, at least in its earlier phase, the activities of the cultural radicals.

Brathwaite, for instance, took the struggle beyond the University campus into Kingston, working in the Zinc Fence movement to explore the connections between music and poetry. The Zinc Fence's activities involved reggae acts, poets, and a range of counter-cultural artists. This movement eventually brought forth a cadre of writers: dub poets such as Oku Onuora, Mikey Smith, Linton Kwesi Johnson, Lillian

Allen and Mutabaruka who wanted to create an art that spoke in the voices of the working-classes to the working-classes.

The Zinc Fence movement in the mid-1970s in Jamaica represented one of the first instances of artists trying to locate in reggae a creative impulse that could permeate other forms. Here reggae artists, writers, painters and dancers converged for discussions and performances in a working-class area of Kingston. In this most creative and open environment, Rastafarian ideology was recognised as an important element of black consciousness and self-awareness. Writers such as Kamau Brathwaite had already brought a strong Afrocentric consciousness to bear on the way artists thought about writing and painting, dancing and making music. The cross-fertilization between the worlds of critical practice and scholarship and the living world of creative artists brought into being a rare and important period in Jamaican culture. It was perhaps only the second time in our history when the culture of the larger community and its political concerns were shaping the intellectual impulse of an artistic community itself committed to communicating back to that wider society. The first occasion had been during the political and social ferment of the later 1940s and 1950s when the *Focus* group, led by Edna Manley, brought together a politically and culturally committed group of artists.[55] In the 1970s the movement began to give voice to the notion of a Jamaican aesthetic, a Jamaican sensibility. There was a perception that within Jamaican society there existed frameworks of cosmology, ideology, and artistic aesthetics that could be applied to the creative impulse across a range of art forms. If there was any doubt about such an assertion, there were the reggae artists to prove that it was possible for the artist to be relevant to the larger community while still exploring and stretching creative and intellectual instincts.

The Zinc Fence Movement began to establish patterns of literary practice that would see their full fruition in the work of writers such as Erna Brodber, Olive Senior and Lorna Goodison in the 1980s. However, such an intellectual community does not exist in Jamaica today. Politically, the hopes engendered by the election victory of the socialist-orientated PNP under Michael Manley in 1972, by the later 1970s had descended into disillusion as tough anti-working class economic policies were imposed at the behest of the IMF, and political warfare between the supporters of the PNP and the conservative JLP brought terror to the lives of the ghetto communities. In 1980, for instance, 800 people died in political violence. In 1980, the PNP was defeated in the elections, and right-wing conservative forces returned to power. As had occurred in the 1950s, a substantial number of Jamaica's writers left the island. Geoffrey Philp, for instance, in his 'Florida Bound' writes bitterly of not being able to go back to his island because 'gunman like bedbug crawl over the land', of the 'parliament of S90s',[56] and even Kamau Brathwaite in time abandoned Jamaica for the USA, but not before being robbed at gunpoint in his own house. Apart from those with university tenure, Jamaica was still a society unable to support writers and artists who wanted to devote themselves predominantly to their work. One senses, too, that, in the end, the struggles within the literary community induced a sense of weariness. As in the 1950s, the possibilities of such a Jamaican-based artistic community were dispersed through emigration. Virtually all the writers involved in the 1970s ferment now either live outside Jamaica or are no longer active.

The cultural polarisation within the literary community had both positive and negative effects on the nature of some of the work actually produced and on its reception. One aspect of this polarisation was the labelling, for instance, of Kamau Brathwaite as an Afrocentric, grassroots writer, in contrast to the Eurocentric Derek Walcott. Brathwaite, the argument went, hung out with the urban poor, in the roots reggae environment of Kingston, performing his poems to a reggae back-beat, wearing the dashiki and the tam, and writing his *The Arrivants* as a recovery of African memory. Walcott produced poems that struggled with his commitment to two heritages – the European and the Caribbean. In 'What the Twilight Says' and in 'The Muse of History', Walcott was seen as taking on those artists who were seeking an essentialist African cultural memory in the Caribbean as sentimentally dishonest and misguided.[57] In particular, he was seen as directly opposing Brathwaite. On the one side, there was supposedly Nation Language, oral public performance, Afrocentric and working-class and folk-centred forms; on the other, there was art which was private, reflective, cultivated, literary, elitist and universalistically 'nonracial'.

While this debate did generate some complex and necessary discussions about race and ideology in Caribbean writing (and some very unhelpful oversimplifications), its very premise was, and still is, constantly gainsaid by the work of the writers in question. Both Walcott and Brathwaite have demonstrated in their work an indebtedness to at least two strong cultural forces. For the Afrocentric evocations of Brathwaite in *The Arrivants* (especially *Masks*) one can find matching concerns in Walcott's *Omeros* or *Dream on Monkey Mountain*. Similarly, parallel to the classical western underpinnings that have given form to Walcott's writing, one may point to the T.S. Eliot influences in the shaping of Brathwaite's long trilogies – an influence that he readily acknowledges[58]. However, what links these two writers together most significantly is their embrace of a dialectic triad in their approach to Caribbean culture and aesthetics. The movement from thesis to antithesis and then to synthesis is recognised by these artists in their constant quest for a voice, for a way to name (and in the process own) what was for years unnamed and silenced. Brathwaite's 'torn and new' expression of hope in *The Arrivants* parallels Walcott's 'New Adams' discourse of naming in 'The Muse of History' and *Another Life*.[59]

Reggae, not surprisingly, was placed firmly on one side in the context of the apparent ideological polarisation between Western and African cultures associated with Walcott and Brathwaite. As a consequence, its actual diversity, its capacity, for instance, to be both public and reflective, was overlooked. A more accurate assessment would be to regard reggae as accomplishing what both Walcott and Brathwaite sought to do in their work, which is to discover a voice that speaks through art to the history and present of Caribbean people. It is within this context that I believe that the elaboration of a reggae aesthetic should be located. My position is quite different from that taken by those who have sought to locate reggae within an aesthetic which draws on only one side of these fixed cultural poles: the African side. This latter position seems to me both restrictive in its perception of reggae and especially limiting in its perception of the potential relationship between reggae and other literary forms. It has led, for instance, to a tendency to see a direct and fairly exclusive link between reggae and the development of the dub-poetry movement, a movement committed to replicating reggae's grassroots popularity in the creation and performance of poetry. This is the characterisation which seems to be expressed by Pam Mordecai in her 1985 anthology of Jamaican poetry, *From Our Yard: Jamaican Poetry Since Independence*.[60]

Mordecai was undoubtedly pointing towards the kind of contemporary discussion then being pursued, but her characterisation appears to be based on a fairly narrow view of reggae, of its aesthetic and of the range of literary expression which could grow from that aesthetic base. This was not a limitation intrinsic to the work of the most significant of the individual artists who found voice in the reggae ethos, including those who pioneered what was labelled as dub poetry, such as Linton Kwesi Johnson, Oku Onuora, Mutabaruka, Mikey

Smith or Jean Breeze. It was a limitation, I feel, which had to do with the actual positioning of 'dub poetry' as a subset of the reggae industry, and its critical positioning as antithetical to 'conventional' scribal poetry. The way Linton Kwesi Johnson's work was seen illustrates this process. Johnson, perhaps one of the most accomplished exponents of dub poetry, was living in England when he conceived an art form that would entail constructing verse on top of a reggae dub track. He had been taken by the authenticity and inventiveness of the voices of the emerging, highly politicised deejays in Jamaica, such as Big Youth, and wanted to locate his poems in this language and texture of performance. He was, though, not a DJ, but a poet who found that the complex rhythms of reggae allowed him a new (and to him more familiar) set of tools with which to construct his work.

These include his appropriation of Rasta-speak, despite being a non-religious Marxist, his use of Nation Language as standard *parole*, his commitment to speaking first to a black working class audience, (and only after to a white audience), his use of reggae musical structures including the dialogue between a defining melodic bass-line and the staccato of the drum in his poetic phrasings, and his belief that the voice he was discovering was adequate for the expression of complex ideas. Johnson's earlier work did not echo all the range of tones and themes in reggae, being in the main deeply politicized and confrontational, but the exceptions – the notes of tenderness and expressions of pleasure in sound – reveal that Johnson was finding in reggae a broad aesthetic grounding that allowed him to write, for example, the lyrical eulogy for his father, 'Reggae Fi Dadda'.[61]

Despite this actual range of voice, the perception of Johnson as a reggae artist working with one of Britain's 'deadliest' reggae units, the Dub Band led by Dennis Bovell, undermined efforts to regard what he was trying to do as something that also belonged to the world of literary aesthetics. It took a while for the critical response to his work to treat it as a valid literary form. The focus on the business of recording and performing and working with full blown tracks, which was only one aspect of Johnson's poetry, served to undermine both the perception of the range of Johnson's work and the idea that reggae possessed a far-reaching aesthetic that could have an impact on the manner in which thought and ideology were constructed in literary works, and not simply on the superficial form of the material. Oku Onuora, perhaps the man who could be fairly described as the originator of dub poetry, tried to expand the manner in which people were perceiving this form of poetic expression when he told Mervyn

Morris that dub poetry was not simply a matter of 'putting a piece of poem pon a reggae rhythm; it is a poem that has a built-in reggae rhythm (so to speak) backing, one can distinctly hear the reggae rhythm coming out of the poem.'[62] But even this definition was clearly limiting. It focused primarily on the rhythmic execution of verse, without acknowledging the lexical, structural and ideological context of reggae music. This business of rhythm is not to be underestimated, and one can see why it has dominated the discussions about the characteristics of dub poetry.

Of course, even when Johnson is heard reading solo or *a cappella* or when his work is studied on the page, one can see one aspect of a reggae aesthetic in its rhythmic foregrounding, but, most importantly, it holds to a reggae sensibility in the language, themes, and ideologies that appear in the work. If dub poetry has been a limiting focus on the theoretical articulation of a reggae aesthetic, it is because dub poetry, for the most part, has defined itself as a 'branch' of reggae music, simply another style of reggae. In reality, the rhythms of dub poetry were often less varied and inventive than those of the best deejay reggae music which often 'rides' or sometimes works against the rhythm. Anyone who listens to a deejay such as Shabba Ranks, working virtually *a cappella* on one of his versions of 'Trailer Load', will understand that the reggae rhythms in dancehall music are often characterised by the considerable flexibility of the deejay's chant style, which is not necessarily located on the back-beat.[63] This is also evident in the way in which reggae deejays, chanting on funk bed-tracks, sometimes suddenly transform the entire rhythm of the piece by the manner in which they ride the track.[64] Dub poetry, on the other hand, in its dogged adherence to the reggae back-beat, quite often phrasing in ways which are counter to the natural rhythms of speech, can sound as if it has been stretched awkwardly to find its way into the grooves of the music. In time, the rhythmic patterns of some dub poetry became quite predictable and standardised. As Gordon Rohlehr wrote: 'Dub poetry is at its worst a kind of tedious jabber to a monotonous rhythm.'[65] While their work is in general rhythmically varied, there are poems by Jean 'Binta' Breeze, Lillian Allen and Mutabaruka that all sound alike, with the same declarative pattern. Unfortunately, it is this rhythmic fashion – the most imitable aspect of their work – which has been picked up, almost as an affectation, by younger dub poets over the years. There is, in truth, a considerable body of work by the imitators of Johnson and Breeze which in its rhythmic sameness, naïve rhyming patterns, and fondness for the declarative statement forces one to the conclusion that, so narrowly constituted, dub poetry represents a limitation of the possibilities of what can come out of the reggae aesthetic.[66] The problem lies in part in the tyranny of the back-beat rhythm which lends itself to patterns of anapaestic and iambic rhythms which have become too easily the stereotyped meters for the 'dub poem'. But this is hardly where the reggae aesthetic is located in the poetry of Johnson and Breeze. Perhaps it has taken the exploration of a reggae sensibility in other forms (in fiction, in poetry which is concerned with the written text as well as performance, dance and drama, and painting and sculpting), to enable us to recognise that there is an aesthetic which crosses forms, and this will enable us to read Johnson's and Breeze's work in the broader way it deserves. Moreover, by paying attention to the efforts of performers such as Breeze and Johnson to find poetic sources in reggae we are able to understand better what writers such as Brathwaite, Goodison or Dennis Scott have been doing in a context that appears much more conventionally literary.

CHAPTER FOUR

THE REGGAE AESTHETIC:

AN EPISTEMOLOGY OF THE SUBJECT

NATURAL MYSTICISM   86

NEW SOUNDS

2

On nights when rum poured golden and sweet
and laughter shook the louvres,
I would be called out in my raggamuffin threads
to skank a magic number to Bob's
rocking reggae sound. And dance,
I would dance, owning this sound, owning
this rasta revolution, my body contorting,
mimicking old moves until the spirit of this pulse
would take root; I would do things I never
thought I could, never dreamt I could,
my face a permanent scowl, my feet cool
on the solid tiles, dancing, dancing.
The applause would shimmer,
and beaming, returned from the sea voyage,
my eyes filled with the souls I had met on the way,
I would withdraw to my cubicle room,
nodding to the sibbling cheers,
still sweating, still floating,
still amazed at this new way of walking.
The record would kick into gear again,
and the voices would rise in deep discourse,
proclaiming this rhygin man the total socialist dream –
a voice of the people, from the people;
and regretting that they can't package the thing,
can't sell the thing, can only watch in awe, and dance.

In this chapter I attempt both a very condensed and generalised description of what I take to be the fundamental characteristics of the reggae aesthetic and an account of how my knowledge of the aesthetic was constructed. I offer the anatomy, which I hope preserves some sense of the aesthetic's inner dynamic, complexity and layered depth, as the context for more detailed discussions of specific elements in later chapters. I offer the personal narrative as an explanation and justification of my particular construct.

I start with the proviso that, like most musical forms, reggae is an evolving one and what I describe as reggae in this discussion represents a necessarily limited pool of songs and instrumentals I have listened to and been influenced by.

My knowledge of reggae and its construction has gone through several phases. When I was a boy, my knowledge took the form of an accumulation of information. For example, during the National Festival activities close to Independence Day, the radio would play all the reggae songs in the song competition and repeat the winners of the previous years. The newspapers would publish the lyrics of all the songs, and it was a ritual for us to learn them by heart. I knew reggae songs, sang the humorous lyrics at school, and paid keen attention to the more philosophical songs. I began to select my minibus by the type of music that was being blasted out through the elaborate sound systems these buses were equipped with. I always picked the van with reggae music pulsing through it. Usually, the songs were not those one would hear on the radio, but the dangerously rude and aggressive tracks, the latest deejay tunes, and that kind of thing. Sometimes a minibus driver would specialise in oldies, tunes from the late 1960s and early 1970s.[1] I already understood the nostalgia of music as these songs reminded me of my good friend, Beverly.

As a teenager, I developed a *functionalist* understanding of reggae's social role and social positioning. At parties ('sessions', 'spots', 'fetes'), the musical rotation was predictable: funk followed by fast R&B, followed by reggae, followed by slow soul music, followed by disco.

I was most comfortable dancing to the reggae, though I enjoyed the faster, funky stuff, but it always bothered me that the slow music was followed by the disco stuff. I wanted to stay dancing rub-a-dub – the reggae dance that I thought was the closest thing to actually having sex: a close pelvic grind that disturbed everything stable in a teenage boy's body.

I discovered bands such as Third World, Aswad, Steel Pulse, and Jacob Miller's Inner Circle[2] from a friend of mine named 'Bird' who lived in Jack's Hill and whose middle-class tastes made him partial to Earth Wind and Fire. Third World represented for him the most palatable type of 'yard' music because Third World were decidedly middle-class boys affecting a working-class posture. But it was also at 'Bird's' home that I first heard Bob Marley's *Rastaman Vibration* album. He wanted me to hear 'Johnny Was', his favourite tune on the album, a tune that even then I regarded as my least favourite.

I was discovering reggae. But it was not until the death of Bob Marley that I began to listen more intently to the music. And I *can* recall where I was when his death was announced. I was in a small room at the university, painstakingly drawing poster after poster advertising the next meeting of the University and Colleges' Christian Fellowship, a four hundred strong student organisation for which I was an executive committee member. I was the publicity director, and my task was to make twenty or more hand-penned posters, complete with design, lettering, and colouring for every weekly meeting. I was working on one such project when I began to notice that the only music coming through the wood panels from the dormitories above was Bob Marley's music – tune after tune after tune. I could tell then that he was dead. I stepped out into the tree-clotted road outside Irvine Hall and experienced a strange epiphanic sense of loss and tragedy at the realisation of his death. It was almost as if I was given permission to acknowledge him, Rastafarian and all, as a legitimate prophet, as a genuine and important voice even in the world of my own Christian convictions. This was an important moment for me.

I began to sneak into the rehearsals of the local bands that practised in the theatre on the campus. The Blood and Fire Posse was one such band that would jam in the theatre[3]. I listened to them, trying to understand the dynamics of arrangement, trying to discern what it was that moved me in this music. I also began to take my older brother's lessons in reggae quite seriously. He had, you see, discovered my illegal entries into his room, so he chose to control the situation by giving me a *formalist* education in reggae. He would sit me down and force me to listen to every percussion instrument in some song that he felt was particularly brilliantly arranged (all of *Exodus* comes to mind). By the time I left Jamaica to go to Canada, I knew reggae like most young Jamaicans knew reggae. I did not understand its aesthetics, nor was I certain of what I felt about the spiritual dynamics of the music – I was struggling with my own spiritual development at the time – but I knew reggae and I liked reggae. In Canada, I became a disc-jockey and producer of a reggae show. That sealed my fate completely. It was in that radio station, CHSR FM, with its most impressive library which had everything in rock and alternative rock dating back to the 1950s on the shelves, that I really began to learn about reggae music. I began to pull out records and piled them up high to chart the progression of the music. I discovered albums I had no idea existed. I started to listen to people such as Lee 'Scratch' Perry, the Abyssinians, The Heptones, The Gladiators, Culture and many more. And I did not just listen. I spoke about this music on the air, I interviewed people who were interested in reggae, and I tried to formulate an intellectual engagement with the music. These were important days. I made sure that the station ordered anything new, and I would enter the studio, turn the lights low, and spin the CDs and LPs, allowing myself to be transported to Jamaica, to another place, to another time. There were some important shows that I produced in this regard. I remember going through the shelves looking for cover versions of reggae tunes – covers done by Jamaicans and by international artists. I did a special show on 'versions' of reggae tunes, and it was in this way that I began to discover people such as Joan Armatrading, Joni Mitchell, Bob Dylan, The Grateful Dead. I already knew of them, but I started to listen to this bedrock rock music, trying again to see the connections and to see the differences. It all made a tremendous amount of sense to me. Reggae was a force, I could tell, and it was a force to which I planned to give serious attention.

While I was growing up in my radical, reggae-focused home, I had probably never fully grasped the extent of the social stigma attached to reggae music. I understood something of it, because I understood the stigma that many Jamaicans attached to Rastafarians and their beliefs. Reggae, by extension, was the product of the 'lazy, no-good Rastas' and amounted to bad bwoy music – street music, music of no cultural merit. There are many who still hold to this view today. In some instances it was mimicking the pattern of colonial thought which gave preeminence to the more classical and elitist conceptions of artistic excellence over more populist forms. But there was also, more often than not, a certain racism at work. Reggae was black. Reggae spoke about blackness and invoked Africa. Reggae demanded that Jamaicans acknowledge a part of their heritage that many were trying to not think about. Rejection of reggae was automatic for people such as these because reggae represented everything that was worthless and meaningless in Jamaican society. Reggae was also local, and we were acutely aware that 'local' things were always substandard and worthy of denigration and dismissal.

At one point I think I was sucked into this vision – I am sure of it – so that I understand the force of this way of seeing. For I could not help seeing that some of the television shows that featured reggae artists, shows such as *Where It's At* and the cabaret or speciality shows, when pitted against the more expensive production values of American shows such as *Solid Gold* and *Soul Train*, seemed embarrassingly quaint. The result was that the appearances of people such as Leroy Smart[4] (a television regular) and Ken Boothe[5] did these artists a disservice, for it immediately placed their work in the category of 'wannabe American' impossibilities. It is still hard to shake that image, even though it was far from the grassroots reality of the careers of these performers. But the stigma on reggae as a local product was one that could only be countered by international success, and it was here that Marley achieved his greatest triumph in Jamaica. He brought excellence, but above all he showed that foreign people liked reggae and liked him a great deal. This is what it took to legitimize reggae for many Jamaicans. My personal experience in this regard was fortunately different. I came to appreciate Marley's music because my father demonstrated that Marley was good. I appreciated the musical abilities of reggae artists because many of them came and performed in my home when I was young. They came with troupes of drummers who performed at the Institute of Jamaica where my father worked, mingling reggae with Rastafarian drumming and jazz horn playing.[6] I understood then that these musicians were valuable and gifted. But I also knew that reggae was a street music – a music with an undeniably dangerous subculture. Knowing that it came from this subculture is central to my understanding of reggae and to the texture of the aesthetic that I have seen evolve from it. I know that it is a way of seeing the world which arises from the conflicts in our social order.

So I know reggae. I know reggae mostly, however, because I started
to play reggae. I started to write reggae songs and perform reggae
songs. I became a reggae musician, and that is when I really began
to know about the reggae aesthetic. I became a reggae musician
with a bunch of white Canadians from New Brunswick who had never
been to Jamaica and who only knew of reggae from what they had
heard on LPs and CDs. But they wanted to play reggae, and they
asked me to work with them. And we all started to learn, to learn
what differences lay in the way the reggae piano was played – the
inverted syncopation; in the way to make that thin, light, and yet
cutting sound of the rhythm guitar, or to achieve the impossible and
create that fat, round sound of the bass. Those were delicate lessons
to learn and we learnt slowly but doggedly. We learnt what reggae
phraseology was about; we came to understand the genius of Marley
in terms of arrangements. We learnt about layering, we learnt that
dubwise has a dynamic that is not easily replicated. We learnt that
drumming reggae is feel, and that feel is not easy to capture. It is a
groove, and when the groove is finally there, there is an epiphany.
We learnt that the reggae lyric is responsible – almost pathologically
responsible – and is constantly aware of its audience. We learnt
that the reggae lyric did not lend itself to abject self-indulgence.
We learnt that solos in reggae were unusual entities and that the
groove, the ensemble groove, was always more critical, more important
than individual genius. We learnt that the drum and bass players
would have to work together alone for hours to find their souls and
to manage the twining that would anchor the music. We learnt all
of this over years of playing, recording, performing, and listening
and listening and listening to reggae music. I became totally immersed
in reggae, and it made me begin to understand a whole lot about
craft, about music and about culture.

Eastern Canada became our touring terrain, driving through blizzards
and brilliant summer afternoons hundreds of miles to perform in
clubs, universities and roadside motels. The crowds had all heard
of reggae regardless of how rural and isolated the town – and while
we had to find polite ways around requests for touristy tunes such
as 'The Banana Boat Song', we rarely had the sense that we were
doing something that was completely alien to our audience. We played
with complete sincerity during the early days and while we produced
some embarrassing music that only barely suggested reggae, we became
increasingly popular and successful as a gigging band. We gauged
our improvement by a simple test: we would cover a Bob Marley

recording and tape it during rehearsal – we would then analyse the
playback, perpetually perplexed at how unlike Marley's recording
we sounded. But this exercise forced us to isolate all the elements
of reggae music: what was naturally and predictably absorbed by
Jamaican musicians living and growing-up with reggae all around
them, had to be studied and dissected by our group, Ujamaa. Sometimes,
the band got desperate. We had a very rigid no alcohol, no drugs
rule for rehearsals and performance. I had played with a band in
which drunkenness was a painfully embarrassing deterrent to good
music. More often than not, inebriation would stir primordial instincts
in the musicians and what emerged was not reggae, but rock and
roll, the music they grew up with and played with instinctive skill.
This was not good for reggae. But at club after club, the band would
be accosted by well-meaning audience members offering us spliffs
of choice weed: it was a ritual perfected by Jamaican reggae artists
who relied on audience members to supply them with ganja when
they played abroad. One Canadian reggae band actually included
a rider that required good herb as part of its performance contract.

Needless to say, the rule against weed seemed completely anti-
Jamaican and anti-reggae. So was my unwillingness to sprout locks;
something I argued would be completely sacrilegious since I was
not a Rasta and did not buy into Rastafarian religious beliefs. But
these were the indices of a reggae subculture which was international.
The other members of the band were not teetotallers as I was, so
there were grumblings about the ban on drugs and liquor. I recall
leaving Fredericton for a conference for several weeks and the band
used the time of my absence to rehearse intensively, trying to really
push the reggae sound into their psyches. It was midsummer and I
arrived back at the Garden Creek Elementary School's gym where
we rehearsed to find the band jamming with absolute pleasure and
indulgence. The music was sloppy, lethargic, and tentative. Gradually,
it became clear that the band had decided to experiment, to see if
the secret pathway to the reggae sound was ganja. In this act, this
all-white band was demonstrating certain assumptions about the
alienness of the music and about its 'primordial' essence. They were,
of course, looking for short-cuts to grasping the technical specifics
and complication of reggae. However, without help from weed, Ujamaa
became a remarkably gifted, pure reggae band that pushed at the
frontiers of reggae composition during the height of our time together.
Our CD, *Chokota*, was popular on independent radios all over Canada,
ranking in the top twenty of albums in the chart produced by Toronto's

largest independent radio station. Our video 'Leave Up the Sky' had fairly good rotation on *Much Music*. On our final tour to Halifax, at the famous Flamingo Club (a venue that had hosted Burning Spear, Judy Mowatt, Lucky Dube, Sugar Minott, and Linton Kwesi Johnson, to name a few), we played an unprecedented four nights of some remarkable reggae, eighty percent of our sixty song roster being original tracks. We recorded the performance, and I still listen to the tapes with a sense of nostalgia, pride, and loss.

The crucible of rehearsal, performance and composition with Ujamaa was what brought me closest to reggae music and to the reggae aesthetic. Understanding the challenge of the music and observing the way it shaped the minds of so many people who had never been to Jamaica convinced me that I was working with an artistic form of some distinction, coherence and power.

It has been six years since I have played regularly with a reggae band. I still buy reggae records, but I am by no means as familiar with all the new material as I am with the roots reggae of the 1970s. I am now relatively green. I know I am, and I know that the music, like the Jamaican language, tends to move off and leave you behind. So I know that what I am going to say about reggae is far more based on the music of the past than on my more limited knowledge of the current characteristics of the music. But what I am dealing with is an aesthetic, and I am convinced that this has a structure of greater permanence than any variations through time of reggae's surface forms. I know that the reggae I know, I know deeply because a few months ago Colin Channer, the Jamaican novelist, and I were travelling through the United Kingdom by trains and tubes and buses and taxis, talking about reggae, writing, our personal histories, and the meaning of existence. We always returned to reggae to entertain ourselves, to find places of reference. And on one particularly long train ride to Leeds from London, we stood between coaches and started to remind ourselves of old reggae tunes, singing them, discussing their shape and laughing at the absurdities in some of the lyrics. It was a moving and haunting experience because we realised how much of our whole sense of self was shaped by the music we listened to, how our sense of identity and confidence as individuals, strangers in a foreign country, was defined by this common memory of the reggae song. We were taking a trip into memory and finding therein answers to our present condition. We might have gone through a hundred songs – I was hoarse when we reached Leeds sometime after one o'clock in the morning. On a BBC late show, a disc jockey was playing world music. A reggae instrumental number we had never heard before was playing. The taxi driver, a burly fellow, was saying good things about this show – he said it kept him awake during the small hours. Channer and I laughed uncontrollably at this serendipitous moment. It is in such moments of reggae's ubiquity that my instinct about the significance of its aesthetic is so frequently confirmed and reconfirmed.

I present this litany of my history in reggae to defend my claim that I know reggae, but also to make it clear that I know my thesis cannot contain reggae, which is evolving into something increasingly different, that is demanding further academic and intellectual scrutiny. Kamau Brathwaite has noted that we have not yet started to write about the crucial period of the 1970s in Jamaica.[7] The context of his comment was political, but he was also referring to the cultural upheavals of that time. He expressed the fear that we might lose what we created then if no one chooses to tackle it now. I am writing about reggae as an aesthetic now because I do fear losing it. I do fear that things will get away from us because the cultures that shape us do not wait for us to understand them before they mutate, before they take new shapes. This book is an attempt to chronicle one aspect of the evolution of reggae as a fundamental and defining phenomenon in Caribbean society. I present myself as a product of reggae, and it is with the confidence born of knowing this that I present this discussion of the reggae aesthetic: this Natural Mysticism.

So, in constructing an aesthetic, I start from the assumption that reggae cannot be approached simply as a musical form that can be examined in isolation from the social and historical realities that give it shape. Reggae is a cultural phenomenon that is rooted in a spiritual and ideological context which has shaped not simply the way in which singers sing or musicians make music but the way in which people talk, the way artists paint, the way dancers dance, the way Jamaicans see the world, and the way the world sees Jamaicans and Jamaica. This expansive conception of the reggae aesthetic must be appreciated if my discussion of the literature that has emerged out of a reggae-influenced culture is to be fully grasped.

I make use of four basic levels of analysis in this discussion. On the first level is the nature of the overarching ideology of the reggae aesthetic. This relates to issues of mythology, cosmology, and the extensive historiographical concerns of the music. Here the influence of Rastafarianism on reggae is given brief but particular attention. This ideological framing of the music is critical to understanding reggae's own shape and identity and in recognising that its influences on other art forms are not merely formal, but exist at the level of its broader discourse. Second, I am concerned with issues of language use since it is the political and formal use of language in reggae that has had the most telling influence on the art of the region. Third, there is the question of the topics or themes of reggae music. Reggae is characterised by a real diversity in the themes it explores, a complexity which is significant in shaping the aesthetic values of the artists who have been influenced by the music. However, it is particularly in the manner in which diverse themes are handled that we begin to see the distinctive quality of the music. Fourth, there is the level of form – the way in which the formal dimensions of reggae can be seen to offer models of formal expression and to have had an impact on the structure of other art forms that have been influenced by the music. This study of form includes a look at the internal structure of the music and the dance patterns that emerge from it.

IDEOLOGY/DISCOURSE/THEME

As early as the 1930s, Caribbean artists were speaking of the need to turn to the folk, to the working-class environment, to find the heart of a nationalistic ideology. This was an expression both of the sense of alienation felt by the middle and upper-class Caribbean artists in relation to the large mass of the population, and of their recognition that it was amongst these people that the most distinctively Caribbean culture and social ideology was to be found. Writers such as Claude McKay, Roger Mais and George Campbell, and artists such as Edna Manley, all in some way sought to turn to this cultural richness to find the language and the aesthetic grounding for their work. However, the work that emerged reflected a pattern whereby middle-class and upper-class artists sought to represent the working-class society, to try and speak on its behalf in a language which manifestly did not emerge from that group. Kamau Brathwaite quotes George Campbell as an example of this instinct in early Caribbean writing:

> We want to identify ourselves with
> Our people; come close to them and they
> Come close to us. People how goeth your

World? Know you with pride in understanding
Or are there hard words in the dark: are you
Formless dust blown in the wind?[8]

Campbell's expression of his desire to draw closer to the people
speaks powerfully of his sense of distance from that group as a privileged
middle-class individual. Most tellingly, in expressing his desire to
find areas of connection and commonality, he reveals his uncertainty
and ambivalence about whether there is anything important to discover.
Reggae completely usurps the power dynamic expressed in this
discourse for it did not emerge as a discovery of the middle-class
but simply established its own terms of value and meaning. The
middle-class individual had to come to reggae and discover her/
his place in the new paradigm. In this way, reggae's assumption of
a Jamaican sensibility, a distinctive voice represents an important
shift in the manner in which cultural identity and cultural value
are defined. Thus the working-class grounding of reggae offered
the emerging artists of the 1970s a sense of nation and a discourse
that was cohesive and self-confident. The value of this shift in paradigms
is not simply, as some would argue, a vindication of a Marxist model
of social liberation (even though this helped to establish a connection
between the middle-class and working-class communities in Jamaica
in the 1970s), but as a paradigm that finally offers the Caribbean a
sense of a realised national sensibility, and one so assured that it
allows for the exploration of other sensibilities without threatening
the viability of the emerging aesthetic.

Emerging as it does from a working-class milieu, reggae is grounded
in the history of working-class black Jamaican ideologies that have
carried across the centuries from Africa through the complicated
cauldron of Caribbean society. Early ska music was clearly shaped
by an attempt to render in song the folk idioms, the proverbs, the
social concerns and the ideological preoccupations of the working-
class community. Thus it is important to understand that reggae
emerges primarily as a music that speaks in the voice of the working-
class community, that speaks first to that community and only then
outside of the community. This makes it quite distinctive from the
imaginative literature which came out of the Caribbean in the first
half of this century, which has been primarily preoccupied with
addressing the western world. Even when efforts were made to speak
of the local environment, the compelling power of a publishing world
situated outside the Caribbean made it almost inevitable that the

paradigm that shaped the work of artists before the arrival of reggae was that of the marginalised individual speaking to the centre. In radically redefining the power dynamics, reggae transformed that model. Built on a very local industry aimed at addressing and selling to the local community, reggae, like ska, and unlike much of the literature, broke away from the economy and philosophy of the plantation society – a cash-crop economy that defines itself primarily in relationship to the dominant colonial or imperial power.[9] This fact represents a shift in the way art is defined and understood and it inevitably affects the language of artistic expression and its sense of confidence and self-assurance.

The emergence of Jamaican Nation Language as the language of artistic expression represents a further crucial development. For the Caribbean writer, finding the language with which to describe experience has always related to the question of the relationship between standard English and the language spoken by the majority of the people. In reggae, the language is almost inevitably and unselfconsciously rooted in the language of the majority. The use of this language naturally affects the cosmological basis of discourse. The fact that reggae from its beginnings articulated complex and varied ideas and emotions in the language of the society inevitably began to affect the way writers regarded language. Prior to the 1960s, dialect or Nation Language was invariably used in quite limited ways. It was most often used in comic sequences, in dialogue and in passages that were very clearly defined as 'character-driven'. In other words, as long as the internal monologue of most writers was in standard English, the implication was that the dialect voice was regarded as inadequate to the needs of philosophical or contemplative discourse. Most importantly, the dominant narrative voice was almost invariably in standard English and so it remained the central negotiator of meaning in these works. There were a few exceptions to this pattern, but even these remained fixed in the pattern of treating the nation language as a language of character and dialogue. Thus in Vic Reid's *New Day*[10], an important work published in 1949, a great deal of the narrative is presented in dialect, but the narrative is in the first person and belongs to a clearly defined character. It is not until Sam Selvon's novel *The Lonely Londoners* (1952) that we begin to observe a West Indian writer trying to explore the use of Nation Language as the language of narrative discourse. But these are isolated examples, and even the poetry (with few exceptions[11]) maintained this pattern. Reggae decisively established a new paradigm.

The Rastafarian role in reggae adds another dimension to the issue of language use, for one of the central characteristics of Rasta-talk is its improvisational quality, which leads to a sometimes deeply complex secret language that is at once confounding even as it is inventive. Rasta speech is particularly adept at word-play, motivated by the desire to usurp the discourse of western society and the language of the 'oppressor'. Thus the transformation of standard English words to correspond with the Rastafarian's literal rendering of language amounts to a very important ideological trope.[12] Thus 'oppressor' becomes 'downpressor' and 'understand' becomes 'overstand' – coinages and puns that seek to argue that language and the control of that language is central to the process of decolonisation and the liberation of an oppressed society. This philosophical dynamic reveals itself in reggae music in most profound ways, for in the language of the deejays, toasters and song writers, language is treated as a weapon of liberation. The use of Jamaican Nation Language in its most inscrutable forms often represented a defiant articulation of the intention of the reggae artist to speak to the people of Jamaica first and the rest of the world next. This presented a situation in which the music was far less easy to appropriate by outsiders, where the terms of engagement were defined by the reggae artist. Above all, however, the reggae lyric, the eloquent and innovative poetic articulations of some of the best reggae artists, gave the Caribbean writer a sense of possibility in the nation language that had not existed before.

Reggae's inextricable connection with Rastafarian discourse also added the dimension of a fully realised sense of aesthetics that speaks to a localised community. Rastafarianism represents a fundamental break with traditional and conventional Judaeo-Christianity. It redefines the meaning of deity and recasts the figure of God in terms that are antithetical to colonial representations of the Christian godhead. By establishing a god in Haile Selassie, Rastafarianism breaks away from the patterns of conventional Christianity that operate in Jamaica, and brings into being a new and very elaborate series of modern myths. Rastafarianism, however, also refashions a complex of myths that are based on Judaeo-Christian texts (the Bible) and radically reinterprets them. This creation of myth is further complicated by the fact that Rastafarianism is as much a strongly political entity as it is a spiritual entity. The language of social transformation, of revolution, is contained within the apocalyptic vision of a grand Armageddon complete with a very clear moral understanding of the universe – one that places the Rastafarian and rasta spirituality at its centre. This lends to reggae a defiant but complex mythology and offers the reggae-influenced artist an approach to art that allows for a dialogue between the political and spiritual. Essentially, this quality in reggae defies the binarism that characterises much of modern western discourse and takes the art back to a multi-dimensionality that is akin to the discourse of African cosmology. Further, by locating Africa as a spiritual homeland for the Caribbean person, as a place of hope and possibility, Rastafarianism presents a mythological shift in the Caribbean person's relationship with Africa. This is very important for it both redefines the terms in which our history is approached and represents a defiant critique of western historical practice. It does this not simply by attacking it and questioning it, but by replacing it with another mythological framework.[13]

Rastafarianism is uniquely Jamaican, and it is this above all else which has determined that reggae is not a Jamaican version of African American music, significant as the influences have been. Reggae and Soul music have two quite distinct ideological bases in Rastafarianism and the African American Black Power movement. These two entities differ in some fundamental ways. Primarily, Rastafarianism is a religion, a belief system rooted in a folk sensibility that plants its social and political discourse, concerning the position of the Jamaican urban black, within a mythic framework that demands a metaphysical reckoning in its construction and apprehension. This fact should not be underestimated.

This focus on history and on race within the Rastafarian ethos is another important shaper of the reggae aesthetic. It has enabled history not only to become accessible to, but defining for the working-class Caribbean person. This embrace of history, particularly in using it to help define the present, is central to reggae and it offers a crucial aesthetic direction. The lyrics of many reggae artists explore the relationship between history and the present, an exploration that frequently redefines both past and present in a radical act of reinterpretation. The very act of retelling history is also important because it brings to the fore the nature of the artist's role, her/his philosophical position in society. In this way, the reggae artist becomes a figure of some importance in Jamaican society, with a symbolic role in the shaping of that society. This represents one of the most important ideological features of the reggae aesthetic.

In the world of reggae in general, there were a number of important and influential individuals such as Mortimer Planno and Count Ossie of the Mystic Revelation of Rastafari[14] who lent a philosophical and ideological groundedness to a host of young and impressionable artists. The Rastafarian association with the ghetto, with working class realities and its fundamental celebration of Black identity made it not simply appealing to reggae musicians, who in the main came from the same environment, but in many cases absolutely necessary for their sense of worth and survival. Within the ghetto community, the Rasta was a leader whose ideas privileged a male-centred sense of self. These factors and their association with such working-class heroes as Marcus Garvey and Claudius Henry gave the Rastafarians status and authority.[15] Rastafarian ideology provided a clear and appealing cosmology for the reggae artist, with highly metaphorical, frequently poetic discourse which fed easily into a working class Jamaican discourse that was already rich in proverbial and Biblical resonance. Rastafarian elders such as Count Ossie and Mortimer Planno also fed into reggae (and before it in Prince Buster's recording of 'Oh Carolina'[16] back in 1959) the African-centred traditions of burru and kette drumming, which can be heard on such Lee Perry tracks as 'Cool and Easy' and 'Well Dread' on *Africa's Blood* (1973)[17], in the music of Ras Michael and the Sons of Negus (*Rastafari* and *Kibir Am Lak*)[18] and of course in Count Ossie's own recordings, *Grounation* and *Tales of Mozambique[19]*). All this provided reggae musicians with a distinctive aesthetic resource which lent weight and force to their music. Perhaps, this pattern is most eloquently demonstrated in the Wailers' song 'Selassie Is the Chapel', which is a version of the sentimental country and western song 'Crying in the Chapel'. The Wailer's version, whose lyrics were written by Mortimer Planno, has soaring vocal lines rooted in a heavy but spacey bedrock of Rastafarian drumming, and is a telling example of the transforming force of Rastafarian philosophy and aesthetic resources on North American musical styles and Christian doctrine.[20]

I present an image of the reggae artist who is both *of* the community and speaking *for* and *to* it and who is also a prophetic figure who sometimes challenges the community from a position of isolation – the isolation of the prophet with an uncomfortable message to give. As such the reggae artist has a role which is at once public and private. The reggae audience lends this range to the artist for it understands the prophet to be both a part of the society and apart from it. But the artist is still reliant on the society for her or his identity and must have the society's permission to exist and function. This dialectic leads to the possibility of the artist being both inclined towards social activism and social commentary as well as to a lyrical engagement with the self, but all negotiated within a dynamic relationship between the artist and the community. Since reggae is also a commodity, very directly answerable to the market force of popular consumption, the reggae artist is forced to be relevant (and entertaining), though this commercial imperative works hand-in-hand with the Rastafarian-derived ideological imperative that the reggae artist functions as, at some level, a moral conscience for society. It should also be remembered that in the 1970s, at least, the economics of record production and distribution was such that it was possible for reggae artists to self-finance the production of their records. The highly influential and spiritually motivated records (in pressings numbered in only a couple of hundreds) of Yabby You (Vivian Jackson) emerged in this way, aided by the fact that leading session musicians such as the late Tommy McCook played for free on them.[21]

I also present the reggae artist as a trickster figure whose distinction lies in a fascinating play with madness and difference. There are a number of very important reggae artists, Lee 'Scratch' Perry in particular, who function in that realm and whose work is seen as maverick, daring and deeply innovative – postmodern in every sense. Such artists are part of the reggae fabric and their presence there is important to the understanding of the reggae aesthetic, for it reveals the extent to which the aesthetic is constantly challenging itself and the extent to which it is open to experimentation and exploration. Again, as with the prophet figure, the community 'owns' such madmen, these trickster, anancy-like antiheroes, and treats them as necessary figures in the social fabric. The trickster figure is an important one for she/he speaks to the relationship between the established order and the working class community – the largely black and disenfranchised people of Caribbean society. Reggae's artists stand as folk figures in the manner of such slave rebels, black rebel leaders and Maroon warriors as Cudjoe, Nanny, Sam Sharpe, Paul Bogle, and Tacky, all celebrated as much for their trickster qualities, their capacity to dupe the white slaveholder or dominant oppressing class, as for their capacities as warrior figures.[22] This sense of the underdog fighting against powerful dominating forces is elemental to the reggae paradigm, for reggae is always situated in the position of the rebel figure, the figure seeking to break free from oppression. But the aesthetic is most affected by the manner of the rebellion: the capacity to use language, discourse and varied forms of posturing to defeat the oppressor figure. The reggae-influenced artist, then, is able to assume a range of postures that will make it at least possible for her/him to survive in an alien and dangerous environment.

But the reggae artist is not to be defined at all times by a strident seriousness, for reggae's social commentary can be absolutely and comically trivial. In this respect, the reggae community is best understood as a village in which the passing on of news and comment is an important act of social solidarity regardless of what its theme or significance might be. The role of the reggae artist as humorist is quite common and offers the writer another dimension to the aesthetic that is not entirely rooted in the fire and brimstone discourse of apocalyptic prophecy.[23] In this vein, too, is the position of the reggae artist as a lover, as a composer of love lyrics that are intended to seduce and to titillate. This is another crucial dimension of reggae, because in the very act of making music that speaks of sexuality and romance, the reggae artist is very significantly redefining the discourse of sexuality along lines that are in keeping with the society in which she/he lives. The reggae love lyric works against the imported modes of romantic expression that have operated in colonised societies for years, modes that are distant from the realities of that community. It is a situation which has left the Caribbean writer with feelings of insecurity about writing about sexuality in ways that are reflexive of her or his experience. Reggae has redefined the conceptions of love and sexuality in ways that can be said to have profoundly transformed the way sexual behaviour is perceived in our society, and even changed the actual modes of behaviour in the Caribbean in the last few decades.[24]

This multiplicity of postures for the artist is critical to the reggae aesthetic. This gives it multidimensionality as a form which defies limiting binary structures and allows for the simultaneous evocation of diverse emotions and ideas within the same artistic statement. In reggae, the profane and the sacred may appear in the same lyric.

The place of dance within reggae is another powerful manifestation of this multidimensionality. The reggae dance, in its many incarnations, can be sensual and sexually explicit, but this kind of dancing can be and is performed to songs that may be celebrating spirituality or espousing revolutionary ideas. There is no contradiction here, but simply a reflection of the Jamaican psyche that allows for these seemingly disparate entities to function within the same moment. Dialectic rather than dualism, then, is elemental to the reggae psyche and to the aesthetic that emerges from it.

It is as part of its ideological complexity that reggae's capacity to draw from other musical forms must be understood. At its core, reggae is distinctive, but it is also able, because of this distinctiveness, to echo and reinterpret other musical forms without in any way compromising its character. This is perhaps the most telling argument for the existence of a reggae aesthetic. Reggae is constantly reinterpreting the work of other musicians, just as it is constantly feeding the stylings of other musical traditions. This it does in a way that suggests that the formal character of the music, coupled with some of the ideological and discursive qualities discussed above, represents a very coherent series of principles and aesthetic values.

Finally, reggae is associated with a certain posture, the expression of an attitude towards the world. This, in many ways, has determined the extent to which reggae has been treated as an aesthetic grounding for other art forms. Reggae's international success came, in part, as the result of a certain arrogance and self-assured sense of mission. Reggae artists were not burdened with self-doubt about the validity and viability of the music they were producing. They knew it was not a music that emerged by accident, but through serious experimentation and hard work. They embraced the notion of international importance without feeling unduly intimidated by the size of their nation, a feeling that was almost certainly encouraged by the strong Rastafarian influence. Rastafarians have no doubt that Jamaica is important because it was in Jamaica that the divinity of Selassie was revealed. This confidence became self-sustaining as the international popularity of Toots and the Maytals, Bob Marley, Peter Tosh, Burning Spear, and more recently Shabba Ranks, Patra, Buju Banton, Luciano and others has fed back into the reggae community a sense of its own importance and a belief in the portability of the art that it produces, regardless of where they are.

FORM

Reggae's distinctive formal qualities are important in the construction of an aesthetic for it is through an examination and understanding of its formal dynamics that we can begin to explore the application of the aesthetic to other art forms. What I offer here is hardly a comprehensive description, rather a highly condensed outlining of what I believe to be most important.

Reggae, as I have argued earlier, is an ensemble musical form that relies on the dialogue between a range of instruments in a way that does not give one instrument privilege over another. The layering – sometimes competing and rhythmically contradictory – patterns of reggae, accommodated within the same composition, is key to the multidimensionality of the music. Each instrument plays its own particular line, but is defined by its relationship to the larger composition. The key figure then in the reggae composition is the 'dub-organiser', the producer or the mixing-board engineer who will take all the elements of the song and arrange them in a manner that allows for the strong grounding of the drum and bass while the lead voice or instrument carries the narrative thread. It is in the manner in which spaces are filled and left open that the special character of reggae is realised. Reggae has an unique syncopation that privileges the offbeat, and it is in this hiccup, this slight off-kilter rhythm that the bop in reggae is located. It is a rhythmic quality that affects the whole music, though within a careful dialogue between the melodic and the percussive. The bass is usually repetitive and melodic – one of the most dominant features of the music – for without the grounding of the bass, the music falls apart. Similarly, the drum is the signature which lends the music its strong African character, its links with the Rastafarian ethos. The absolute importance of drum and bass is revealed in the way that most of the significant innovations in reggae (which have nearly always been to do with rhythmic change) have been driven by drum and bass teams such as Aston and Carlton Barrett, Sly (Dunbar) and Robbie (Shakespeare) and more recently Steely and Clevie. The other instruments, which range from guitars, organs, horns, harmonicas, melodicas, to violins, pianos, traditional drums, flutes – literally any other instrument – find their way into and around the spaces created by the drum and bass. The reggae band on stage marks its credentials in the way that this 'dub-scape' is created without a cacophony of sounds battling each other for space.

The reggae composition is structured around a circular, non-linear pattern that stands in clear contrast to the more climactic patterns of rock music for instance. The reggae composition is almost always consistently moderated in tempo and intensity throughout its entirety. The result is a music that makes for excellent dancing with its consistency of rhythm, one that has a certain hypnotic quality. The absence of a dynamic of climax suggests an ethos that is rooted in the notion of continuity. The reggae song fades out in recordings because it is designed to continue to ride the same rhythm for as long as possible. This does not mean that the music lacks variety in texture, but the projection is circular and not linear. The manner in which this affects the application of reggae to aesthetic principles is something that I will return to later, but it should be clear that the possibilities are quite interesting for narrative structure and narrative meaning.

Variation in reggae therefore takes place within the framework of the drum and bass. On top of this assured base, reggae can be extremely flexible. Indeed, the patterns of reggae are often established by silence and not sound. The listener is aware of the rhythm for it has been established early in the track, and so when it is pulled out, the listener is still hearing it despite what is going on above. The creative game is to explore how long that invisible, silent throb can sustain itself despite the improvisations that are taking place above it. Indeed, this game with absence is an integral and almost expected part in many of the dub arrangements that accompanied regular forty-fives. The tangible absence of drum and bass is like the sensation of feeling in the amputee's absent limb, and, correspondingly, the re-arrival of the rhythm section amounts to a moment of relief and a signal to throw oneself into the earth-centred throes of dancing.[25] The often repetitive sound of the bass might appear to be monotonous, but in the throes of what becomes a spiritual dynamic, the repeated sound gains in dimensionality, for the listener, the dancer, is looking for spaces, is looking for ways to make the body cleave to this sound until there is a submerging of the listener/dancer in the sound as the reggae pulses to the body's internal beats.

The experimentation within that framework can be highly complex as artists such as King Tubby and Lee 'Scratch' Perry have demonstrated with their distinctly postmodernist experimentations in the studio.[26] Here the dub-organiser is self-reflexive in his borrowing of samples from a complex range of sound worlds to create a new and dynamic soundscape. The postmodern patterns are reflected in the centrality of technology in the creating of the music and the melding of sensibilities which are both national and international within a single musical composition. Reggae nationalism cannot be defined by any recourse to culturally essentialist explanations but by the central vision of the artist who takes in a range of styles and voices and distils them into a singular vision. Thus, while the community's embrace and acceptance of the music is critical to reggae's success, the community relies on the artist, the innovator to stretch the limits of the music and to bring fresh and innovative stylings to challenge its sense of meaning and identity. Perry frequently speaks of his willingness to drag into the reggae composition a range of musical styles not normally associated with reggae.[27] The sampling of sounds on top of a reggae bed-track leads to an aesthetic model that is at once conventional and yet deeply innovative. This dialectical image speaks of reggae's capacity to embrace multiple ideas and forms without necessarily compromising its fundamental ethos. Within that ethos, reggae is textured and sometimes mutated by these influences, and this is perhaps what lends the music its constant capacity to reinvent itself. While the casual listener might wonder whether some of the recent, sparsely instrumented ragga actually is reggae (or at least reggae as defined by the roots reggae of the 1970s), the capacity of recent ragga albums such as Buju Banton's *Inna Heights* (1997) or Anthony B's *Universal Struggle* (1998)[28] to incorporate both ska and roots reggae within utterly contemporary arrangements reinforces my thesis that there is a fundamental aesthetic which persists through such changes.

While reggae has not introduced any really new instruments to the musical world (as, for instance, did steel pan music), it does introduce new ways of playing instruments and its experiments with new hierarchies of sound can be seen to have altered the way in which popular music throughout the world has developed in the last thirty years. For instance, the reggae bass with its strong yet involved melodic lines that run in circles through the composition, coupled with the invariably low-ended mixing of the bass, has come to affect the bass work of many African American artists in the last few years. Reggae's bass is almost always married to a lead guitar played with a muted, ticking tone that closely follows the bass-line, offering the muffled bass an edge that helps to define it.[29] But this muted guitar lead also plays varied harmonies with the bass, thus complicating the bass sound. The organ frequently functions as a rhythm instrument and as a kind of subterranean bubbling sound that rumbles below the whole composition. The syncopation of the keyboard work is largely an inversion of the way the left and right hands work in conventional western musical patterns. So while reggae's instrumentation uses the tools of western culture, they have been adapted to speak the language of the people making the music, to the extent that some of the variations render the instruments almost unrecognisable to the uninformed ear.

While I have stressed the collective quality of the reggae sound, instrumental solos do occur, but they are always very firmly integrated within the whole. If you listen to some of the best instrumental solos in reggae, you will hear a profoundly melodic and almost vocal counterpoint to the repetitive structure of the drum and bass. Cat

Coore's solo on '96 Degrees in the Shade' is an eloquent example, as is the violin obligato on Justin Hinds 'Sinners'[30]. Here the delicate melody line functions as a plaintive lyric, a blues-like lament which reflects the pathos inherent in the song. It counterpoints the aggressive sounds of drum and bass, for in the act of memory there is the threat of revolutionary action. This kind of counterpoint owes its presence in reggae music to the pioneering soloing style of the great trombonist, Don Drummond, during the days of ska. Drummond's signature was a laconic, easy-tempoed voice that was plaintive, jazz and blues-tinged, but also heavily soaked in the music of the black churches and the lamenting strains of much Jamaican folk music. This strikingly introspective lament was always in counterpoint to the frenetic energy of the ska back-beat. The ska solo was the thematic core of the ska tune. Drummond's most characteristic recordings, such as 'Green Island', 'Schooling the Duke' and 'Addis Ababa' were almost always instrumentals which demanded the lyrical interpretation of theme by the soloists.[31] Thus, while the rhythm section held the tempo, tumbling along with an energetic and dangerous pace and drive, the soloist settled above the fray and spoke, sang, lamented, and considered. This pattern has continued into reggae, the solo almost always functioning as a comment, as a reflective interpretation of theme. Thus the guitar/keyboard solo in 'Concrete Jungle' is completely and appropriately blue; the trombone solo in Linton Kwesi Johnson's 'The Anfinished Revalueshan'[32] (which echoes with uncanny effectiveness, the solos of Don Drummond in 'Eastern Standard Time'[33]), has distinctively varied phrasing, an interplay between long drawn out notes and the sharp bursts that replicate the timekeeping rhythm-guitar licks; and Lucky Dube's 'Trinity' has a clever dialogue between violin and guitar.[34] What reggae offers these solo voices is not simply space, but a dialogue between assertion and reflection that encourages variations in texture and shape for the soloist.

But unlike the rock or modern jazz solo, the reggae solo never entirely dominates the track. It is a variation on a theme, but it is the bed-track, recognisable and defining in its shape and tempo, which always dominates. This is what has made some rock artists very unsuited for the reggae ethos, for the rock guitar is an assertive egotistical force that is reluctant to remain submissive to the rhythm section. In most of Marley's compositions, and especially in his live performances, the solo is rarely in the foreground as it is in blues or in jazz. Indeed, what the organist or guitarist or horn player does in reggae, in tiny soloing moments, can best be described as variations on the rhythm track. These subtle variations layer over each other to create a complex of ensemble sounds with a powerful and cohesive effect. The instrumentation of reggae is about being part of a larger picture and trying to determine where the particular instrument or voice best situates itself. The well-seasoned reggae band, well practised in the common arrangement cues, often performs what seem to be fairly involved arrangements on stage that are in fact improvised.

The reggae lyric is also characterised by formal patterns that are a key element of the aesthetic. There are a variety of forms which relate to the variety of postures adopted by the reggae artist, but consistent within this variety of lyric form is a dialogue between the artist and the audience. The artist speaks to the community and assumes the community and as a result the language of the lyric reflects shared values and a shared discourse. The call and response pattern of reggae, with the backup vocals functioning as the response to the lead singer's call, enacts that relationship between artist and community and no doubt has its roots in the call and response patterns of West African music.[35] There are times when the reggae lyric takes the form of a prayer or a psalm that has a close resemblance to the Judaic psalms of the bible. There the lyric speaks to God, often on behalf of the community. At times the lyric is directed at an assumed audience (the generalised oppressor) or to a symbolic person who represents a particular group. Thus, Gregory Isaacs' 'Mr. Brown'[36] speaks from a black sufferer's perspective to a representative figure of the brown middle classes. In other instances, the lyric is largely self-reflexive and represents an overheard internal monologue. Storytelling is crucial to the reggae lyric. Many of the lyrics of Bob Marley function as parabolic lessons that begin with a narrative and culminate in a homily of sorts. There are love songs that represent a private dialogue between an individual and her or his lover. These pieces often function as communal celebrations of love but maintain the privacy of lyrical verse to ensure that the erotic or romantic character of the work is sustained.

The range of genres within the reggae lyric is, indeed, almost limitless, including, for instance, the praise poem[37], the warrior poem[38], the exhortation poem[39], the social commentary poem[40], the insult poem[41], the boasting poem[42], the blues lamentation[43] the celebration of music[44], the dance instruction piece[45], and the lesson in history[46]. But in all these genres the overriding pattern is of a dialogue between the community and the artist. Thus, even when the artist is being self-reflexive and exploring seemingly private constructions, there is always an awareness of audience and of the artistic form that is being used. Reggae is not a purely private vehicle for poetic expression, but a public one. The private is negotiated in that environment through the use of metaphor, simile, and other figurative devices.

From the days of the ska songs of the 1960s, the popular music of Jamaica has used folk idioms to describe the artist's world, the use of proverbs, sayings, riddles, current street slang and biblical verses serving as signature patterns of poetic expression. The songs of Justin Hinds and the Dominoes contain excellent examples of this pattern.[47] An important and sometimes undervalued feature of the reggae formal pattern derives from the Christian church music of the revivalist and African-centred churches of the black working-class. Much of ska was founded on such patterns, with songs of political and social commentary that borrowed the discourse, melodies and formal structure of these gospel songs. The entry of Rastafarian ideologies into popular music further reinforced this pattern because Rastafarian songs themselves were frequently modelled on the music of the revivalist churches, though with a translation of the name of the deity and other lexical items into the language of Rastafarianism. It is no accident that artists such as Bob Marley, Peter Tosh, and Toots Hibbert of the Maytals all had strong gospel or Christian roots and produced music that reflected that connection.[48] The impassioned styling of this revivalist-influenced music, coupled with its strong Afrocentric syncopations, were powerful influences on reggae composition and arrangement. In later incarnations of reggae, the revivalist patterns of drumming and trumping have had significant effects on the dancehall and ragga music of the last fifteen years. There are strong elements of the African-centred Pocomania cult in some current dancehall music, which makes use of rapid and non-Rastafarian drumming patterns associated with revivalist and kumina drumming. Reggae constantly seeks to ground itself in the culture and values of the folk and working-class milieu of Jamaican society. This willingness to translate the rhythms, lyrical patterns, and motifs of rural folk experience into what is predominantly an urban form represents an important characteristic of reggae. In this respect, reggae musicians reveal themselves to be interested in speaking for the whole of their society, in creating a discourse which links rural and urban, Caribbean past and Caribbean present.

Any discussion of the formal patterns of reggae must also include a look at the dance stylings that reggae has spawned over the years, for these represent important indications of the way that reggae has interpreted and expressed a dialogue between the body and the mind, the sensual and the spiritual, as well as exploring the metaphorical relationships between the individual human body and the body politic.

Dance is the way in which the listener actively participates in the reggae performance. Albert Murray, in talking about African American song and story, points to the role of the listener (in the blues) and the reader/hearer (in storytelling) as adding to the composition by a physical and psychic involvement in the performance. His concept is very much applicable to the reggae track for the listener/dancer assumes the role of an instrumental soloist when the dub track is being played. Indeed, the instinct to deejay or to scat, or to sing improvisationally over a reggae bed-track points to the participatory dynamic of the music.

It is a dialogue and interaction about which the reggae artist is intensely aware. From its beginnings in ska, reggae has 'worked' on the listener as dancer. For instance, the great ska trombonist Don Drummond would force the listener to be simultaneously engaged in the energising force of dancing and in deep recollection and reflection. In many ways, this dialogue helped to define ska music and the way it was received. It was also ska's most essential influence on reggae. In the context of Jamaican society, dancing is not simply an act of recreation, but a statement, an articulation of reality. If it suggests flight and escape, then it is flight and escape from a very realised pain. Reggae goes further than ska in not allowing the frenzied madness of escape without an act of consideration. Reggae is so carefully tempered that the dancer must consider each posture, each move, and each such move articulates something about him or her.

Dance has always been central to reggae, and particular styles have come and gone in the same way that dance crazes have entered American culture with each new musical innovation. But there remains a fundamental reggae dance-step that has remained constant over the years. All reggae dance represents a dialogue with that basic movement which is the skank – a kind of offbeat walking on the spot that requires very limited movement and exertion and is so generic that it allows for multiple variations according to mood and context. The skank is hip-centred, but the extent to which the hips gyrate depends on the nature of the interpretation of a given song. The skank manifests a 'dread' articulation of the individual's walk through society, and the manner in which the individual dancer varies and alters arm movements, facial expression (cool blankness or the screw-face scowl), the emphasis of stepping, the height and depth of her/his bop, and the extent to which the hips gyrate speaks volumes about what the dance seeks to communicate. This sometimes self-involved movement is a lyrical expression of posturing, or what Henry Louis Gates has called 'signifying'[49]. I use the word 'posturing in the sense of an acting out of a created role rather than with any connotation of insincerity. The skank can be at once a solo movement and a duet. It has evolved into a variety of related moves which have surfaced over the years. They include the Eastman skank, Water Pumpy, Cripple, S90, and so on. In each of these, the body becomes the vehicle for the metaphorical interpretation of the music and the 'body politic'. The body contains in it the history of a society and its connections to a past of hybrid influences. Reggae dance styles are much more than the fashions of a particular era, rather they are definitions of the way the body interprets society's changes. Much of reggae dancing is founded on folk-dance patterns such as are found in the dinkie mini, kumina, brukkins, revivalist trumping, and so on. The strong pelvic-centred movements owe their presence to the African retentions in the Jamaican psyche and the Jamaican body. Further, reggae's more erotic elements are particularly defined through dance and the way in which, through dance, sexuality is enacted in the public and private forum. The most recent dancehall incarnations have transformed the rub-a-dub of the 1970s and 1980s into dance moves such as the bogle and the butterfly, which are both explicitly sexual in their orientation, and yet also represent other elements of the complex mix of history and sexuality that characterises Jamaican dance. The bogle is named after the national hero Paul Bogle, and the dip and sway action is reminiscent of the limbo, dance associated with slaves being exercised on the decks of the slavers while crossing the Atlantic. The bogle involves the use of very expressive hands that point and communicate, making statements of danger, aggression and embrace. Here, then, even a largely sexual dance begins to have other dimensions, all of which are possible in the same poetic space. Within the aesthetics of reggae, the politics of gender and sexuality are not necessarily divorced from the politics of society.

While this notion of posturing has been explored effectively in the Rhygin/Ivan figure in the film of *The Harder They Come*, and in Trinidadian Earl Lovelace's portrayal of the bad-john figure in *The Dragon Can't Dance*, in the context of Jamaican writing the profundities of this posture/dance phenomenon are yet to be plumbed by our novelists and playwrights.

In the deeply violent and sometimes sadistic edge of some ragga, we encounter another element of the reggae sensibility that affects its aesthetic form. The rude bwoy sensibility has evolved into the almost anarchic and destructive world of the 'gun-talk' of recent dancehall expression[51], and the laconic sensimilla pace of 1970s reggae gave way to the more frenetic and cocaine-fuelled rapidity and convulsion of 1980s and 1990s Jamaica. It is a pattern akin to gangsta rap, though one which has its own roots, predating gangsta rap, in the rude bwoy music of the late 1960s and early 1970s. (Listen to the Trojan compilation *Rudies All Round*.) Here the dance moves are shaped by the posturing of gun-toting criminal types. The gestures of gun salutes and the dance moves that reveal a macho 'gun-in-the-waistband' pantomime indicate how the aesthetic must be seen to include this deeply disturbing discourse of violence, one which reflects the actual violence of the political and cocaine wars that have exacted such a heavy toll in Kingston. Yet this articulation of violence cannot be kept separate from another formal characteristic of the reggae sensibility, which is the urge to explore the strange humour of Jamaican society. This is a pattern of 'taking serious t'ing mek joke', the pattern, perhaps developed during slavery, of making a mockery of the pains of living as a way of coping. Thus the gun-talk of dancehall culture is notorious for taking profoundly disturbing ideas and rendering them with wit, using inventive metaphor and imaginative language coinages which seduce the listener into laughter and enjoyment of what is, in reality, the description of sordid violence. This pattern of using inventive and entertaining language play to draw the listener into complicity is one that artists such as Marley and Tosh used to make the most cutting social commentary. It is all contained in the lines 'one good thing about reggae music/ when it hit you feel no pain'. But it does hit. It is central to reggae's form: a seductive, danceable and seemingly benign form that carries a deadly and deeply serious articulation of truth and meaning. Reggae believes in the entertainment value of art, but it does not create a dichotomy between entertainment and social or political commentary. This quality is crucial to the formal character of the music and consequently to the reggae aesthetic.

CHAPTER FIVE

THE REGGAE LYRIC:

A LITERARY MODEL

SOME TENTATIVE DEFINITIONS XIII

'Blow them the full watts tonight'

When the sound kicks in gear,
everything jumping,
the dance hall rocking,
that high hat shimmering,
the bass drum thumping,
and Mr. Bassy unfurls a cord
of spiraling sounds
causing the bodies to spin
like tops unleashed,
what else to do but dance.

And when the brilliant strike
of the guitar licks
like sparkle and tinsel
and the knife blade's edge—
impious, peevish, obstinate,
yet whimsical, and seductive—
straighten the back,
cause the heart to look
to see where it is coming from
this sound, this sound
what else to do but dance.

There is a casket of light at the edge of the garden
that glimmers with the possibility of better times.
From far, it shimmers bright, like the familiar sound of the guitar:
chekeh   chekeh   chekeh   chekeh   chekeh   chekeh

In many ways, Jamaica at large began to understand the history of slavery, oppression, and the connection to Africa through reggae music. Of course, for many Jamaicans, Africa was always an important and proud heritage to be celebrated. The sense of pride in Africa assumed various forms ranging from the strong sense of memory and dignity contained in the Maroon culture, to the strong Afro-centric consciousness of leaders such as Paul Bogle and the Baptist preachers during the nineteenth century, to the highly explicit pan-Africanist ideology of Marcus Garvey in the 1920s and 1930s. In the nineteenth century there were a significant number of Jamaicans who travelled to Africa as Christian missionaries devoted to the task of winning their 'motherland' to the Christian faith. My paternal grandfather was one such missionary who travelled in the early part of this century to the coastal regions of Nigeria. Augustus Dawes was, from all the photographs that I have seen, a stolid black man with a passion for education and a venturesome spirit. It is hard to know if there was any sense of pan-Africanist passion in what led him to Nigeria with his wife, Laura, or whether it was wholly his zeal and faith in the Christian God, but I can't help imagining in him a profound affinity to Africa, one passed on to him through generations of free and enslaved blacks in Jamaica. My father was born in Wari, Nigeria, and so too were at least two of his siblings. I have seen photographs of my grandparents returning to Jamaica, posing proudly for the newspapers flanked by masks, shields, spears, and the pelts of wild animals; two people effectively suited in the Victorian rigidity of missionary attire while proudly declaring a connection to Africa. A few years ago, my eldest sister, Gwyneth, travelled with her mother to Nigeria. They lived there for eight years, and during that time, my sister managed to visit the town where our grandfather had lived and worked, the town of our father's birth in the Calabar region of Nigeria. The Dawes name was immediately recognised. There was a Dawes Island, and there were people still alive who had been educated by my grandparents. My sister attended the funeral of an elderly woman whose obituary included an extended tribute to our grandparents for their teaching, their generosity and their goodness. It is clear that Africa was a part of the consciousness of my family long before my father moved there in 1950 as a teacher, long before he met my mother, a Ghanaian, and long before I was born as a Jamaican/Ghanaian.

For some of the poorest Jamaicans, with little access to education and even less to travel, Africa remained a place of inner spiritual journey. Adherents to pocomania and other Afrocentric syncretic religious beliefs held to a fairly elaborate sense of connection to Africa that would eventually come to shape the thinking and practices of Rastafarians in the 1950s and 1960s. Kamau Brathwaite demonstrates this when he quotes from an interview with a woman called Queenie (or Kumina Queen) in *The Arrivants*. She describes her sense of history and heritage in a manner that suggests the spiritual connection with Africa has been a part of her own sense of self for as long as she can remember:

Well, muh ol' arrivance ... is from Africa... That's muh ol' arrivants family. Muh gran'muddah an' muh gran' fadda. Well, they came out here as slavely... you unnerstan'?

Well, when them came now, I doan belongs to Africa, I belongs to Jamaica. I born here.

Well, muh gran'parents, she teach me some of the African languages an' the rest I get it at the cotton-tree root ... I take twenty-one days to get all the balance...

So I just travel right up to hey, an' gradually come up, an' gradually come up, until I experience all about... the African set-up... [1]

What she learns is the centrality of Africa in her consciousness. But this awareness was not an acceptable middle-class preoccupation in a society so deeply fixated on the principles of lightness of skin as a sign of quality and darkness of skin as a sign of abjection. So while Africa has always been a part of the Jamaican consciousness, it was frequently a carefully submerged element. In addition, the dominance of British-derived cultural models of what constituted civilised society – models in which the construction of Africa was alien, exotic, and best forgotten – ensured that those who held to a view of Africa that was positive were either not heard or regarded as belonging to a not yet civilised underclass or misguided mavericks devoid of class or culture. It is clear that such views were not limited to the middle and upper-class, but permeated those sections of the working-classes who were seeking upward mobility and 'respectability'.

Compounded by such miseducation and ignorance, the place of Africa in the Jamaican psyche in the 1960s and 1970s was not a universally positive one. Derek Walcott's lament about being unable to reconcile his sense of split loyalty between the British heritage and the African heritage is made sophisticated by the facade of intelligence and the deceptive posture of being informed. In truth, the persona of Walcott's poem 'A Far Cry from Africa'[2] is deeply inscribed in colonial cultural norms, and his symbolisation of Mau-Mau (perceived through the screen of the colonial propaganda of atavistic savagery) is as ill-informed as the view of the average schoolchild of that period. Walcott's poem is, though, less about the politics of the Mau-Mau, than it is about his own anxieties about embracing a history that is so strongly associated in the canons of Western Literature with animist darkness.

Reggae challenged these notions in a direct and aggressive manner by constructing a rhetoric around the dignity of the black race and of Africa as a utopian heaven, a place of ultimate beauty and peace. In this process of myth-construction, there was an instinctive recognition that only the condensed power of myth could counter the malignancy of the other myths that prevailed about Africa. But this construction of Africa did not simply stop at viewing it as part of the Jamaican's past, or even as the ultimate spiritual home, but sought to trace the journey of the black person from Africa through to the present reality of poverty and struggle. This act of historical retrieval, the ownership of the slave past, and the declaration that rebellion was an appropriate response to that history – all this condensed in the declaration of Rastafarian faith – amounted to an decisively affirmative encounter with history. This affirmation distinguishes reggae and the fact that it speaks to modern Jamaican realities even as it recalls the past is what gives it such a potent immediacy.

What is not often recognised is that reggae's expression of this awareness of history is not uniformly one of outright anger and rebellious fire, but one that is textured and varied. The process of unearthing this history drew from reggae artists deep sorrow (Marley's 'Redemption Songs', Spear's 'Slavery Days'), calls to action (Marley's 'Catch a Fire', 'Revolution'), the sober recounting of the history to keep it in the imagination (Third World's 'Ninety Six Degrees in the Shade'), the revelatory analysis of contemporary events within the context of history (Steel Pulse's 'Klu-Klux Klan'[3]) and a range of other emotions. It has been a genuinely sophisticated encounter with the past. But it is perhaps in the way that reggae has conflated history with present realities that were part of everyday consciousness, expressing this in language which had the immediacy of the contemporary street, that gave so many reggae lyrics mythic weight.

Bob Marley's narrative in 'Burning and Looting' (*Burning*), illustrates this connection of the present with history with consummate skill:

> This morning I woke up in a curfew
> Oh God, I was a prisoner too
> Could not recognise the faces standing over me
> They were all dressed in uniforms of brutality
> Yes, how many rivers do we have to cross
> Before we can talk to the boss,
> all that we've got it seems we have lost
> We must have really paid the cost.

Beginning with the narrative of the very plausible personal experience of being caught in one of the many curfews that held Kingston in a vice during the 1970s, Marley is able, through the art of metaphor, to construct a larger narrative of the plight of the 'sufferer', the 'we' in the song. Thus the shift to the biblical allusion in 'rivers do we have to cross', opens the poetic construct in a psalm aimed at the people. This shift is signalled by the change in person, from the first person singular to the first person plural. The rivers are symbolic barriers to progress and they connect with the rivers that held up the progress of the children of Israel in their flight from slavery in Egypt. But the river is more – it is the huge expanse of the Atlantic that carried the Africans to the Caribbean; it is the water that the limbo dancer must weave his way under in burial and out of in resurrection ('limbo, limbo like me'). After the crossing of the river, the 'boss' who awaits could be both the grand divinity who is promised to the pilgrim and a metonym for the remoteness of the society's rulers, protected from the anger of the people by those in 'uniforms of brutality'. Then Marley uses a deeply-rooted idiomatic expression which looks back to slavery, concerning the ubiquitous presence of suffering in Black lives ('We must have really paid the cost'), a statement of sometimes resigned puzzlement about why suffering and blackness should appear to go together. However, in Marley's construction ('seems' and 'must have') the statement is transformed into a kind of question which is answered by the refrain so that the revolutionary or anarchic action is all too understandable: 'We gonna be, burning and a-looting tonight/ Burning and a-looting tonight.'

Marley then achieves another trick of language by stretching the metaphor again. For what appears to be, and is intended to be, a cry for actual violent insurrection and social defiance is elevated to an act of intellectual and spiritual guerrilla activity: 'Burning all illusion tonight/ Burning all pollution tonight' so that the 'weeping and a-wailing' that is prophesied for the recipients of this action is not merely a response to the physical pain, but a metaphysical cry of psychic pain in response to an act of sacrificial burning. This is a cosmic expiation of the sins of the oppressor and enactment of the 'fire next time'. Thus, when Marley turns to the next verse, it is clear that his request for 'food' to 'grow' is symbolic, and the 'me' now represents the larger suffering populace. It is, after all, 'the music of the ghetto' that he is creating, a music that locates its ethos within an urban space that is both creative and destructive.

The way the internal sound structure of the reggae song supports this kind of dialogic expression – the pattern of simple lyrical lines intertwining until a fabric of complex harmonies and disharmonies is created – is worth noting here. Much of early reggae vocalization borrowed significantly from the doo-wop stylings of black American music. In much of their early work in ska and rock steady, Marley, Tosh and Bunny Livingston devoted their time to trying to perfect the eloquence of the three-part harmony structure. This sweet melodic harmonizing, normally associated with love songs, then gave way to a harder, less soothing sound in their more political material. But always, there was the interplay of voices, working with each other, dialoguing, calling and responding, to construct a communion of sound that is deeply African in its ethos. Anyone listening to a reggae song will note that the vocal lead is announced less by any particular vocal smoothness or purity of tone, than by the capacity of the singer to phrase imaginatively around the fabric of the music. Thus reggae vocalization is never 'straight', but often indulges in a play with rhythms, entrances, exits, complex pauses and takings of breath. The Wailers displayed this kind of improvisational virtuosity from very early in their career. In a track such as 'Concrete Jungle'[4] we hear the strains of doo-wop in the use of long, carefully harmonized 'oos' and 'aahs', but it is the phrasing of the song that shows the greatest innovation. Here Marley carries himself through a series of acrobatic turns that reveal the voice as being as daring an instrument as any of the other instruments used in the song:

> No sun will shine on my day today
> The high yellow moon won't come out to play
> I said [pause] darkness has come on my life
> And has changed my day into night
> [pause] where is that love to found
> Won't someone tell me, 'cause life [sweet life]
> Must be somewhere to be found (*my square brackets*)

It is almost impossible to transcribe the complex dialogue going on between the vocal 'back-up', ('back-up' fails to indicate how central the 'supporting' vocals actually are), and the lead, that dances around the harmonies, and the bass-line, that is constantly shifting from a melodic smoothness to a syncopated staccato tone. This is complex music which, to be fully appreciated, needs close attention to be paid to all its various parts. Lyrically, 'Concrete Jungle' contains all the multiple perspectives that are characteristic of the reggae ethos. The 'I' is at once the autobiographical ego of experience and at the same time the communal 'I-and-I'. The deeply personal nature of the lyric almost hides the fact that Marley is constructing an archetype. As a griot-artist he is drawn into the myth-making process, and the landscape and metaphysical reality of Kingston's slums come to assume mythic proportions. As such, the narrative, reinforced by the metaphor drawn from slavery, is able to address issues of identity that embrace a whole people, without overtly stating this:

> No chains surround my feet but I'm not free
> I know I am bound here in captivity
> But I'll never know what happiness is
> No I'll never know what sweet caress is
> I'll be always laughing like a clown
> Won't someone help me 'cause
> I've got to pick myself from off the ground
> In dis ya concrete jungle
> Where the living is hardest
> Concrete jungle, man got be the very best

But this is not a song about abjection and defeat, but a postcolonial assertion in which the individual, while acknowledging the end of slavery and colonial domination (and the gaining of political independence), is projecting the need to transcend the new tyranny ('mental slavery') by an act of self will. The cry for someone to 'help me' is a personal plea which expresses vulnerability, a call for social and political change, and an invitation to the community that he is singing for to share in the song for freedom. In many ways, Marley's cry for help here is similar to that in 'Redemption Songs': 'Won't you help to sing,/ these songs of freedom/ Cause all I ever had...'

The lyrical call of 'Concrete Jungle' is bolstered by an instrumentation that borrows from a range of musical styles, though all are subordinate to the very steady and consistently articulated rhythm section of drum and bass and the sharp off-beat cut of the rhythm guitar. The lead guitar engages the organ in a blues-inspired wail that enters and exits as a kind of preface to the song, an opening few bars that do not immediately distinguish themselves as reggae. This trope is one that is used a great deal in reggae – in the work of Peter Tosh and in much of Lucky Dube's music, such long, involved introductions are almost signal patterns.[5] But then these stylings are slowly and subtly undermined by a rhythm that becomes more and more distinctly a distinguisher of reggae – the off beat. Then the sharp cut of the tightened snare signals that this is indeed a reggae track. These are signals that are grounded in reggae as a dance-based genre where the appearance of the drum and bass in solid reggae tempo amount to a long awaited familiarity, the pulse that will allow the dancer to begin to move.

Apart from the 'dub-organizer' (the arranger/engineer/producer) of the dub, instrumental or even some vocal tracks (such as Lee Perry's production of *Heart of the Congos*[6]), the dominant and central figure in the reggae track is the vocalist, the lyricist whose words become the defining force in the music. At its most essential, reggae is founded on the construction of the prophetic voice, the voice crying out in the wilderness, the griot voice speaking to society, the psalmist's voice. This centrality of the word is inevitable because, as I argued in the previous chapter, reggae is so connected to Rastafarianism, and Rastafarianism is founded on the notion of the word as power. The spoken word is not merely a way to express internal angst, but the means to speak into a society and to try, by the rhetoric of vocalization, to transform that society.

Urban discourse in Jamaica is a constantly mutating and dynamic entity. Were I to go to Jamaica now and exclaim 'blouse an' skirt' or 'a blow wow', or to refer to women as 'beef' or 'bat', or to refer to a nervous person as being 'bummy', or to describe someone in dire straits as being 'salt', I would immediately date myself, locate myself as someone caught in a peculiar 1970's time warp, someone who had left and been cocooned in the static world of *foreign*, protecting and preserving their Jamaicanness as one would an old record or a favourite, memory-steeped shirt. I have not lived permanently in Jamaica for over ten years; consequently there is some distance. However, through the music, through talking with friends, through brief visits, I have managed to hang onto some sense of the changes in the language – enough at least to avoid embarrassment – but I have missed out on the immediacy of language shifts and the jazz of watching the shaping of new words within the discourse of the community. This process of change, reinvention and renewal is part of what gives the Jamaican culture its vitality.

These elements play a significant role in the construction of the reggae lyric, for if nothing else, the reggae lyric must be current, aware and relevant. This is even more acute for the deejay where verbal dexterity and the capacity to coin and shape a phrase is as critical to success as riding a rhythm with flair. This is a further way in which the reggae lyric has played a significant role in shaping the discourse of the scribal or literary writer who is open to influence from reggae culture.

Anything more than a casual examination of the reggae lyric reveals varying degrees of the lyricist's awareness of its 'art', a consciousness that her or his role is not simply to replicate the socio-political 'realities' of society, but to amuse, entertain and educate through a heightened form of language. The reggae lyric, like every recorded popular musical form, is limited by a number of things. Its length is related to the capacity of the playback medium and to powerful conventions about duration which relate to its context in the dancehall or on the radio, and most critically to the expectations of its listeners. The classic lyric, then, must have poetic brevity and clarity, it must complement the music, and it must be current, relevant and meaningful for the listener. The fact that many vocal tracks will also have dub versions is pertinent here, where fragments of the lyric may be mixed into the drum and bass version. The haunting effectiveness of Lee Perry's dub mix of Junior Byles's 'Curley Locks' comes not least from the way in which fragments of the lyrics continue to focus the meaning of the song.[7] Whatever impulses there might be merely to list the woes of the world or the suffering of Rastafarians is in the main countered by reggae's situation in a culture with a strong storytelling and rhetorical tradition. There is a quest for the art of saying things, and saying them uniquely in a language that is current and dynamic. The pressure of relevance should not be underestimated because it plays a major role in the establishment of reggae as a distinctive form.

The inextricable interconnection between Rastafarianism and reggae means that the reggae lyric is frequently trying to give voice to a metaphysical vision that is founded upon a localized series of mythic and archetypal agendas.

When Haile Selassie died in 1975, something significant happened in Jamaica. Selassie, most Jamaicans knew, would at some point die, and his mortality would force the Rastafarians to contend with the divinity of their God. We knew Rastafarians regarded Selassie as God, and this was a dogged belief that went against all reasoning, all contemporary rationalizing. This issue was of particular importance to me because I had the questionable privilege of being an African in Jamaica – an African to whom the Rastas I knew showed grace and deference, an African of whom the Rastas I knew were in some awe. When I was being insulted and abused by my non-Rastafarian school friends about my Africanness, Rastas wanted to talk to me, to listen to me describe Ghana and to reason with them about Africanness and things African in the context of Jamaican society. But even in those early discussions, I was sceptical about a faith that held a figure whom I regarded as an oppressive tyrant, Haile Selassie, as a God. I knew that I could not adhere to such a faith, and I found this to be a strange conundrum since I found much in the spirit and tone of Rastafarianism admirable and attractive. In these 'groundings' and 'reasonings' I would express my doubts about the divinity of Selassie, and the dreads would admonish me gently as a youth who had been brainwashed by the western media and western history books. The accusation was not unfounded, but I never did manage to reconcile the two conflicting images of Selassie.

So when Selassie was reported dead, I wondered what this would mean for Rastas. I anticipated that many Rastas would deny the news, but I also knew that after a while, the death could not be simply dismissed as a fabrication. The silence from Selassie and the change of political power would be far too telling. I was young (thirteen) and, in some ways, quite a cynic, and I decided, on the night of the announcement of Selassie's death to reason with a Rasta about the news. My older brother and I were on a bus heading down Red Hills Road on our way home, and we broached a conversation with a dread who was on the bus. There must have been a mocking condescension in our tone because the dread exploded and called down fire and brimstone on our heads. He was not hurt, not crushed, but deeply annoyed, and his righteous indignation frightened us.

We got off the bus earlier than we normally would, laughing all the way home. Selassie was dead – what would the Rastas do now?

Yet, it is in such moments of deepest tragedy that the mythic transcends 'reality' and assumes a sublime quality that is poetic and contains a larger truth about the human condition than the unfortunate and shameful display that I enacted with my brother on the #35 bus heading for Red Hills. What I recall of the magic of that time was that a day after the announcement of the news, a brilliant new Marley song was on the airwaves. 'Jah Live' became an immediate hit. I never understood the significance of that act of creativity until years later when I was reading Timothy White's book on Bob Marley, *Catch a Fire*.[8] The meaning of this moment was also reinforced when I saw the moving documentary footage of Marley and the Wailers recording this new song late into the night. This was a moment of legendary proportions, and it brought out of Marley what is the fundamental value of art – its capacity to express the pathos of a moment, and its capacity to transcend the tyranny of the present reality and enter into mythic sublimation. 'Jah Live'[9], a song co-written and produced by Lee 'Scratch' Perry, is a statement of faith that parallels the narrative of the earliest Christians when they met after the crucifixion to assert their faith, to reconstruct the meaning of their faith and to offer a way forward. Marley was not involved in a political struggle, but in a spiritual struggle, a metaphysical dynamic of no mean order. This became a quintessential moment that elevated reggae music beyond its socio-political context and towards the grandeur of myth. As a reggae lyric, 'Jah Live' is important because of the context that shaped it, and because of the craft involved in creating it. In this singular moment, Marley and Perry were not simply writing a hymn, but offering a salient tenet of faith, actually shaping a faith. The artist who witnessed this moment, and who continues to witness this moment, may not be moved to have faith in Selassie as a God who still lives, but will have faith in reggae's capacity to engage in the most profound issues of human existence. It is through such moments as this that writers who have been affected by reggae music have found a confidence in the language, discourse and aesthetic of reggae.

Lyrically, 'Jah Live' falls into the same mystical/trickster pattern of the work Perry and Marley did in *Kaya*. It is the enigmatic form of proverbs linked to each other that shapes this lyric, which is framed by a simple but deeply profound assertion: 'Jah live, children, yeah' – an affirmation offered both as a statement of defiance to the nay-

sayers and as an admonition and encouragement to the faithful to
keep believing. These two trickster figures – Perry and Marley –
imbue the Emperor with a godlike trickster quality, so that while
no overt or explicit denial of Selassie's death is offered, the suggestion
is made that Selassie has confounded humanity and the heathen
with his inimitable wisdom:

> The truth is an offence
> And not a sin,
> And he who laughs last
> Is he who wins,
> It's a foolish dog
> Barks at a flying bird
> But one sheep must learn
> To obey the shepherd.

The 'truth', of course, is that 'Jah Lives', but the test of the assertion
will come in the 'fullness of time' when those who laugh and mock
are proved wrong. The trickster stands at a distance and watches
the heathens laugh and question the faith of the Rastafarian. The
futility of their laughter is caught in the third proverb of the stanza,
which argues that truth, wisdom and understanding are as elusive
as birds, mysteries the unbeliever cannot comprehend. In the final
proverb, the implication must be that the shepherd is still alive.
Constructed in these mythic terms, Selassie's death becomes a spiritual
mystery that can only be open to metaphysical interpretation. Thus
in the second stanza, after reiterating the Old Testament proverb of
the fool who says in his heart, 'There is no God', the 'dread' reality
of the Rastafarian apocalypse is evoked, suggesting that there is a
grander design at work here. This is made evident in the last verse
where Marley and Perry enact a resurrection, a poetic and spiritual
resurrection, which makes the final refrain of the chorus resound
with meaning:

> Let Jah arise
> And let his enemies be scattered
> Let Jah arise
> Now that his enemies, his enemies are scattered
> Jah Live
> Children, yeah
> Jah, Jah Live
> Children, yeah!

But despite the defiance and optimism of the song, one is struck by its pared-down starkness, the almost dirge-like one-drop and the seeming lament of Marley's voice. It is in these contradictory elements that we discover the tension of the piece and the moment. There is little doubt in my mind that the news of the death was devastating for Rastafarians. The singer Junior Byles, who also worked closely with Perry, attempted suicide following the news of the Emperor's death, explaining that 'I wanted to die with His Imperial Majesty. They was tellin' me that He could die, and I was sayin' that He couldn't die. So at that moment I told them it would be best if they could take my life then...' [10] Marley and Perry would have been closely aware of Byles's distress. So in the act of writing and recording this song, they attempt to offer hope to others, even as they try to write themselves into hope. It is a powerful reggae moment.

For me, there is another lesson to be drawn from this significant creative moment in Bob Marley's life, and it rests in the very absurdist brilliance of reggae music and Rastafarianism. There is a certain arrogance, an almost Quixotic doggedness that adherents to the Rastafarian faith possess, which, ultimately, becomes a quality that leads to a strong and assured sense of self. Their 'faith', in the complete and very Christian sense of the term ('substance of things hoped for, the evidence of things not seen') is buffered by the value placed on the 'foolishness' of God which works in direct opposition to the 'wisdom of this world'. Rastafarianism situates Jamaica as the centre of the universe, or, at the very least, the spring from whence a profound truth about existence derives. So while Ethiopia and Africa are, in some ways, far more privileged in Rasta cosmology and iconography, Jamaica, as at once the source of the new faith and the Babylonian space of captivity for the dread, is written explicitly into the doctrine and the imagination of the those who adhere to the faith. Thus Rastafarianism, in all its creativity and dynamism, represents a source of confidence and assurance. Where the colonial looked to Britain for a sense of tradition and legitimacy, Rastafarianism suggests an indigenous centre. This very fact is revolutionary, and its attraction for the creative writer in Caribbean society should not be difficult to imagine. Even those who have not come to accept the beliefs of Rastafarianism have embraced the spirit of confidence and almost nationalistic assurance that comes from the arrogance and clarity of self displayed by the Rastafarian. Even for those wholly resistant to the mystical centre of Rastafarianism, there is a tendency to see it as a continuation of the insurrectionary Jamaican sensibility, one that produced people such as Nanny[11], Paul Bogle[12] and Marcus Garvey[13], people willing to take on the colonial establishment in their assertion of self-worth and pride.

It is this deeply rooted and distinctive ideological and aesthetic base which gives the reggae artist the confidence to borrow, steal, and allude to styles and practices that are wide ranging and seemingly distant from the reggae ethos. The reggae lyric, then, is eclectic even as it holds to a series of communal expectations. Here I need to qualify my argument and admit that it is impossible to try and define the essence of the reggae lyric as a generic entity because reggae music falls into a broad range of camps, of styles and of lyrical expectations. In many ways, my comments in this discussion are shaped largely by the 'Roots Reggae' genre, a style that predominated in the early to mid-1970s; the style that the world was introduced to when reggae started to spread outside of the country. But even as this form of reggae – heavily steeped as it was in Rastafarian doctrine – existed and thrived, there were other, sometimes locally more popular forms of reggae expression that were far more secular and far more devoted to commenting in a secular way on the society from which it emerged. There was, for instance, the love lyric in reggae which featured such brilliant reggae artists as Dennis Brown, Ken Boothe, Marcia Griffiths, Gregory Isaacs, Bob Andy, and Leroy Sibbles. As is discussed at greater length in Chapter 6, these artists, along with Marley and Jacob Miller, would bring a vernacular to the expression of love that was not steeped in or dependent on the rhythm and blues love song that offered one of the few other models of love expression in the Caribbean.

There were also the largely secular lyrics of the dance and deejay music of the period. Indeed, though there were religious/rastafarian deejays such as Jah Stitch and Tappa Zukie, deejay music has in the main tended to distinguish itself from roots reggae by its focus on non-religious themes, on themes that are located in social commentary that must be fresh and always current. So it is important for me to admit that while I, as a teenager, always acknowledged the seriousness and regality of Marley as a prophet, I was equally familiar with the many popular deejay hits which had little to do with Rastafarianism. Tracks such as General Echo's 'Arleen'[16], Ranking Trevor's 'Love Bump'[17], Ernie Smith's 'Life is Just for Living'[18], Pluto Shirvington's 'One More Jamaican Gone Abroad'[19], Dr Alimantado's 'Best Dressed Chicken in Town'[20], Michigan and Smiley's 'Diseases'[21] remain central to my reggae memories of the late seventies and early eighties. I danced to those songs, learned the lyrics by heart, and enjoyed their wit and currency, their catchiness and their unquestionable popularity.

Thus, my assertion that Rastafarianism is central to reggae, while largely valid, must be tempered by an expansion of the discussion that at least acknowledges that much of the reggae produced during the 1960s and 1970s was not about Rastafarianism nor founded on its cosmology. Even among artists who were very much 'roots', whose songs were concerned with social and spiritual realities, there were both popular and significant figures who were not Rastafarians, such as Toots Hibbert, Jimmy Cliff (who was a Muslim) and Vivian Jackson (Yabby You) who was a devout Christian. In fact had Bob Marley and the Wailers not openly and publicly situated themselves as Rastafarians and established the Rasta ethos in their music, it is conceivable that the growth in Rasta-centred reggae would not have taken place.

Even so, I return to assert the importance of Rastafarianism because its impact and influence was not always blatant, but sometimes quite subtle, and, in fact, linked more to the formation of the aesthetic than anything else. Artists who sang political songs that acknowledged a divinity at the centre of existence were more than likely being influenced by the theo-political ethos of Rastafarianism. Throughout Jimmy Cliff's classic 'The Harder They Come'[14], there are appeals to 'Lord', to some divinity – this despite the fact that the song's central ideology explicitly rejects the 'pie-in-the-sky' repressive theology of orthodox Christianity, and celebrates the very humanist and materialist thesis of 'getting mine on earth', not unlike the appeal of the Wailers 'Get Up Stand Up'[15]. This capacity to make such strong political and largely temporal complaints, while at the same time appealing to a divinity, is endemic to the theo-politics of Rastafarianism and present in much reggae music, even of a non-Rastafarian persuasion.

So I understood that reggae's *de facto* spiritual home was Rastafari. Whether this was a product of genuine spiritual insight, my desire to be part of a street culture which regarded Rastas as not just legitimate but cool, or the sheer fad of deadlocks as symbols of reggae in Jamaica and abroad I am not quite sure, but I knew that almost all references to a deity in reggae music were directed at Jah, Haile Selassie I. This, indeed, became a problem for me when I became involved, at the age of eighteen, in the Charismatic Christian movement. Within this movement, Rastafarianism was demonic, a cult: totally antithetical to Christianity. Caught within the metaphysical crucible of guilt and redemption, the message was clear: put away reggae. The rub was that the music of the Charismatic movement was largely derived from American country and western music, less than successful mimicking of Jewish or Yiddish musical forms, a good deal of rhythm and blues and soul, rock and roll – all somewhat toned down, and of course, traditional black gospel and white Southern gospel hymns. Quite clearly it was All American and reinforced the deification of things foreign. There were peculiar hypocrisies at work here, for while I was not warned against listening to black American soul music – the preference then of middle and upper-class Jamaican youth – reggae was anathema, dangerous and demonic. It was not just the lyrics; there was also a great deal of anxiety about its rhythms, and its tendency to encourage pelvic-centred dancing that was deemed to be too sexual for the precincts of the church. Reggae's capacity to function both intellectually and viscerally rendered it dangerous, whereas the clearly ecstatic and no less sexual emotiveness of the gospel concerts held during those days were apparently quite safe. I remained defiant and continued to listen to reggae. My one compromise was to stop dancing to reggae and all other forms of music at parties. The church was right about my intentions there. Sex at that age was paramount.

But I began to encourage the Christian musicians I knew and worked with to start including reggae in their repertoire. My ideas were merely a part of a trend that would blossom in the 1980s when almost all the Christian music groups, including New Creation, David Keane and the Sunshine Singers and Birthright were writing and performing Christian songs in reggae. The quality of the reggae was not always high, but it was apparent that the music spoke strongly to the community of believers, and many of the compositions began to assume a stronger political and race consciousness – a shift that can only be attributed to the force of the reggae aesthetic.

The reggae lyric, then, with its connection to Rastafarian ideology, is rooted in an ethos and aesthetic space which encourages dialogue between the temporal and the eternal, between politics, issues of current social interest, sexuality and spirituality. Most critically for the region's writers, this dialogue in the reggae lyric was conducted in Jamaica's vernacular, suddenly enhancing the status of that language and allowing it to be the basis of literary innovations. Ultimately, however, the fundamental dialogue in reggae is that between the artist and the Jamaican people. This is perhaps what has been most inspirational for Caribbean writers over the past thirty years.

CHAPTER SIX

'STIR IT UP'

THE EROTIC IN THE REGGAE AESTHETIC

SOME TENTATIVE DEFINITIONS V
'Feels so ... right could it last another night'
Ziggy Marley

Watch it when the rapid riddim
bubble like a poco tambourine
over the sound system trembling.
Watch how de dawta dem squat
with dainty decorum of Victorian queens
without the propping of hoops and bones
about to make water in an open field,
and the shape they make
with legs like that
is the frame of a house,
a doll's house with no walls.

Like the way the wave dem come
and go, or two loose windows,
flapping tongues in the wind,
the girl dem causing ripples
on the dance floor.   Pure style!
See the coy tilt of the head to the side,
hand resting there on the knees
to keep it all together,
all that water in the waistline;
I can't imagine who call it a butterfly,
what I see is too wet for that,
too water for that, to earth for that.

This vision is a stumbling block,
you know, and if you reading this
you must pray for mercy rain afterwards,
for there is nothing straight and narrow
about the sweet symmetry of this vision.
Me, I am leaning too far forward.
I fall over into the water. It is warm.

I was about ten when I began to understand the dynamic relationship
between reggae music and sexuality. I think I understood that
relationship before I understood the political call of reggae. I had
a primary schoolfriend called Mark who lived on Red Hills Road
in one of those fifties-styled homes with elaborate awnings and a
tiled verandah clotted with potted plants and various other bushes
that darkened the entrance to the house. After school, Mark and I
would go to his backyard to compete with gigs, or marbles, or to
play an impromptu game of cricket. We also raided the black mango
tree in his backyard and would eat ourselves to sickness. One day,
Mark came sprinting around the back to tell me I had to see something.
He instructed me to bring one of the cement bricks that we used to
sit on in the backyard. He took one for himself and we made our
way quietly to the side of the house. I could hear the strains of Ken
Boothe singing a rock steady song coming from the window. Mark
placed his brick beneath one of the windows and climbed up and
peered into the room. I followed his lead. What I saw startled me
and remained with me for a long time. Mark's brother was lying
naked on top of a light-skinned girl who lay there, spread-eagled
and twisting her body, while Mark's brother's sweating back and
buttocks moved slowly and deliberately to the music of Ken Boothe.
I was fascinated by the evenness of his movements, the roundedness
of everything that he did, and the manner in which the picture could
not have been as seductive and arousing as it was without the music
coming from the gramophone. I am not sure how long we stood there,
but the girl must have noticed us, for she pulled violently away from
Mark's brother, reaching for her clothes. I saw him moving towards
us, his awkward member bobbing stupidly, and in the split second
that I stayed suspended on that brick before leaping into mid-air
and sprinting for dear life I caught a glimpse of the dark v of her
pubic hair. We hid in the gully behind Mark's home giggling and
talking about what we had seen. I did not have the language then
to speak of the sensuality of the music and the movement, but it
became an expectation of mine, during the ensuing tumultuous teenage

years, that sexual activity would be accompanied by reggae music – slow, easy reggae music. Indeed, it was, for a long time, hard to hear Ken Boothe's voice without associating it with that image in Mark's brother's room. Later, from my experience of parties and dances during my teenage years, I added to this connection between sexuality and reggae by noting that the closest and most erotic kind of dance available to us as teenagers was the rub-a-dub. It superseded the slow soul dance because rub-a-dub demanded a simulation of the sexual act, and it became a deep and abiding desire of mine to be able to rub-a-dub with a woman near the end of the night at a dance. This close connection between reggae music, dancing and sexuality has long been part of my imaginative landscape, but I have since concluded that it is both elemental to the meaning of reggae and its aesthetic and the literary aesthetic which I am attempting to construct.

Reggae's inherent sensuality is, however, at odds with the strong social conservatism and the Protestant ethic embedded in Jamaican and even Rastafarian society, a conservatism which I feel has restricted the capacity of Jamaican literature to explore sexuality, still less celebrate the erotic. It is in the way that reggae resolves the tensions between the equally Jamaican voices of righteousness and sensuousness, in the very structure of the music, that I see a powerful model for our literature.

When I made a personal exploration of those tensions in my collection of reggae poems in *Shook Foil*, I felt the need to construct some working definitions of reggae through the dynamic form of poetic utterance. The decision made sense, because, for me, the poem is the most apt vehicle with which to construct a definition for something that is so non-linear and so layered with nuances of meaning. What became clear in writing these definitions is that while I had always regarded reggae as largely a music of protest and political and religious energy, it is, at its most essential, a deeply complex music that walks the peculiar tightrope of the sacred and the profane – the holy and prophetic and the erotic. This apparent dichotomy or dualism is, however, a construct that grows out of the binary system of semantics and the linear syntactical structures of the expository English prose I am using to try and define it. Reggae, on the contrary, seems to me to function in a dialectical and non-linear manner. Indeed, reggae music eschews the climactic structure of the western mythos by constructing an idiom of circular movement. The reggae composition never explodes into a climactic end – it walks out of the room with the same kind of assured poise (or casual skank) as it enters it.

The communication that comes from the listeners' encounter with this circularity is subtle; it involves capturing their pulse and then taking them on a journey through sound. Once the listener becomes drawn into the pulse of the music, which enters the imagination like plumes of smoke, engulfing and consuming mind and body, the listener is transformed. This dynamic points to the centrality of the rhythms of drum and bass in the music and indicates that the notion of circularity must be an essential dimension of the reggae aesthetic. There is no place of ultimate completion and ending – the reggae jam will go on and on and on, for what sustains it is the bottom-beat, the undertow of the music, the tidal pulse of the rhythm section.

Anyone who plays reggae will recognise this principle in the construction of the bass-line. Here a singular theme is repeated again and again, creating a circle of sound that becomes a mantra. After a while, the bass line has no clear beginning or middle or end. It is a rounding, a manner of taking us always to the end and the beginning at the same time. For the uninitiated, this can appear to be a monotonous sound – an absence of innovation, but it is the effect of the chant, the repeated phrase, the circle of comfort that comes from the familiar that serves as the bedrock for improvisation and the emergence of the self-defining solo voice. In the same way, the reggae dancer is able to rest in the circular motion or venture out into improvisation, outside of that circularity, only to return to it at the end. Metaphorically, the sexuality of the reggae composition is female rather than male, for while the orgasmic moment may be written into the composition, the orgasm is not a male-defined explosion followed by a period of post-climactic rest, but represents rather a orgasmic construction which is female-derived, in which the pulse of living, the bass-line, continues to ground the individual even as she/he finds orgasmic moments – heights, if you will, which do not completely overwhelm the larger pulse of existence. The bass-line keeps things in place. The circle remains unbroken.

Reggae vocal arrangements often share this pattern as well. The typical reggae song ends in repetition – the repetition of a single line, with multiple variations – and the fade is standard in the reggae recording because there is little that one can do to replicate the circularity of sound but to fade it out in a way which suggests continuity. The pragmatics of the reggae dancehall play a big part in this notion of circularity too. Reggae is not consumed as a symphony is consumed. The reggae composition is consumed in the context of the dancehall in which dancing is more central than listening to the lyrical expression of the song. Dancing, in this context, is continuous, and the sound that comes from the system must be one that allows for the dancer to continue to groove through a series of compositions. The disc-jockey's or the mix-master's excellence is marked by her/his capacity to make a seamless transition from one composition to another, thus allowing the dancer not to miss a step, a beat, but to continue on this journey that is rooted in the drum and bass. This pattern is caught in some recent dancehall and ragga recordings, where the fade has given way to the continuous segue from one song to the next, a feature most prominent in such single rhythm albums as *Pepper Seed Jam* (MadHouse, 1995), but also in Gussie Clarke's *Hardcore Ragga, The Music Works Dancehall Hits* (Greensleeves, 1989). This may be why reggae does not encourage a great deal of overt rhythmic change in the body of a composition. Changes will occur, a doubling up of tempo from verse to chorus or a predictable shift in drum and bass lines around a version stretch (a quality that we note in many of Burning Spear's live performances)[1], but even then, while the dancer is being carried along to new complexities of rhythm and consequently of movement, there is the assurance of the familiar bass-line to guarantee safe passage from one episode to the next. The eroticism, then, of reggae is rooted in this circular construction. Thus any attempt to read the reggae composition as a replication of the patterns of male coitus, where coitus is constructed around the Aristotelian construction of dramatic action – introduction, exposition, complication, climax and denouement – will prove disappointing. This construction, incidentally, is one that we see operating in much western rock music and much classical music. The frenzied guitar and drum cacophony at the end of many rock compositions somehow attempts to replicate the explosiveness of the climactic moment – a metaphorical rendering that is largely masculine. In traditional blues, we do not see this pattern at all. As in reggae, the assured sound contains its own erotic pulse and energy. There is no end in sight. Loving will go on all night.

The circularity of the music has a strong physiological impact on the dancer. The music calls for a stepping motion that is easily transformed into a pelvic-focused and belly-grounded movement. Reggae is music that is especially suited to the steady repetition of sexual action, and reggae dancing reinforces that concept. The dub or the rub-a-dub, in which a couple stand belly to belly and slowly roll their hips in a circular fashion to the pulse of the bass-line, is the quintessential reggae move.

The sensuality in the reggae composition is not usually contained in the lyric of the song, but in the music itself. Distinguishing these two elements of the reggae piece is important because it is often their contradictory impulses within a single composition that give the music its unique form. I return to Marley's assertion that when music 'hits', the listener 'feel no pain'. The reason that there is no pain is not because lyrically the music has nothing painful to say, but because the painful lyrics are riding a sound that demands an awareness of the pleasure of possibility, the rejuvenation of dance, the inherent creativity of the erotic that is contained in the heart of the music itself.

It is this quality that Albert Murray seems to be pointing to in his analysis of the blues – his distinction between the music and the lyric:

The words, magnificently poetic as they can sometimes be, are only a part of the statement of the blues pattern. The spirit of the music is something else again. The lyrics almost always have tragic implications. They tell of disappointments, defeats, disaster, death, trials, tribulations, mistreatments, losses, separations, frustrations, and miseries. The music, however, does not by any means create an atmosphere of unrelieved suffering, wailing-wall lamentation, chest-beating, and gnashing of teeth. To be sure, there is always an element of regret and sobering sadness that life should be this way, but the most characteristic ambiance generated by the sound and beat of blues music is not despondency, but earthiness and a sense of wellbeing. The verbal response to a blues vamp, whether in a ramshackle honky-tonk or a swanky midtown New York nightspot, is not 'Alas!' or 'Alack!' but rather, some expression equivalent to 'Hey now!' or 'Yeah now!' or 'Lord, am I born to die?' When 'Lord, have mercy' means 'Lord, enable me to endure the good times that this music is already generating.' Indeed, once the music gets going, the words may be mumbled, jumbled or scatted.[2]

In reggae it is possible to dance and contemplate revolution, anger at oppression, the cruelties of life, the beauty of sexuality, the humour of human existence – all at the same time. This is the potential that is inherent in the creative centre of the music, what generates its meaning and life. This sensuality is part of the construction of the music, its earthiness and willingness to engage in the pulse of human existence. This is why Peter Tosh is able, on his *Legalize It* album[3], to place two seemingly incongruous songs back to back. The sacred anthem 'Let Jah Be Praised' is followed hotly by 'Ketchy

Shubby', full of barely masked sexual double-entendres, which is funny and quite 'unholy'. This kind of connection is basic to the reggae sensibility.

The value, for me, of this erotic dynamic in reggae has to do with something I touched on in an earlier chapter. There I suggested that my encounter with West Indian literature was to some extent precipitated by a desire to find literary fodder for my sexual imagination. Just as much as I wanted to recover my landscape, my physical environment and the political realities of my existence in the language that I knew and spoke, I also wanted to express love and sexuality in a language that I could recognise. In this I was struggling against the fact that in Jamaica, no less than in other parts of the world, the American love song had come to dominate the language and discourse of romantic expression, so that for many Jamaicans the perfect backdrop for a wedding or a romantic interlude was not reggae music, but something soulful from an American singer. This was true in the 1970s and may still hold true today.

Despite the emphasis within the reggae music produced during the 1970s of strongly religious and political music, a significant proportion of the songs recorded and sold in Jamaica were love songs or songs that worked around the theme of relationships. Indeed, there is a clear sense in which reggae's pop credentials were established around the love song or the love lyric. The early work of Marley and the Wailers, for instance, was almost entirely devoted to the love song or the song about relationships. From Marley's early recording, 'One Cup of Coffee'[4] to the blues-like lamentations of Peter Tosh in 'No Sympathy'[5] there was cut after cut of love tracks such as 'I Made a Mistake', 'Love and Affection', and 'Lonesome Feeling'[6] which were the mainstay of the Wailers in the sixties. Reggae brought with it a shift towards more overtly political songs, but the love song is as elemental to the formation of the reggae ethos as Rastafarianism, poverty or a strong anti-colonialist inclination. While these love songs often modelled themselves on American R & B and rock and roll love songs coming across the airwaves to the island in the 1960s, what was different was the shift in accent and the transformation of the rhythm carrying these lyrics. Eventually, reggae lyrics became increasingly localised and topical to the extent that the idea of their imitating American love songs became absurd.

The most popular artists in the seventies were usually artists with the capacity to render a love song with force and passion. Alton Ellis[7], Ken Boothe[8], The Heptones[9], the juvenile Dennis Brown[10],

Gregory Isaacs[11], Leory Smart[12], Bob Andy[13], Marcia Griffiths[14] and, of course Bob Marley were immensely popular artists because of the love songs they produced. These songs spoke to the dynamics of male-female relationships in a language that we could connect with. They all offered a largely male-driven perspective on these relationships, but they gave voice to what the music itself was doing.

Reggae's sensuality lies, as I have argued, not simply in the lyrical sensuality, but in the very shape and texture of the music itself. The dances associated with reggae have always been predicated on the business of the party – the spot, the session, the dance, the bashment. In this environment, while the desire for escape from the difficulties of life are important, there is also a strong need to find a communal language of sexuality and self-affirmation in the music. The dancehall is a venue for sexual behaviour – it is part of what dance is about. The world established in the dancehall over the years has been overwhelmingly heterosexual and defined by the negotiation of sexual dynamics between males and females. This dynamic is manifested in the dance patterns. Skanking is often a largely solo exercise, but when two people are skanking together, there is something more than a suggestion of a sexual walk, a movement that seeks to reveal the importance of synchronicity in the sexual act. Men and women express the language of this sexual act even when they are not touching. The very acts of role-playing – flirtation, posturing and attention seeking – are part of the milieu within which this music finds its primary audience. Dancing is not an incidental part of making the music, or composing, mixing and arranging, but is, in fact, an elemental part of it. This means that reggae is as much interested in making people dance as it is in articulating ideas. In reality, though, the two are not distinct, for what reggae is about is making people recover a sense of self and identity through the act of dancing. The love lyric of reggae music, then, is rooted in the call to dance, the call for people to work together in the dance, and this dance is almost always rooted in the sexual politics of the dancehall.

> I'll play your favourite song, darling,
> We can rock it all night long, darling,
> Mellow mood has got me,
> Let the music rock me...[15]

Here the rocking is an unsubtle euphemism for the sexual act, but it literally refers to the act of dancing on this date. Toots and the Maytal's call to 'Do the Reggay'[16] is also a call to dance the rough, street dance of Kingston that is very suggestive of sexuality. The very term 'rock steady' is directly predicated on dancing – a steady rocking, a steady grind that goes along with the swoop and turn of the music itself. Peter Tosh, in his song 'Ketchy Shubby', referred to above, makes use of a children's ditty to simulate both the sexual act and the act of dancing. The music establishes the give-and-take principle that is addressed in the song:

> Come mek we play some, ketchy shubby
> And when me shubby
> You fe ketch I
> And when you ketch I
> Don' mek it drop
> For if it drop
> Den it will pop....

'Shub' is a Jamaicanism for 'shove', and 'ketch' is of course, 'to catch'. This catching and shoving is a play on the sexual act, but as the chorus begins to chant the refrain 'We a go ketchy, ketchy, shubbi, shubbi tonight', in this call-and-response fashion, it is clear that the music itself is enacting the sexual act. In the 1980s, Bunny Wailer took the dancehall as the venue for one of his more explicit articulations of the close relationship between the music he is making and the sexual act.

> No one didn't tell you was to roam the streets
> Cause that's what happen when the rub-a-dubbing get sweet
> Yuh lock so tight you don't even know when it's morning
> The music so right you don't even care bout the dawning
> Well how does it feel to have been on the ballroom floor
> And yuh deh feel like yuh deh rock some more
> Cause a strickly rub-a dub for sure
> And de dub an de wax galore. [17]

Here the working metaphor is the dancehall where a range of dances are enacted and each of them carries its own sexual language, a language that places the male and female in a sexual union that is buoyed by the music itself.

But given the dominance, to date, of men as reggae performers, it is not surprising that the reggae lyric has shown a particular fascination with the male's position in the sexual dynamic. In the Heptones'

'I've Got the Handle', the song's blatant chauvinism is almost standard in the reggae lyric which is often predicated on a conception of the woman as seductress or betrayer of the male.

> I got the handle baby
> You've got the blade
> So don't try to fight, girl, cause
> You'll need first aid. [18]

The Wailers, in an early rock steady tune offered their own 'understanding' of the position of the woman in the sexual dynamic. It is true that Marley would mature from these sentiments, but they offer an interesting insight into the nature of Jamaican sexism with its roots in the misogynistic undertow of the Protestant ethic. After outlining the Genesis narrative of the Garden of Eden, the singers conclude, 'I wanna know why they sinned/ In the Garden of Eden/ It's a devilment affair / in the shape of a servant./ They broke the fruit of life/ And everyone of us is living in sin/ And any, anywhere you go/ Woman is the root of all evil./ Eve was the first one to break the fruit/ And everyone of us is living in sin.'[19] The principle is continued in numerous songs that position the woman as a dangerous kind of antagonist that men can't do without. Yet, this view is counterpointed by the language of a more equal kind of sexual play that we see in artists such as Gregory Isaacs, Dennis Brown and, of course, in later Marley himself.

There are numerous examples, but I choose to focus on Marley because his work is so easily available and known. 'Stir It Up'[20] is a classic reggae love lyric, as is 'Is This Love'[21]. In these two songs, Marley locates the sexual and emotional moment in the Jamaican landscape by his use of imagery and nation language. In 'Stir It Up' the conceit is that of cooking – a domestic conceit that captures a working-class circumstance – over an open fire. This moment becomes erotic through sweetly suggestive and delicately rendered verbal play:

> I'll push the wood
> Blaze your fire
> Then I satisfy your heart's desire
> Said I'll stir it
> Every minute
> All you got to do honey
> Is keep heating it.

The 'wood' is an unsubtle Jamaicanism for the 'hood' or the penis
in its erect and ready state. But the lyricist does not abandon the
romantic picture of a man and a woman cooking around a fire, sharing
the give and take of sexual intimacy. In the next verse, the language
of thirst is employed to suggest sexual hunger and longing:

> Quench me
> When I'm thirsty
> Come on cool me down, baby
> When I'm hot
> Your recipe, darling
> Is so tasty
> And you sure can stir your pot

The pot-stirring is at once a metaphor and a literal instruction
to the dancers to stir, in a circular motion, their respective 'pots'.
Riding a slow-tempoed beat with a round circular bass-line, 'Stir
It Up' is one of the most sensual of Marley's love lyrics, but it represents
only one of many love songs that are as germane to the reggae ethos
as the Rasta praise song or the political protest song.

In 'Is This Love' Marley is again careful to locate his lyric concerning
the flight of love in a very 'known' Jamaican space. This groundedness
of the love image is an important feature of the reggae aesthetic. It
offers the writer a confident and assured model for articulating
erotic experience. Through the example of Marley's poetic, the writer
is no longer constrained by Walcott's concern that a West Indian
fruit is less literary or poetic than a European fruit. This is the power
of the reggae aesthetic:

> I wanna love you
> and treat you right
> I wanna love you
> Every day and every night
> We'll be together
> With a roof right over our heads
> We'll share the shelter
> Of my single bed
> We'll share the same room
> Oh Jah provide the bread
> Is this love, is this love
> Is this love, is this love that I'm feeling?

The world that is created here is one of economic poverty, but in this 'real' space, the poet has found the metaphors for romantic expression. The 'single-bed', the symbol of poverty, as Carolyn Cooper points out in her very insightful introductory essay to reading Marley's lyrics,[22] and the lack of means becomes the 'shelter' of their love. Food will be provided by Jah – all modest expectations, void of material wealth, but ultimately these become truer expressions of love. Carolyn Cooper sees in Marley's work a fairly unusual desire to write seriously about relationships between men and women and erotic love in the context of Jamaican society. It is true that a blatant and often macho sexuality became the hallmark of the dancehall slackness movement, and this is indeed elemental to the reggae imagination, but the return to roots in the music of Garnett Silk, latter-day Buju Banton and Morgan Heritage has also seen a return to sensitive and erotic love lyrics[23]. But even in the dancehall idiom, one is recognising a strong sense of owning and constructing an imaginative sensibility that is rooted in the Jamaican environment.

At the heart of this constant exploration in reggae of sexuality and the notions of romantic love is an important national truth. The discourse of romance is one of the important areas in which a society defines itself and asserts its own identity. Through reggae, Jamaican society has begun to find its own language of romance. By contrast, the literature emerging from the Caribbean has been strikingly void of this kind of sexual play. Apart from Edgar Mittleholtzer, the occasional sex scene by Hearne and Mais, the notions of love, of romance and sexuality have not been treated to a great deal of attention by our writers. Lamming's exploration of love in *Water with Berries*, for instance, is a study in perversion and one finds nowhere in his work any indulgence in the sheer pleasure of sexual play and sexual behaviour. V.S. Naipaul's sexual discourse, cramped by a strong brahaminical conservatism, seems rooted in the idea that sex functions as a metaphor for something else, some other deeper psychic preoccupation. The notion of sex for its own sake, for the pleasure of sex, has not been a prominent theme in West Indian writing. The recent exceptions to this tendency are, in the main, those writers working outside of the Caribbean, novelists such as Dionne Brand, Opal Palmer Adisa, Marlene Nourbese Phillips and the poets Ramabai Espinet, John Agard, Lillian Allen, and Lorna Goodison. What is also clear here is that these writers are predominantly women. However, in his *Waiting in Vain*, Colin Channer offers one of the first novels by a West Indian in many years that is a sophisticated and sexually uninhibited love story. *Waiting In Vain* is, significantly, rooted in the discourse of reggae and founded on the principle of the novel itself as a moment of seduction, a play between the author and the reader. In this work, Channer assumes an understanding of the language of reggae – the seductive language of reggae which is based in an understanding of Jamaican culture, the culture of the dancehall and the narratives of reggae artists. In a passage from the novel, Channer describes a scene of seduction and he paints this moment against the backdrop of Bob Marley and his music.

'I said you remind me of Bob Marley,' she repeated. 'I saw him at the Garden with the Commodores. I'd never seen such charisma in my life. And ... wow... I remember taking a hit off my first joint and thinking. Oh shit, I've never wanted to get involved in a concert this way before. Whenever he would call out, I'd cup my hands over my mouth and scream loudest. Wo-yoyi. Wo-yoyi.   Wo-yo-yo-yo-uh. Wo-yo-yo-yo-uh. There was a sensuality to him ... not plain sex appeal ... but a spiritual magnetism ... as if he were a shaman ... as if he had the power to draw people out of themselves into this new space ... his space. I guess ... and make them do things they'd always wanted to do or thought of doing before.'

'Bob,' Fire said, wondering how this was related to the discussion. She began to hum, and he recognised the bluesy air of 'Turn Your Lights Down Low', which the band on the barge was playing now, guiding the ballad with a torch of shimmering guitars. She turned her body to him and drew her knees in to her chin, wrapping her arms around her shins. 'You look like the picture on Natty Dread,' she said. Her voice was soft but buzzy like the ripping of damp silk. 'The hair is the same ... not locks ... but a mantle of Spanish moss. And your nose is similar and your cheekbones ... they're like fragments of rock. Your eyes are different, though, and your forehead. But especially when you're sleeping, or thinking, the resemblance becomes uncanny.' Her lisp, now that she was tired, was becoming more pronounced, investing even the most common words with an erotic sibilance. The mention of sleep aroused in him the memory of her nakedness. And as he thought about watching her through the doorway, he began to undress her with his narrowing eyes, drawing his lids closer so his lashes could coordinate more fluently as his eyes slipped the straps of her dress over her shoulders.

'Did you ever meet him?' she asked.

'Who?'

'Marley. Are you listening to me?' In his mind she was lying on her back with her legs apart and his tongue was engaging her clitoris. Whispering to it. How are you? Nice to meet you. Are you shy? Is that

why you wear this hood all the time? Here... let me help you slip it
off. I want to see your face so I can kiss you...[24]

The seduction is being enjoyed for the pleasure inherent in it,
with reggae as the basis of the language of seduction, and as the
sensual backdrop for the actual seduction. In this instance, Marley
becomes the archetypal sexual figure whose sexuality is not rooted
in the simply carnal, but in something more spiritual. And yet, in
the same moment of spiritual revelation, Sylvia, the woman who
tells the story of her first Bob Marley concert, is aware that she is
engaged in a seemingly contradictory act of chanting to the Rastaman
yell from 'Rastaman Vibration' – not a love song by any stretch of
the imagination – in a manner that is completely sensual.
    Channer's debt to Marley lies in the manner in which the very
language of his book, the images he uses, the rhythm of his lines
are deeply rooted in an inclination to indulge heavily in the senses
– the feel of things, the smell of things, the taste of things. The richness
of this kind of tactile imagery is perfectly suited to the deeply sexual
themes that the novel deals with. And yet, even when the themes
are not overtly sexual, when he is, for instance, dealing with the
suicide of Fire's friend, Ian, Channer's writing has the same sensual
richness, a sensuality that seems to belie the tragedy of the moment,
and yet becomes the very meaning of the loss, the sense of death.

The mist was melted away by now and all was green before him –
green and wet with dew and life. The low sunlight was dripping off the
coffee plants. And the orchard blazed with pulsing colour – yellow papayas,
orange mangoes, fat magenta plums....
    He asked himself what time it was. Around five by the sun, he thought.
A crowing rooster confirmed this as an army chopper shot across the
sky ... thukkering ... thukkering ... whipping a breeze, bending plants
and shaking trees and stirring dust and grit.
    He closed his eyes. Fuckers, he thought, dissing the dead like that.
His face was wet when he looked again. It must be the wind, he thought.
These could not be tears because my heart's too dry to make them. I
have no blood left. No sweat. I haven't pissed or shit in days. Maybe I
too have died. Maybe I'm dreaming. Maybe this is how it feels when
the plane goes down or when you come in a flutter of flailing limbs
into arms that do not know you.[25]

Reggae, then, becomes a place for Channer to root his own poetics,
his discourse and he is constantly making allusions to reggae's sexual

politics, arguing with them, agreeing with them and exploring their validity in the novel. As I have argued above, the possibilities inherent in this kind of writing have not been exploited greatly by West Indian writers, by novelists at least. In Jamaica, the yard playwrights did, however, discover the dynamic possibilities inherent in reggae's sexual play through a series of 'slackness' plays or 'yard theatre' pieces that proliferated in the 1980s during what can be described as the 'Restoration' period in Jamaican society after the austerity of the 1970s. This movement coincided with the emergence of the slackness lyric in dancehall and its dominance in Jamaican dancehall culture.

Caribbean poetry has, in the main, been as chaste in its exploration of the erotic as the novel. There are exceptions, and these come tellingly almost wholly from writers infused in a reggae sensibility. In Kendel Hippolyte's 'Antonette's Boogie'[26], the paradigm of the fused duality of reggae music, at once sensual and profane, is captured with eloquence and deep feeling. This is a classic reggae poem that contains within it much of what I have been trying to define here in its dynamic interplay of language, movement, sexuality, spiritual rejuvenation and hope in the midst of an emotional crisis. It is such an important piece that I feel compelled to quote it in its entirety:

> i could do wid one o' dem boogie tonight
> a deepdown spiritual chanting rising upfull-I
> a Bunny Wailer flailing Apollyon with a single song
> i could be in a mystic dance tonight
> when every tramp I tramp I stamp de dragon head down into hell
> and every high step lifting my leg one more rung upon de Jacob ladder
> and dark as de place be, it have a light
> it have light, sweet Jah, more beautiful than fire!

The high-stepping (militant steppers) dance is the posture that speaks the language and spirit of the 'dragon-defying' reggae sound. The ritual of stepping and tramping becomes a metaphor for resistance and dreaming and a spiritual encounter with God. The light in the dark is not only hope in the midst of struggle, but an apocalyptic flame of purging, cleansing and righteousness.

> I miss dat kinda boogie tonight
> where your heartbeat is de bass-line
> and everything so still within de centre of de music
> although to an outsider it sound noisy
> but doh mind, out dere is de wilderness

and here alone in dis place is de voice of prophecy
wailing in de reggae riddim for our time
telling us to flee, to forward, doh look back
and wo! right in de middle of de song
Bob singing stop – de rams' horns start to wail
and dis dance-hall is an ark
dis dance become a journey

This moment is magical because of the protean nature of the imagination that is at work. The music and the movement are working together, and the poetic transformation occurs in response to the musical arrangement. Marley's voice is withdrawn from the mix, and in this pared down version, the horns blaze, taking the dancer into the poetic conceit of Biblical discourse. Outside, 'the wilderness' is the world of Sodom, the world of Babylonian exile, and the chant to keep going forward becomes a chant to resist the temptation of falling back into the Babylon of despair. This deeply spiritual moment is to be found at the centre of the music, created by its circularity. This is the mystical moment when the journey onwards and the still place of arrival become one. For Antonette, this spiritual moment is not just a part of the human condition, but indissolubly bound to the sensuality of the human body:

One o' dem kinda dance i want
where flesh to flesh is serious business
where de rubber and de dubber making one
a dance where music is priest
and de deejay from the tribe of Levi
and all our voices from de valley of de dance floor
rise up in jubilation everywhere upspringing children of Jah
chanting psalm unto psalm unto psalm unto psalm
night into morning, praising and raising every heart higher
until de light
and den we sight Jah face

i miss dat kinda boogie tonight
where de dance-hall is a holy place.

The world of the dancehall becomes, then, a space in which the rub-a-dub dance that ritualizes erotic movement expresses sexual energy as a sacred force. This paradigm, which moves away from the protestant ethic that pits sexual behaviour **against** holiness, is

part of what characterises reggae, and this is significant because
the protestant ethic is so much a part of the Jamaican mindset. The
tension between the 'openness' of reggae and the 'closedness' of
the Protestant system of ethics is part of what is realised in the
literature that emerges from writers working within the reggae aesthetic.
Lorna Goodison's poetry, for instance, explores the tension between
dualism and dialectic inherent in this dialogue. At its most powerful,
the effect is not to create poems of torn sensibilities, split along a
fault-line of ethical division, but, instead, poems which express an
acceptance of the multidimensionality of the individual psyche. There
is, for example, a good-humoured acknowledgement of this complexity
of human emotion in the poem 'Farewell Wild Woman (1)':

> I seemed to have put distance
> between me and the wild woman
> she being certified bad company.
> Always inviting me to drink
> bloody wine from clay cups
> and succumb to false promise
> in the eyes of slim dark men.
> Sometimes though when I'm
> closing the house down early
> and feeling virtuous for living
> one more day without falling too low
> I think I see her behind the hibiscus
> in dresses competing with their red,
> and she's spinning a key hung on a
> cat's eye ring
> and inviting me to go low riding[27]

In my own quest for a familiar language with which to articulate
my own actual and imagined romantic and erotic encounters with
women, I found what Marley did in his music especially empowering.
This began when I found that being able to quote Marley during
my rather tentative high school romances satisfied both my precious
youthful nationalism and gave me, I hoped, more plausibility than
I might otherwise have had. By the time I began to write poetry,
the love songs of *Kaya* and *Exodus* offered me a model by which I
could shape a lyric that spoke at once to our own landscape and
our own constructions of sexuality. Indeed, I suspect I evolved a
poetic pattern that personified Jamaica as mistress, as a kind of
reggaefied woman whose contradictions represented for me an appealing

poetic type. But my exploration of the erotic in poetry has not been
focused entirely on this kind of voyeuristic projection of male desire
onto the female, but is, I believe, more tellingly located in the complexity
of trying to speak of the sexual and the spiritual in the same voice.
At the heart of my work is a real effort to find a language that articulates
and reconciles the spiritual and emotional values that have supported
my imagination for the past eighteen years. As I have suggested
elsewhere, it is reggae's aesthetic that offers a poet such as Lorna
Goodison the language with which to be at once a self-defining,
assertive feminist voice, confident in her sexuality and quite explicit
about her attraction towards men, and a voice which assumes the
cadence and convincing righteous weight of an Old Testament prophet,
a voice which has an assured authority in speaking of the pain and
spirituality of human experience. Popular music in Jamaica, with
its unwavering commitment to comment freely on any and every
issue of concern in the society, presents artists in whatever form
with a license to engage in a wide range of themes and types of
discourse. I think too, that while reggae has been dominated by
male voices, it has had a significant role in the emergence of the
female Jamaican literary artist. Reggae's vast topical range has created
a distinctly nationalistic audience, at ease in the place of the island
as ample subject matter for creative expression, and this has, I believe,
helped to establish the space within which women writers can address
whatever issues they wanted to explore. By the time of the emergence
of women reggae and dancehall artists in the 1980s[28], the corresponding
explosion of women's voices in the literary world was already underway.

The politics of sexuality are most explicitly explored in the dancehall
today by artists who seem aware that such discussions are important
to the public. These artists are quite explicit in the descriptions of
sex and frequently explore the details of sexual activity in a manner
that is literally pornographic. Yet there is, as Carolyn Cooper has
argued in her work on this issue[29], a clear sense in which the sexual
candour constitutes a revolutionary development in the gender dynamics
of Jamaican society. Beyond such social developments in the politics
of gender, something equally important has taken place, through
reggae, with regard to the possibilities of the treatment of the erotic
in literature. Reggae offers models of how to speak of love in the
Jamaican language, models that did not quite exist before. Reggae
also offers, as do rock and roll and rhythm and blues for Americans
a collective treasury of the romantic and the erotic that becomes
the bedrock of much of the literature of nostalgia and the literature

of sensuality. This common discourse – of a shared history and of shared moments of self-realisation – is part of what helps to forge a shared literary language, a shared sense of imagery, allusion and metaphor.

I began this chapter with an anecdote about my childhood and the manner in which Ken Boothe's music began to establish for me a language of sexual experience that would affect my writing for the rest of my life. I return to this moment to end the chapter because it is in this quality of reggae that I have found one of its more significant principles of beauty. Reggae music is predicated on the dialogue between the body and music, and this is inevitably sensual. This dialogue, when translated into literature becomes an open door to the exploration of the contradictions and collusions between the body and the language that is used to explore that body. That I can find in my own writing, and in the work of Lorna Goodison, Rohan Preston and Colin Channer, a strong inclination to explore the sensuality inherent in the imagery and language of Jamaican and Caribbean society assures me that it is important to read into reggae a capacity to shape the way in which both literary form and content can be developed. Reggae's sexual politics are sometimes deeply reactionary and disturbing, yet it is through its discourse, its willingness to explore the pleasures of sex itself, that some of the most daring and sexually challenging writing is beginning to emerge in West Indian writing.

CHAPTER SEVEN

DON DRUMMOND — THE FORERUNNER:

JAZZ AND THE REGGAE POETIC

ARCHETYPE

SOME TENTATIVE DEFINITIONS II

'brutalize me with music. . .'

Into this sweet, well-made bed
slips the high tenor
of the lead man, dream man,
front man, don man,
face guy, lover guy,
with lyrics like water,
washing down, washing down,
fingers slow on the skin.

'Baby but yuh jus' won' let me'

He makes a poem of grunts,
the impromptu gutturals
framing the lyric's clean edge.

This is poetry walking a bass line,
this is poetry darting sweetly
around the rigid lick of the rhythm guitar.

Pungent like a wet mango,
the smell lingers in the skin
when the sound has passed.

While it is true that Marley represents perhaps the single most important figure in the development of an effective postcolonial aesthetic emerging out of popular culture, there are several important individuals who, even before the advent of reggae, had begun to create an art that reflected the evolving sensibilities of the society. Toots Hibbert and the Maytals, Prince Buster and Justin Hinds and the Dominoes are among the artists who were pioneers in this respect.[1] However, I believe that for a variety of reasons Don Drummond represents the most important of such figures.[2] I understood very early in my exploration of reggae that Drummond could be described as the forerunner, the artist who drew upon the language and idioms of the working-class environment to transform the dynamics of jazz music into a distinctly Jamaican form called ska. Even without the sheer and iconic drama of his life – his troubled childhood, his prodigious gifts, his clinical schizophrenia, his engagement with Rastafarianism, his relationship with a nightclub dancer, Marguerita Mahfood, his repeated sojourns in the Bellevue Sanatorium, his inscrutable silence, his murdering of Mahfood with a kitchen knife, his celebrated court case, and his death, allegedly from suicide, in Bellevue – Drummond's genius as a trombone player, his innovative use of Rasta drumming, folk melodies, and African syncopations to create a danceable but completely realised Jamaican musical form situate him as a creative genius and forerunner to Marley and Lee 'Scratch' Perry.

Drummond represented one of the first clear instances in which urban ghetto music, street music, was being inextricably linked to the spiritual complexities of Rastafarianism. His compositions were largely instrumental tracks, but their titles, and his characteristic use of minor keys, suggest a poetic journey into issues of identity and selfhood. Africa and Pan-African sensibilities were critical to Drummond in a way which presages the political inclinations of Marley and roots reggae. Titles such as 'Addis Ababa', 'Beardsman Ska', and 'Marcus Junior' point to these concerns in Drummond work[3]. Marley's movement towards the politics of postcolonialism and pan-Africanism were not a sudden break from the colonial past, but grew out of his contacts with people like Drummond and the Skatalites (with whom the Wailers recorded the first version of 'Simmer Down'[4]) in the recording studios of Kingston.

While in Canada, I was pushed into digging more deeply into Drummond's life by a filmmaker friend, Errol Williams, a Guyanese transplant who was very interested in doing a feature film on Drummond. He wanted me to co-write the screenplay. In my research I found newspaper clippings and some anecdotal material on Drummond's life. I used these 'texts', filled with the contradictions and revelations of a complicated man, together with a series of Drummond poems written by Jamaican poets, to construct the play which I called 'Valley Prince', borrowing the title from Mervyn Morris's poem. I subtitled the piece 'A Bellevue Sonata'. What was clear to me after writing this was that in Drummond we see the emergence of the Jamaican artist, struggling with issues of class and race and yet laying the foundations of an indigenous artistry that has spawned many more aesthetic excursions. Drummond was an early representative of this possibility, and I would like to argue that his music and iconic life offered a number of writers their first encounter with a working-class sensibility that forged works of genius that were both steadfastly Jamaican and peculiarly universal.

The music of Don Drummond has fascinated a number of Jamaican poets, and at least one American poet, and has generated several very important poems that speak to the notion of an aesthetic that emerges from Jamaican popular culture. But it was also Drummond's most tragic life as an artist, living and creating in relative poverty, suffering the tensions of the isolated artist, yet imbued with a strong sense of community, that has fascinated poets such as Mervyn Morris, Anthony McNeill, Lorna Goodison and Norman Weinstein. For my part, the Drummond story has spawned in me the still unproduced full-length play referred to above, several poems, published and unpublished, and a strange fixation with trying to discover the spirit of Drummond's music in contemporary Jamaican music.

Don Drummond was a border at the Alpha Boys Academy, an approved school established for working-class delinquent youths by the Catholic church in Kingston which became a musical nursery for some of Jamaica's finest musicians.[5] His mother placed him there to ease her already heavy family responsibilities and because she expected him to secure a good education and some discipline. Drummond went on to acquire remarkable skills as a trombone player and became the leading light in the immensely popular and innovative ska big band, The Skatalites. He is said to have recorded over a hundred compositions before he was placed in an mental asylum at the age of twenty-eight. There remains some uncertainty over Drummond's age. Some have estimated that he was in his mid-thirties when he was finally committed to the Bellevue asylum after the murder of Mahfood. Prior to this most tragic moment of his life, he struggled with what has come to be accepted as chronic schizophrenia. Drummond was an isolated figure, notorious for his silence and his intensity.

Early in his career, Drummond developed a tempestuous relationship with the rhumba dancer and cabaret star, Marguerita Mahfood. Their relationship was complicated by Drummond's apparent unwillingness to accept her performing in clubs, carrying out a role that was largely predicated upon her attractiveness to men. The details of their relationship, like much in Drummond's life, needs to be properly documented and explored, but it is enough for our purposes here to say that their disagreements reached a head one Christmas night when Mahfood decided to perform at a club against Drummond's wishes. When she returned home, he stabbed her brutally with a large knife, killing her. Drummond gave himself up and was defended by a cadre of lawyers including the now Prime Minister of Jamaica, P.J. Patterson. Drummond was deemed guilty, but his plea for insanity was accepted and he was committed for life in the Bellevue asylum in Kingston.

His life was the subject of much media attention and popular interest. His killing of Mahfood was a national tragedy for some, and a confirmation, for others, of the seedy brutality of the Jamaican working-class environment. Their story became an elemental part of folk culture, largely because these two individuals were known and celebrated artists in the community, who, despite their fame, remained working-class icons because they never achieved the financial security that would have taken them out of that class. They lived in a lower middle-income area and survived on very meagre earnings. It is important, then, to understand that Drummond's position as an artist was characterised by a clear association with the working class black experience. His interest in Africa, Rastafarianism and blackness is, as noted above, evident in many of the titles of his songs. His association with the Rastafarian guru and musician, Count Ossie, deeply affected his perception of Jamaica in the postcolonialist

1960s, and in turn Drummond was appropriated by Rastafarians and by working-class youth as an icon of popular working-class culture.

But what fascinated Jamaican poets has been the disturbing relationship in Drummond between creativity and madness, between the beauty of his music and the brute ugliness of the murder, between his sense of communal responsibility and a strained and disturbed egocentric psychosis. The notion of the artist as a madman, the prophet as slightly off-kilter, is one that appears in each of the poems discussed below. But ultimately, what writers located in Drummond was a genius of creativity, a seed of poetic force that would germinate into the reggae blossoming that overwhelmed Jamaica in the 1970s.

> ...
> Hold
>
> an image of a horn
> man playing before
> ruins of Neruda's 'All
> for Art's Sake' mansion
>
> sending herons onto Saint
> Marley's rock
> steady dance floor. Watch
> their flickering body
>
> English. Drummond's
> practising a scale
> created by stomping
> oxen parading in lines
>
> as long as the epic
> lies (lines) trailing
> the wake of the Santa
> Maria...[6]

Norman Weinstein links Marley and Drummond in their use of related sources. They are both founding their work on a tradition from which they can generate a contemporary reality, and this tradition is contained in the Caribbean history of exploitation and slavery and of survival. But they are also sharing a musical history which they add to, the one building on the other. Drummond was building on the folk idioms of Jamaican society, building on the church songs,

the mento music, the calypso; and he was also drawing upon the
blues and jazz, fully aware that these forms opened the way for him
to interpret, recast and reshape a music that would become increasingly
distinctive and distinctively Jamaican. Here, then, was an artist
who was listening to the historical framing of his society – in terms
of sounds that came from that historical space, while also listening
to its current sounds – the popular films, the street talk, the chanting
of the Rastafarians, the drumming, the violence in the streets, the
rumours of revolutionary action, and so on. He was bringing those
things to bear on his own jazz-inflected sensibility to create something
which, while it retained the improvisatory inventiveness of jazz,
transformed what was both an American and a minority form into
something which was both popular and wholly Jamaican. Drummond's
relationship to jazz and its transformation within the body of ska
provided one of the earliest models for Caribbean writers in their
relationship to the metropolitan literary tradition. In Weinstein's
poem, Drummond is positioned aesthetically as eschewing the western
maxim of 'Art for Art's sake' to embrace a more provocative and
engaged sensibility, finally realised in 'Saint/Marley's rock/ steady
dance floor'. Neruda's old 'mansion' or plantation is usurped by a
new artistic mandate, one that will be picked up by the reggae artists
of the 1970s.

Anthony McNeill's encounter with Don Drummond in 'Don: For
the D'[7] is especially revealing in the way in which Drummond's persona
comes to define for McNeill the persona of the poet seeking a 'way
into praise'. The epigraph that McNeill uses for the poem – 'To John
Coltrane, the heaviest spirit' – positions it as a jazz piece. In evoking
the figure of the jazz saxophonist, McNeill is defining the Drummond
persona as a visionary artist trying to contend with the weight of
the human condition as it burdens his soul and spirit. Like Coltrane,
Drummond becomes the possessor of the 'heaviest spirit', and it is
this heaviness that McNeill is drawn to. A pained sensibility becomes
the basis for creativity and vision:

> May I learn the shape of that hurt
> which captured you nightly into
> dread city, discovering through
> streets steep with the sufferer's beat; (p. 137)

In some respects this is a partial view of Drummond's actual music,
which focuses on the isolated, 'misunderstood' persona of the avant-

garde jazz musician, whereas the reality of Drummond's music is in the popular transformations of ska and its frequent joyousness.

Even so, in McNeill's language there is a clear sense in which Drummond, even as an artist who predates reggae, is imbued in the reggae ethos. The city as a dreadscape in which the 'sufferer' must find meaning is a motif found in many poets who are working out of the reggae ethos. The language is Rasta-centred, and the prophetic artist, in McNeill's rendering, is set apart from suffering, even as he has to witness it and feel it. In what is an almost masochistic anthem, the persona (McNeill's, one presumes) desires not simply to witness this pain and suffering, but to make it part of his own sensibility. In this quest, McNeill is demonstrating something important about the class dynamic as it operates in Jamaican literature and Jamaican culture in general. Like most established writers in Jamaica, McNeill was not a working-class individual. He was from the educated middle class, and his movement towards a strongly reggae-based or 'sufferer' sensibility amounted to a conscious act of trying to connect with the working-class milieu. What, in fact, the ska of Drummond brought home to many middle-class writers like McNeill was a strong sense that the 'real' action, the real grounded space of vision was being developed among working-class artists, the popular musicians and folk artists. In his poem to Drummond, McNeill is asking for the language that will allow him to enter the reggae space and understand the shape and dynamic of the Jamaican culture in a way that he has not done before, something that could offer him the kind of aesthetic foundation he so desperately needs:

> teach me to walk through jukeboxes
> & shadow that broken music
> whose irradiant stop is light;
> guide through those mournfullest journeys
>
> I back into harbour Spirit
> in heavens remember me now
> & show we a way into praise,
> all seekers to-gather, one-heart: (p. 137-138)

As the poem progresses, the language begins to assume the lexicon of the prophet voice, and in this instance it is Rasta-derived. In the third stanza, the expected 'me' of standard English, is usurped by the ubiquitous Rastafarian 'I'. The poet, not averse to a certain

cynicism, is here asking for faith, for the capacity to find the calm
centre of Rasta ideology, which is the communal place of 'one-heart'
or what Goodison terms 'heartease':

> and let we lock conscious when wrong
> & Babylon rock back again:
> in the evil season sustain
> o heaviest spirit of sound. (p. 138)

The language is clearly inspired by the reggae lyric, and the poem
becomes, in fact, a vocal track to Drummond's instrumental music.
Here 'Babylon' is an established icon of oppression, and the potential
for hope in the midst of suffering is eloquently captured in the last
three lines. Against Babylon and the 'evil season' that it connotes,
it is the heavy sound of both suffering and creativity that 'sustains',
that offers hope. Thus, in 'For the D', McNeill is writing a reggae
poem that functions, in many ways, as a manifesto for his own poetic
position.

Mervyn Morris in 'Valley Prince'[8] also elects to situate Don
Drummond in a narrative that explores the dynamics of the artist's
existence in society. He too discovers in Drummond's enigmatic
and deeply introspective personality an example of the alienated
artist whose creative output is born out of an intense and deeply
isolating psychic angst. The artist is not only alone, but mis/not
understood by people in the community. In many ways the artist
has been abandoned because the community is unwilling or unable
to appreciate him:

> Me one, way out in the crowd,
> I blow the sounds, the pain,
> but not a soul
> would come inside my world
> or tell me how it true.

Morris in this passage conveys the paradox of the artist existing
within a community and yet in complete isolation because of some
spiritual or psychic distinctiveness. Like Mais's misunderstood and
mystic Brother Man[9], the persona in this piece is both 'in the crowd'
(belonging) and 'way out' (isolated). He is therefore able to articulate
himself in the language of the crowd and at the same time convey
feelings and ideas that push the boundaries of creative expression.

It is into this turbulent, insular world that the 'melancholy baby' enters. Like the proverbial muse, this melancholy baby evokes absolute emotions from the artist, driving a creative expression that is suicidal:

> Cool and smooth around the beat
> she wake the note inside me
> and I blow me mind. (p. 146)

The artist becomes so intensely involved in himself that he understands all external experience through a limited self-reference. The reader who possesses the extra-textual details of the death of this 'melancholy baby' is invariably struck by the poem's inversion of murder into suicide. Thus the killing of the melancholy woman, the whore, becomes an artistic statement, yet another misunderstood expression of self-destruction. Morris does not allow irony to reside in the narrative. The woman is painted in simple but absolute terms. She is a spiteful whore whose apparent infidelity has driven the poet to distrac/struction. Morris takes up a male perspective in dealing with this narrative: that of the cuckolded male, driven to violence by the inconstancy of a 'loose' woman. Such a perspective makes literal and naturalistic sense of the anguish of the persona. In the voice of the Valley Prince, Drummond, Morris encodes a masculine subjectivity which the reader is encouraged to accept as the expression of a tormented and paranoia-filled mind. The Prince's desire to blow his mind at the end of the first movement becomes, therefore, an expression of frustration and desperation. It is insanity brought on by external pressures: the artist is out of control. An important shift takes place in the second movement:

> Inside here, me one
> in the crowd again,
> and plenty people
> want me blow it straight. (p. 146)

'Here' is the world of insanity, the introspective and closed world of the mind locked in its own isolating psychosis. More literally it invokes the asylum in which Drummond spent the last few years of his life. Yet, 'In here', the artist becomes more confident of his voice. It is a voice that has been discovered after the abandonment of reason, but a voice that expresses completely the persona of the individual. Despite its 'twistedness' the artist is convinced that his voice's

distinctive quality must be protected from the demands being made
by the society at large. The persona asserts the alternative nature
of his direction: 'straight is not the way'. By accepting and protecting
the deviance inherent in his choice of artistic expression, the artist
moves towards an explosive kind of creativity that is at once artistically
brilliant (it blows you away) and destructive (it blows his mind).
Importantly, the artist/persona has realised that there is a world-
view, a subjective reality, that is his alone. He seeks to give voice
to that reality:

> and plenty people
> want me to blow it straight.
> But straight is not the way; my world
> don' go so; that is lie. (p. 146)

Rhythmically, the piece becomes less predictable and controlled
at this point. The pauses indicated by semicolons represent unusual
rhythmic breaks which reflect the now involved struggle to find meaning
in the artist. There is shift from the calmer 'matter-of-fact' narrative
cadence of the first movement, to the more direct and confrontational
explosion of the last three lines in which the artist addresses the
reader/viewer/hearer. He demands the right to create his own psychosis,
to discover his own art through a willing engagement with insanity.
The desire to 'blow [his] mind' in the second movement is expressed
as a protest, an expression of artistic angst which cries for the freedom
to create, even against the values of the community at large. And
in this moment, the poem assumes the kind of individualism that
one associates with an artist like Lee 'Scratch' Perry, whose cultivated
'madness' and desire for isolation represent an elemental part of
his reggae ethos.[10] This madness, this posturing that places the artist
outside the pale of society's expectations is repeated in reggae music
again and again. We hear it in the aggressive and sometimes
incomprehensible discourse of Peter Tosh in interviews. Tosh was
known to be a defiantly confrontational individual capable of strange
and dangerous acts. Again, Bunny Wailer's dark persona of the 'Black
Heart Man', the man with the capacity to make use of folk magic to
see into and take action against people, fulfils the picture of the
reggae artist/poet as a maverick but inspired creator.[11] These are
enigmatic figures with a very distinct awareness of the importance
of the posture of the individual. Reggae creativity, therefore, derives
from the tension between a certain engagement and a desire to forge

a distinctive voice, which is what Morris excavates here in the model of the artist as isolated and persecuted soul. Implicit in the request of the Drummond figure, 'Oonu gimme back me trombone...' is the suggestion that the community is withholding from the artist the tools with which to create. Drummond, deprived of his trombone, is rendered helpless. The artist is being punished for his deviant expression by being silenced. If he hopes to produce again, he must obey the tenets of the society – he must follow the 'straight' path.

Morris's artist is a loner and is granted the intent, if not the capacity, to chart her/his own creative and ideological course, expressing emotions and acting out of felt experience. The artist is not easily defined, nor does she/he desire to be reduced to the position of 'the voice of the people'. Morris is attracted to Drummond's difference, the unique vision which allows him to act against the mainstream in a personalised manner. Others have appropriated Drummond's position as an icon of the working-class artist to produce a more politically explicit reading of the artist's experience.[12] Tributes to Drummond on his death and after focus on his position as a black artist charting new courses in working-class artistic expression. Morris, significantly, eschews such readings of Drummond's life, and instead creates a piece that celebrates the alienated position of the artist. 'Valley Prince' becomes an important archetype for Morris the poet. The artist, while existing within the society, remains an enigmatic observer. The artist is not easily defined and will ultimately resist the urge to follow the 'straight' line. Despite her/his vulnerability, the artist remains in control because she/he has understood what is her/his truth. However, this control must be qualified. The artist does not have control over the art that evolves within her/him. There exists in the artist's psyche a creative core which has a life and will of its own. The artist will struggle both with the pressures of the external world (the crowd) as well as the inner muse (the melancholy baby). It is important that she/he rejects the demands of the 'crowd' and resolves to accept the 'melancholy baby'. But there is a tension between this rejection and the attraction of an audience, to speak to the 'crowd'. In this there appears to be an expression of Mervyn Morris's own struggle with the role of the artist. What the reggae sensibility allows is a complex dialogue which is deeply involved in resolving such ideological and aesthetic concerns. For even as the poem celebrates the individuality of the artist, it does so in a language that seeks to 'reach' the mass, a language that seeks to connect with the working-class ethos.

Morris is not a poet who can readily be seen as a reggae-inscribed artist. But this poem, among others, reveals that Morris was aware of the impact that reggae music has had on the ways in which the artist must see herself/himself in the context of Jamaican society. More particularly, Drummond offers Morris an entry into the discussion of the role of the artist in society. The poem, then, is as much about Mervyn Morris the poet as it is about his own understanding of the tragedy of Don Drummond. Morris in 'Valley Prince' is quite convinced of the insanity of the Drummond figure, but, as with McNeill, it is clear that he links this madness with the weight of his artistic mission, that his madness is directly associated with the pain that he has to consume and then express. In the long run, then, the madness that grips Drummond and makes him at once a creative genius and a tragic figure is the same one that looms over the artist working in Jamaican society. Morris is aware of this, and in this sense, it is fair to say that Morris speaks out of an engagement with what I have described as a reggae aesthetic.

The way in which Don Drummond is constructed as an iconic figure in relation to which Jamaican writers have expressed their aesthetic engagements with postcolonial Jamaica can be clearly seen in the differences between McNeill's and Morris's 'Drummond' on the one hand and Lorna Goodison's 'Drummond' on the other. Her 'For Don Drummond'[12] is an early and defining poem in which she manages to capture the image of Drummond both as the tragic figure of his own narrative and as a prophetic voice; a representative prototype for the modern Caribbean artist. The language of the poem itself introduces a different kind of dialogue with its subject. Goodison's poem is in patois, like Morris's, but unlike Morris's her use of patois is not simply a way of constructing a character. It is the voice of the poet which slides easily along the continuum of Jamaican talk. In the same way, Drummond's visionary difference is located within a Jamaican continuum – born that way, and constructed by the magic of folk beliefs – rather than defined through the archetype of the alienated modernist artist of western culture. In Goodison's poem, Drummond is born into a place of difference, born to see things, to make things known, but nevertheless born into a community:

> Dem say him born
> with a caul,
> a not-quite-opaque
> white veil

> through which he visioned
> only he knew (p. 84)

The story of Drummond is established, then, as a myth carried
by the community. 'Dem say' is a quintessential assertion of the
communal ownership of a narrative. Goodison, the poet, does not,
at any point in the poem, detach herself from the community voice
– she speaks in the first person plural, and yet her encounter with
the Drummond narrative is deeply personal. In this moment, she
too assumes the prophetic role: a role in which she is isolated and
personal in her vision, yet inextricably linked to the community
and to the collective sensibility that is the community.

The world that she creates in this poem is quite precisely cast.
This is the landscape of Drummond's march into the world, which
is anthemed throughout the poem by her rendering of some of his
most important horn lines. The memorable line she relies on here
is that laconic phrase in the composition 'Far East' which is at once
a hymn of lamentation, filled with long melancholic phrases that
carry a certain nostalgic longing, and yet shifts into the vamping
bursts that start to lock in, step-by-step, with the frenetic beat of
the ska:

> Taptadaptadaptadada...
> Far far East
> past Wareika
> down by Bournemouth
> by the sea,
> the Angel Trombone
> bell-mouthed sighs
> and notes like petals rise
> covering all a we. (p. 84)

Goodison lets this music become a part of her own poetic line:
the combination of short observations, tidy compressions of syntax,
and the longer lines of memory create a fabric that is analogical to
Drummond's genius. The music is functioning not simply as an
inspiration for the poetic exercise, but as a frame, an aesthetic grounding
for what the poet is doing.

The prophetic 'voice' of the horn player is a balm for the people,
for 'all a we', but the prophet is tormented. This is the complexity
that Drummond offers the poetic moment – that conflict and agonized
dynamic felt by the artist. In many ways, the reggae aesthetic is

rooted in these sometimes conflicting roles of creativity. There is
the quest to speak truth, to be the standard-bearer of meaning in a
chaotic world – the voice crying in the wilderness; yet there is that
very personal quest to exorcise, through writing, through creativity,
the demons that haunt the psyche – a deeply personal agenda that
ultimately leads to the explosive brilliance of the art that is created.
Goodison's narrative for Drummond is, then, empathetic and locates
Drummond's homicidal act as a part of the tragic psychosis of the
artist. There is, in truth, little exploration in any of the poems of
Drummond's apparent misogyny, his violent inclination to control
what he thought of as *his* woman. Instead, his movement towards
violence is predicated on his position as a haunted and tormented
artist:

> Not enough notes
> to blow back the caul
> that descend regularly
> and cover this world vision
> hiding him from we. (p. 84)

Madness, then, distances the prophet from the community. This
madness is that personal angst that shapes one element of his psyche
and his creative reality. We can observe in much of Goodison's work
this tension between the artist's role as a voice speaking to the
community and the confessional stance of trying her best to speak
the trauma of the soul's truth.

The Marguerita figure that next enters the poem arrives as a mythic
construct, a kind of muse of rescue who offers to transform the artist.
The muse figure is especially tragic because her hopeless task is
to try to transform the artist and prophet from what he has to be – a
seer, a troubled seer because of his destiny. In this movement, the
musicality combines sweetly with the sensuality of language:

> Find a woman
> with hair like rivers,
> a waist unhinged
> and free;
> emptied some of the sorrow
> from the horn's cup;
> into the well below her belly.

> She promised to take the caul
> from his eyes:
> to remove the cold matter
> that clouded his eyes;
> and stand between him
> and
> the trombone tree duppy.
> The promise dead like history.
> Dead like she.

The earnestness of the exploration of tragedy finds voice in the erotic figure of Marguerita, creating a moment that is archetypal to the popular music of Jamaica: that combination of the sacred in the prophetic and the profane in the erotic and sexual. As was discussed more fully in Chapter Six, reggae music is as much predicated on the basic human condition of sexual desire and sexual articulation as it is on the Rasta ideology of faith and prophecy. Reggae is sensual, and the reggae dance slides comfortably along a continuum of political posturing, personal self-assertion, and explicit sexual articulation. These things cannot be extricated from each other.

The drama of the narrative then begins, but this is not climactic in the sense that a crescendo of images and moments normally are. Instead we enter a chanting construction in which the dirge-like lament produces the pathos of the moment. History is defied, for history is completely usurped by the compelling present. Drummond's act of murder is a very present reality – he is blinded by his prophetic role, his role as a visionary, and the last strains of music that he creates are distorted ones. His 'caul', then, becomes the wash of schizophrenia which Goodison suggests is the source for both his creativity and his self-destruction. Here, Goodison shares the same paradoxical grasp of the historical moment as does Morris. Both of them recognise that the 'straightness' of sanity is a force that dampens the creative instinct and that the true tragedy of Drummond lies in the fact that the very demons that give breath to his brilliant compositions are the demons that defeat him, that lead him to madness, self-destruction, and brutal murder.

But the artist/prophet still captures the imagination of the community, and the crowd takes up the sound of Drummond and carries it forth. In this, Goodison situates Drummond at the heart of the reggae revolution, the culture of the Jamaican popular sphere. This sound that comes out of the urban madness is what she reconstructs in

the chant of the people: 'One gone.../ Don gone/...', a sound that
she then places in the mouth of a reggae toaster. At this point, Goodison
shifts into the first person as does Morris at the end of the poem,
but the voice that is assumed by Goodison is far more complex.
The voice of the 1970's deejay toaster who enters the music frame
– the version frame – and begins to chant lyrics is the construct
that is at work here. Goodison is enacting the layering of reggae
composition through the use of various voices that are distinct and
seemingly incongruous. But 'mixed' right, they begin to create a
complex mesh of musical meaning. We are thus hearing the phrase
from Drummond's 'Far East' dancing above the bass note of the crowd
of people chanting 'One gone.../ Don gone.../', and above this version,
we hear the toaster cast in a Perryesque surrealistic gesture:

Lay me down for the band must rest/ Yes, Music is my occupation.
I tired a hold this note/ you hold this memory / For J.F.K., For Me
Mek the slide kotch/ is right here so I stop
Belleview is the view I view. /Sometime I think the whole world mad too.

In the early 1970s, a number of reggae songs contained similar
articulations that served as caesuras in the music's fabric. These
became signature articulations of the arranger, for instance, Glen
Brown. The words were spoken into a vacuum that still pulsed with
the shape and echo of the compelling drum and bass:

Hold it mister T
Dis dawta cyaan keep up to dis ryddim
Ask me no question
I tell you no lie
Ask me no question
I play music[13]

In this Glen Brown instrumental composition, 'Merry Up', the melodica
of Joe White leads, with a trombone playing obligato behind the
line, reggae echoing a Drummond composition, and the voice that
speaks into the vacuum represents the only vocal articulation in the
composition. Goodison models her poem around a similar structure,
so that Drummond's voice, cast as the voice of the 'dub-organiser' in
retreat, achieves a poignancy and tragic sadness that constitutes something
akin to sheer genius.

The 'music' returns after this interlude. The madness of the whole world assured, we have almost come to accept the passing of the prophet/genius. Goodison retires into a slower, far more reflective moment that contains the ritual actions of burial. The language register shifts slightly even as she shifts towards an imperative construction in tense. She addresses the community as she addresses herself:

> Behold the house of his feet,
> the brown booga
> tongue ajar, a door that blow open and close no more.

The biblical 'behold' speaks to a religious moment, but the image that meets us is sad, hopeless, and bereft of the musical genius. Drummond is at rest, and his existence is now captured in the absurd juxtaposition of the sacred ('Behold the house of his feet') and the banal ('the brown booga').

The community is then called upon to carry out the ritual burial of the artist/prophet. This detail of domestic activity – the pressing of the suit under a newspaper and collecting of his effects, the felt hat that was a signature item of clothing for Drummond – all offer an example of how Goodison tries to construct a world in which the community becomes one with the prophetic artist and begins to exist in this world of empathy even in the midst of tragedy. The imperative that ends the poem is a cry for the society to understand that the artist, as visionary and as a tragic figure of madness and genius, demands only one thing from the community – its indulgence in the spiritual destiny of the artist and a respect for that spiritual existence:

> And this time do the burial right fi we
> Bury the Don under the Angel Trombone Tree.

Goodison is alluding to the apparent scandal that surrounded the burial of Drummond. The Catholic Church was apparently reluctant to bury Drummond with full rites as his death was apparently judged as suicide. His mother managed to convince the church to carry out the burial somewhat clandestinely. But Drummond's Rastafarian brethren were convinced of Drummond's Rasta faith and wanted the right to grant him a Rasta burial. They invaded the cemetery when he was about to undergo a Catholic burial. The burial was abandoned at that point, and eventually Drummond was buried in secret, at night, by the Catholics. As I write this, I am aware that much of this information is legendary, and I am not even certain of the origin of the strange knowledge that I have of this moment. But, in terms of the dynamics this piece is exploring, it is hardly important whether this narrative constitutes a mythic telling of events that have been passed down by word of mouth or if it has 'historical veracity'. What is important is how it serves as evidence of the mythic place held by Drummond in the Jamaican psyche.

Ultimately, I regard Goodison's poem as centrally situated in the reggae ethos because of what she seeks to do in her use of language and her creation of the 'prophet/artist' paradigm so critical to the reggae posture. While Drummond's genius as a musician is assured, it is not this that fascinates Goodison. It is his role in society, his impact on the community, his capacity to be a folk-figure whose art has an impact on the way the society sees itself. This is the genius, then, of the reggae aesthetic. It offers a way for the community to write itself into its own imagination. This assured capacity to see a coherent pattern in the creative instincts that emerge from the community is a critical feature of the development of an aesthetic, a way of seeing and knowing things. I am suggesting that while Drummond was a ska artist and not a reggae artist in the strict sense of the term, these poets have encountered him in a language and philosophical framing that is reggae-based. It is in reggae that the dynamic between the artist and the community is most fully realized in the Jamaican culture. The poets I have discussed above recognise this and write from that premise.

CHAPTER EIGHT

BURNING SPEAR:

ARCHETYPE OF THE REGGAE PROPHET

SOME TENTATIVE DEFINITIONS XV

'play I some music...'

The *chekeh* of a guitar lick
is the marshall ordering of the troops,
the high cutting edge of sound
like a stick beating you to get up,
to stand to the call, the call,
to grow a callous on your soft soul
so hard it makes the shedding of blood
painless like river-flow to sea.
This is the militant perpetual
of reggae, roots reggae.
Now you can find the blood of Babylon
in the sky; and hear your voice,
cutting the clutter of other voices
with an irrepressible brilliant licking,
a stiff tongue rubbing a knife edge:
chekeh, chekeh, chekeh, chekeh.
This is the bright outer garment of reggae
catching the noon day light.
Ride on, people, ride on.

Christmas is, strangely, the most productive time of the year for
me. I write quickly and energetically during the last three weeks
of the year; often birthing works that have gestated all year. I have
no good rationale for this peculiarity, all I have is a track record.
But there are some speculative possibilities. Despite the intense
commercialism of the season, Christmas somehow draws me back
to a delicate place of spiritual sensitivity. I am aware of the shape
of myth and its centrality in my temporal existence. I am acutely
aware of the rituals that give meaning to myth, the rituals of faith.
I am constantly transported to old home spaces – the memory of
my father making souse and marshalling the entire house in the
slaughter and roasting of a pig for Christmas meals in our home in
Ghana; the ritual of going from house to house, my parents drinking,
we children eating sweets until nauseous. And there are other memories,
other rituals of living in Jamaica, trying to retrieve the community
of Ghana in the poinsettia-blooded, sun-hot days of Kingston: the
memory of family cohesion and of rupture and absence. I remember
also the almost extremist enthusiasm of my early days as a convert
to Christianity, when I rejected all pagan trappings of Christmas:
the trees, the gifts, the ivy, the holly and the absurdly anachronistic
artificial snow on the dried-up Christmas tree. In this desert, the
water of faith, of hymns, of the Bible was always the sustenance.
Christmas, for me, then, is a place of metaphysical charm, the meeting
of memory and faith, of myth and the pain of history.

For some reason, I write best during that season. I wrote the long
poem *Prophets* during the Christmas of 1994; the following year it
was *Jacko Jacobus*, another long poem, and in 1996, I drafted the
first lively and rugged version of this book. The three works are
closely linked, for in each I have sought to express the most telling
feature of the reggae aesthetic: the idea of natural mysticism, the
metaphysics of faith and memory. In many ways the three works
are rooted in reggae's anatomy; all represent an effort to write work
that emerges from a coherent aesthetic. In *Prophets*, the startling
narrative of competing prophetic voices in the distinctive Jamaican
landscape was what fascinated me. The poem was permeated by

the language of reggae, the psalmic, the prophetic, the sensual. But it is in *Jacko Jacobus* that I find the most realised articulation of the reggae ethos. Jacko emerged from a longtime desire to put into verse the twisted and earthy narrative of Jacob and Esau. I was amused at the fundamental contradiction of Jacob's existence: his duplicity, his human frailty and his position as Israel, the ultimate and most unlikely progenitor of the nation.

Perhaps my attraction to Jacob was entirely personal; a sense that if someone as unscrupulous as he was could be taken beyond his frailties and failings and made, by the sheer audacity of God's will and wit, the father of a whole nation of elected people and the root of at least two significant world religions, then I could assure myself of the illogicality of God's grace and embrace it as mine. Much of this appears in the poem as I wrote it; all those psalms of bewildered faith, those articulations of almost prevenient and labourless grace reflect this preoccupation. But I suspect that the greater attraction of Jacob is his trickster status. The familiarity of that remarkable Anancy quality suddenly shifted the poem from a meditation on faith to an exploration of history, a study of culture and intimate portrait of a man all too close to my imaginings. When I saw this, Jacob's very essence had to be founded in the complex cast of reggae archetypes, for in him were located the poet, the patriarch, the lover, the journey man, the don-man, the ginal and the rhygin warrior. Above all, his humanity, his capacity to fail, his capacity to be tricked even as he tricked, all made him the quintessential reggae figure. As the poem evolved during those cooler, dry December days in Sumter, scribbled out quickly onto a Churley note pad in orderly two-line stanzas, a pattern began to emerge, one that linked perfectly to the music I was listening to while writing. First, there was Winston Rodney (Burning Spear) wailing away on 'Mek We Dweet',[1] the bass-line hopping along, his voice carrying the cadence and authority of the prophet. His dignity connected well with the old Jacko, remembering, speaking to the Jamaican nation. Then there was the insanity of Lee 'Scratch' Perry's *Greatest Hits*,[2] loaded with Perry's sardonic wit, the seeming madness that belied a certain genius. Finally, there was the Anancyism of Marley caught in Jacko, the founder of nations, the deft tale-weaver, the assured leader. It all made sense to me. I was connecting with individual and highly distinctive artists; but I was also salvaging from their voices a shared aesthetic base which gave me the encouragement to offer in verse the sinewy sensuality, the sexuality, the proclaiming tones of prophecy, the surreal mysticism of the Jamaican and South Carolina landscapes, and the unabashed spirituality of salvation and damnation. I tried to make clear this approach in a sequence of poems dedicated to Winston Rodney, Lee Perry and Sister Patra which break the narrative of Jacko's journeyings. I called these poems ('Trickster I, II, III and IV') 'Home Melodies'. Placing this sequence in the middle of the narrative allowed them to function as a bridge, a musical interlude that was intended to create a moment of rest, of poetic reflection, and to be a prelude for the second flight of the narrative. They formed a bridge between Jacko's American exile and his return to Jam-Rock, his place of birth and the promised land of his destiny. The 'Trickster' sequence, then, served as a choric reminder to me, the poet, working in America, about the idiom I was working with, about the language that was shaping the poems and, most importantly, about the basic aesthetic that gave them possibility. I must explain this more. The reggae impulse that is central to the 'Trickster' sequence – the 'Home Melodies' – is also central to the conception of the entire poem because it was this trickster element that attracted me to the Jacob narrative in the first place. In the Biblical Jacob I saw a quintessential postcolonial figure, an individual forging a new language, a new sense of nationhood, and a new sense of identity. And this pattern amounted to something at once eloquent and sublime, and yet something deeply flawed, profoundly human. Jacob gains his right to found the nation by way of trickery and, throughout his life, he tenaciously resorts to trickery, 'brain-work' and ginalship to get what he wants. And in terms of a sweetly poetic justice, he attracts trickery to him: the devices of Leah and Laban, of Joseph, and of his other sons, all conspire to make him as much a victim of trickery as its perpetrator. His heroic status is assured in the narrative, for Jacob is the father of Israel. This title is granted him by God, so that his antics, his devices, amount to classic moments of human futility and meaning, the existence-defining acts of one who is overshadowed by the 'divinity that shapes [his] ends'. And yet, for all this predestination, Jacob makes his own narrative and constructs it around action, around an admirable tenacity. His overnight struggle with the angel and his dogged desire to be blessed are not simply cases of someone seeking domestic advantage, but of a person who is willing to do anything to fulfil his destiny. But that kind of drive does suggest a certain insecurity, a human anxiety that forces him to hedge his bets, to make sure that the deal is not reneged upon. No one, not even an angel of God, is going to dupe him out of what is his. And, as a trickster,

Jacob is acutely aware that people do dupe others over things of eternal importance – his entire life testifies to that reality – so that his suspicion of all, including his sons, is an instance of acute psychological realism in the Bible.

It was not an especially grand leap then, to see in Jacob the elemental character of another archetype – Anancy – a figure whose journey Kamau Brathwaite has effectively charted from West Africa, as a deity, a peculiar man/god with creative potential and human frailty, to the Caribbean where he loses some of his status as a deity, but retains the spirit of hero, of the trickster who has learned how to use his wiles to eat, gain power, win women and, ultimately, succeed against the power of plantation society.[3] This trickster figure is a crucial one in Caribbean society, founded as it is upon the principles of brutal subjugation and the exploitation of a disenfranchised people. Trickery, in the context of slave society, was one of the few weapons available to the slave to resist the oppressive colonial apparatus. The celebration of this figure who uses his brain, his audacious understanding of human behaviour to win for himself or herself a degree of power in an oppressive environment has now become endemic to Caribbean society. Even over the thirty years after the withdrawal of the British colonial system from Jamaica, there still remains an admiration for those who appear to defy the ruling class, an acknowledgment that someone who is able to use 'brain-work' to bilk the 'system' is worthy of admiration. This is the folk hero who is not constructed around ascendancy and pedigree, but within the context of poverty and oppression. It is this figure that Derek Walcott offers to us as heroic in his play *Ti Jean and His Brothers*.[4] Ti-Jean uses trickery and common sense to defeat the white devil/plantation owner and to restore the dignity of the community represented by the animals in the forest. Ti-Jean stands as distinct from his two brothers Gros Jean and Mi Jean who rely on brute force and book-learning respectively. Both of these have a complete disregard for their community and the wisdom of their elders; but above all, they fail because they lack the wit, the daring, and the tenacity to dupe the devil.

It is little wonder then, that this trickster figure is often linked, in her/his modern incarnation in Jamaican society, with the reggae artists and Rastafarians who begin with the premise that they are the 'small axe[s]' coming against the 'big t'rees' of the world:

> Why boasteth thyself
> Ole evil men

Playing smart and not being clever
Ah say yuh work iniquity to achieve vanity
But the goodness of Jah Jah i-dureth for-i-ver

If you are a big t'ree
We are the small axe
Ready to cut you down
Sharpened to cut you down.[5]

The 'big t'rees' is, of course, a clever Marley pun about the top three recording giants in the late 1960s and early 1970s who were notorious for exploiting the talents of the young reggae upstarts like Marley and the Wailers.[6] It is, therefore, not simply a metaphorical boast of intended violence (with the hint of an actual threat) against those whom he saw as conspiring to exploit him, but a threat made in the prophetic language of the Old Testament that elevates the battle from one between artist and record producers to one fought between the forces of good and evil. The capacity of the small axe to cut down the big tree is granted by the 'goodness of Jah-Jah', and so the tables are turned in favour of the small man, the 'stepping razor', the 'stone that the builders refuse':

These are the words of my master
Telling me dat, no weak heart shall prosper
And whosoever buildeth a pit
Shall fall in it, fall in it
And whosoever buildeth a pit
Shall bury in it, bury in it.

At the same time, the singer, in using the veil of spiritual pontification to construct a very disturbing threat, deflects responsibility for the threat from himself to the feet of his 'master', to God himself. Thus the threat of burying this man is not a specific threat on his life – at least not in a way which could be legally upheld – but a prophetic utterance, though the listener is in no doubt about its implications. Marley is constructing a classic trickster song of resistance and defiance through the sheer wit of 'brain-work'. The ultimate act of defiance is located in the very recording and airing of the song, for every time it is heard it plays out the defeat of the 'evil men', its presence on the airwaves and in the record stores an act of 'cutting down' the monopoly of the 'big t'rees.'

As Rohan Preston has rightly pointed out,[7] this style of 'trickery' in the articulation of violent threat is particularly characteristic of a certain period of the reggae lyric. Such delicacy, which demands a degree of creative genius, has been replaced by a far more blatantly aggressive and barefaced articulation in the 'gun talk' of the dancehall scene of the late 1980s and early 90s. But even in this context, violence becomes its own kind of metaphor for other rather less malign intentions. Here the bravado, at its best expressed with a degree of self-reflexive irony, represents yet another facet of the trickster persona: the word-spinning trickery of the braggart. This is nicely illustrated in another Marley song, 'Bad Card',[8] where reggae becomes a weapon to disturb the class-conscious neighbours that he has acquired when he moved uptown:

> I want to disturb my neighbour
> Cause I'm feeling so right
> I want to turn up my disco
> Blow them the full watts tonight
> Inna rubadub style,
> Inna rubadub style.

Reggae becomes the flag of revolution to wave in the face of the scornful uptown neighbours who have, unusually, drawn a rare poor hand in the battle of society. Marley has the good hand; he is here to stay in all his creative ubiquity:

> Dem a go tiaad fe see me face
> Me seh dem cyaan get me outa de race
> Oh man I said I'm in your place
> An' den you draw bad card

With impish smugness, Marley, who had bought a colonial mansion on Hope Road, a few hundred yards away from the Prime Minister's official residence, declares to his new neighbours that he is now 'in their place', not as someone taking over a space left vacant, but as someone who has crashed a party, moved into someone else's space and come to own it. Marley's justification for driving only BMW's is part of this spirit of 'throwing words' at 'society', the snobbish upper classes of Kingston. The BMW, he argued, stood for Bob Marley and the Wailers; so how could he ignore such cosmic contrivance? In this act, among others, Marley understood himself to be playing the trickster hero, the anarchic trickster slave who is challenging the authority of the slave master, and he understood that this was central to his connection to working-class people.

This trickster image was undoubtedly part of Marley's persona as a folk hero. His famously enigmatic interviews were brilliant examples of the kind of proverbial advice old folks would give to young people about how to make the bigger person fall to the smaller. Marley was notorious for being deliberately unintelligible at points in his interviews, choosing often to wax densely philosophical when faced with a question he felt it was prudent not to answer. The density of his language at such points was invariably compounded by a heavy injection of Rasta-talk which, to the uninitiated, was decidedly inscrutable. He made few attempts to adapt to the language of those who tried to interview him, most of whom addressed him in a very standard form of the English language. Marley spoke street patois, and was uncompromising about this. The effect, which I am certain he recognised, was to gain the power of enigma, the persona of the otherworldly prophet. I recall one moment in an interview, conducted by Neville Willoughby for local television, when Marley was asked about his marital status and about women. His response, accompanied by a grin, was: 'Who, me? Me? Me 'ave nuff queen, seen?' And when asked about Rita, he simply said, 'Me 'ave nuff queen, seen?' The discussion ended there. I recall this because for years I was under the impression that the fact that Rita Marley and Bob Marley shared the same name amounted to a simply coincidence, and that the suggestion that these two were married was merely a rumour. I am sure that many Jamaicans knew the truth of it, but as I had arrived in Jamaica as a preteen in 1971, I had a lot of catching up to do. But when Marley died, Rita Marley must have recognised that there were others, like me, who might have had the impression (aided, of course, by Marley) that they were not married, and so she ensured that one of the first photos to be published in *The Gleaner* to accompany the news of Marley's death was one that depicted the Marley family (with Rita as wife) complete with the immediate clan of children (now the core of the Melody Makers) posing for a photograph taken in the late 1960s. We soon saw pictures of their wedding as well, as Rita assumed so effectively the role of grieving widow. Marley's 'trick' had come back to play itself out with a certain poetic justice.

These were the kinds of stories that I wanted to evoke in the character of Jacko, and I found that, in the reggae sensibility, it was possible to speak of the trickster figure and yet still be speaking of God,

destiny, faith and fate. This combination of realities seemed to me
to be more available in the ethos of reggae than in any of the literature,
Caribbean or otherwise, that I knew of. In reggae the posture of
trickster can be a dignified one, born out of suffering, and the strong
instinct to survive it and with the capacity for the sublime. In his
deeply melancholic song, 'Time Will Tell'[9], Marley is the trickster
figure who speaks proverbs against those whom he sees as trying to
work against him:

> Jah will never give the power to a baldhead
> Run come crucify the dread
> Time alone, oh time will tell
> Think you're in heaven but yuh living in hell.

   This is a Davidian lament, a cry that calls upon the order of God
to prevail against the wickedness of the baldhead, the quintessential
evil-doer who lacks any moral scruples, the antithesis of the locksed
Rastafarian. While the song suggests that the cards are stacked against
the oppressor – the evil man shall not prosper, the evil man shall
crumble – Marley, like David, is speaking into an abyss, a Babylonian
reality which seems to defy these truths. But as he sings his psalm,
he finds healing, he finds the capacity to tell the 'children' (his
people) to 'weep no more'. The refrain is most important for it indicates
proverbially that the wise trickster can see beyond immediate realities:
'Think you're in heaven, but yuh living in hell'. This is the other
side of the trickster persona. Along with her/his gifts for deceiving
the powerful goes an acute awareness of their machinations and the
ability to 'see through' them. As with Walcott's Devil in *Ti Jean
and His Brothers*, this 'baldhead' is unaware of his destiny, seduced
by his position of power. The trickster has the remarkable capacity
to read through the apparent impregnability of the powerful and to
recognise this failed figure for what he is. The trickster will prevail.
And so it is in this sense that the trickster is also a prophetic figure.
Like Jacob, he has a connection with God. His fate is assured. This
was the figure I saw in reggae, and which made me recognise that
in *Jacko Jacobus* I was writing a reggae poem. I saw, too, that reggae
gave me a language to narrate this Jacko narrative in a manner that
was believable. In *Jacko Jacobus* I discovered I could write about
the political, the spiritual, the sexual, the mundane, and the sublime
within the same narrative structure. As literary antecedents for what
I wanted to do, I knew only of Roger Mais's *Brother Man* and *Black*

Lightning and those of Wilson Harris' early novels where the mystical and the socio-political are in some kind of balance[10]. Of these only *Brotherman* really begins to chart a connection between a spiritual ethos and a socio-political reality. There were also two notable poetic expressions, Lorna Goodison's *Selected Poems* and Kamau Brathwaite's *The Arrivants*, in which I felt there were genuine intimations of an equal engagement with the meaning of faith, with political reasoning and with a sexual dynamic. But all this I found over and over again in reggae.

In 'Interlude', then, there are variations on the reggae theme which try to point to the range of notes I was sounding in the narrative. The sequence opens with 'Trickster I', an homage to Winston Rodney, aka 'Burning Spear', a veteran reggae artist who has been unwavering in his commitment to his political, spiritual and artistic vision. He is a prophetic voice who has found his spiritual and ideological sensibility in the teachings of Marcus Garvey and in a vision of Africa as a utopian source of grounding and identity. His compositions are notable for their incantatory structure and for their very dread and driving drum and bass-led arrangements. But what drew me to Spear in this instance was at once strange and yet strangely appropriate. A few years ago, he was one of the many world-class 'rock' artists selected to cover songs by the Grateful Dead as a tribute compilation CD. Spear offered an incredibly affecting version of the Grateful Dead's tune, 'Estimated Prophet'[11]. I heard the piece while sampling the compilation and I was terribly moved by the manner in which Spear completely owned this originally rather multi-chorded tune. He had stripped the song down to his signature two chord arrangement, and then imbued it with a pulsing, driving bass and drum pattern that served as the engine for his controlled and profoundly committed rendering of the lyric. It was as if the song and its lyric had been written especially for him. I say this not because of the style of the Dead version or because of the lyrical form used – for in many ways, this is one of Spear's most 'wordy' songs, at least in his repertoire of the last ten or fifteen years. It was because the content, the meaning of the song, served as an eloquent expression of the Spear figure, the genuine prophet who can claim to be a 'preacher preaching on the burning shore.' This image, when rendered by the Grateful Dead, feels exotic, a playful romp with mysticism that is not free of a certain ironic distance. The prophetic 'I' is not convincing in Jerry Garcia's voice because he carries with him the full baggage of a relativism endemic to rock culture, a quality of necessary cynicism about any claims for the truth of prophecy. (Compare Paul Simon's attempt to deflect the position of the prophet away from himself in the 'Sound Of Silence': 'the words of the prophet are written on the subway walls'. Even Dylan must turn from rock to reggae to truly express the essence of his conversion to Christianity in his Sly Dunbar and Robbie Shakespeare driven 'I and I' or the declarative 'Joker Man'.[12]) It is impossible to be a rock and roll iconoclast and not sound pompous and self-important when claiming the position of prophet. For the reggae artist, however, such a position is elemental, and Spear represents one of the most distinctively effective of such voices.

In his rendering of the song, Spear translates the song into nation language. This was both necessary – Spear would not have attempted a standard English approach – and an act of genius. His process of covering the song is to simply transform it until it becomes completely credible in his voice. The translation is not lexical, it is a translation of sounds, of the pronunciation of words, of intonation and of syntax:

> My time coming,
> Any day now
> Any day now
> Don't worry 'bout me, no
> It's gonna be just like dey say
> Dem v'ices tell me so

Spear then places his 'brand' of authority on the recording by infusing his most recognisable horn riff, the line from his signature composition 'Marcus Garvey' into the laconic strains of the horn line written for the new recording. The act is a profound one because it at once offers Spear's justification for covering the song: this is a song about a prophet, and thus, it is a song about the ultimate prophet of black identity, Marcus Garvey. If there is any question about Spear compromising on his devotion to Garvey in his use of this song, it is dispelled immediately by this simple musical allusion. Suddenly, not only does Spear own the song by transforming it musically, but also acknowledges that this song is now one of his many anthems to the great Garvey. And it is in this act of ownership, this brilliant and respectful transformation of an American rock anthem into a totally Third World and Jamaican construction, that we see again the distinction and distinctiveness of the reggae aesthetic. Reggae transforms any sound that comes towards it, making it something new and distinctive. It is clear that reggae has its own deep structure and essence that allows it to accomplish something like this. This was not merely the accomplishment of a brilliant musician – Burning Spear – but is integral to reggae as a musical phenomenon. For me, Burning Spear was doing to the Grateful Dead's song what I wanted to do with the narrative of Jacob in the Bible. Like Spear, I could see within the frame of the Jacob story and within its essential self, a story that translated effortlessly into Jamaican culture.

'Trickster I' begins with an acknowledgment of the eldership of Burning Spear, his position as reggae's elder statesman who contains within himself, within his imagination, within his presence, the fulfilment of Psalm 133 which has become a signal expression of Rastafarian social doctrine: 'Behold, how good and pleasant a thing it is: brethren to dwell together in unity!...' or in a more modern but equally eloquent rendering:

> How good and pleasant it is
>   when brothers live together in unity!
> It is like precious oil poured on the head,
>   running down the beard,
> running down on Aaron's beard,
>   down upon the collars of his robes.
> It is as if the dews of Hermon
>   were falling on Mount Zion.
> For there the Lord bestows his blessing,
>   even life for evermore.[13]

It is to this psalm that Marley also alludes in the first lines of his anthem 'Africa Unite',[14] a song that served as a statement of homage for the freedom fighters in Zimbabwe's struggle for independence:

> How good and how pleasant it would be
> Before God and man,
> To see the unification of all Rastaman
> As it's been said already
> Let it be done
> I tell you who we are
> Under the sun....

And Jacob Miller in his 'A Chapter a Day'[15] offers the same psalm, maintaining the pattern of reggae/Rasta discourse which is located squarely in the Psalms of David.

'Trickster I' evokes the same pattern of discourse:

> Geriatric, wizened, ancient man
> with a beard constantly damp
>
> from the flow of good and pleasant
> nectar; our cedar of Lebanon,

Another, perhaps more revealing rendering would allow for the foregrounding of the punning in the first line: 'Jerry-a-trick, wise-and, ancient man' – the play on Jerry Garcia's name is a tad juvenile, but represents an appropriate and sincere homage or 'props' (respect due) to Garcia. It is also a way to establish the trickery of the piece. The word 'geriatric' suggests a certain weakness, a place past usefulness, yet the 'trick' embedded in the word undercuts that suggestion, offering an image of age as an image of wily strength. Placed beside the pun 'wizened/wise-and', I hope that it becomes clear that the play is to undermine the stereotype of age. His 'ancient' mantle is the truest and purest descriptor, harking back to another time, a time of the prophets.

In Winston Rodney, I locate the prophetic voice, the creative voice and the explosive revolutionary voice. These are contained in the images of the evergreen, the cedar of Lebanon, and in the volatile, but equally creative image of the volcano. The volcano image allowed me to draw on Spear's own iconography which is contained in one of his seemingly benign renderings of a nursery rhyme, 'Fire Down Below'.[16] Here, Spear takes the ditty about the teapot and creates a revolutionary statement:

> Fire down below
> Fire down below
> And the people dem running around
> Yes the people down running around
>
> All who nah sleep
> Shall get a cup a tea
> All who nah sleep
> Shall get a cup a tea
> I'm a lickle teapot
> Short and stout
> This is my 'angle
> Here is my sprout
> When I get my tea, yeah
> I will shout

> You got to tip me over
> And then you pour me out
> Fire down below... etc.

Here the volcanic eruption images the kind of apocalyptic revolution that figures so prominently in 1970's reggae: 'And if a fire mek it bu'n/ And if a blood mek it run...' ('Revolution', Bob Marley[17]); 'Burning and a-looting tonight/ Burning and a-looting tonight,' ('Burning', Marley[18]), or 'An' when de right time come/ Dem a go bawl fe murder', ('Right Time', Max Romeo[19]), and a plethora of other songs about fire, brimstone, blood and the crumbling of Babylon and its evil system, of which, perhaps, the most famous of all is Niney's 'Blood and Fire'[20]. In my 'Trickster I, I alluded to such apocalyptic images, in the above and in Spear's songs-:

> evergreen griot, since forever chanting
> fires down below, blowing up
>
> like volcanoes, revolution:
> hearing you now chanting,
>
> isolated prophet on the beaches,
> preacher preaching on the burning shore...[21]

I used the griot figure to suggest the position of the reggae artist in Jamaican society. It is not incidental that the griot, keeper of the society's treasures of knowledge and memory, is West African, the figure within whom are contained the roles of prophet, preacher, artist, politician, warrior, priest and historian. The griot epitomises a non-western conception of the individual not fragmented by divisions between the secular and the spiritual. Indeed, the griot is necessarily spiritual and necessarily political and social, for the griot is defined by her/his community, even as this griot stands outside of this community. The reggae artist's capacity to speak about the divine and the political, to see in the history of a society's experience an elemental spiritual pattern, is an aesthetic model that differs significantly from the secular construction of the contemporary western artist. It is this, too, that I try to locate in Jacko, who, while not being an artist, must function with just such a world view. It is not a monolithic view, and there are tensions and variant positions within it. Winston Rodney, for example, assumes the role of griot with terrible sincerity,

and his position as spiritual, single-minded priest, when it comes
to his music, is evident from the fact that he has recorded few, if
any, 'love' songs[22]. In this, he stands as an interesting contrast to
Bob Marley. To borrow a Biblical construct, Marley represents the
Davidian figure, the psalmist of passion whose very narrative is
constructed around his capacity for prophecy, warriorhood, regal
leadership, and sexual potency (and David, is, of course not without
a capacity for tricksterish duplicity); whereas Burning Spear belongs
to the company of 'isolated' prophets of the Old Testament: Elijah,   .
Elisha, Jeremiah, Ezekiel, and Haggai, all men who demonstrate
no erotic side, but who remain devoted to the stern business of bearing
the news of God to the nations. Burning Spear's lyrics are always
founded on the vocation of the teacher and the teacher's rhetorical
strategies:

> Do you remember the days of slavery?
> Do you remember the days of slavery?
> ('Slavery Days'[23])

or

> My roots I'll never forget
> I'll always remember the road I travel
> My roots I'll never forget
> I'll always remember the roads
>
> I travel all over
> Do the works of Jah
> One thing I know for sure
>
> My roots I'll never forget.... [25]

Burning Spear's voice speaks into an apparent void of history,
but in truth it is a void that existed only in the world dominated by
colonial education. He, like many of the reggae artists who emerged
in the 1970s, encountered the teachings of Marcus Garvey not through
the orthodoxy of the education system, but through the folk history
of communal memory, memories that retained a sense of Garvey's
days as a powerful speaker/prophet in Jamaica in the 1930s and
the tragic history of how he was betrayed and destroyed by the colonial
Jamaican and U.S. governments. In a number of reggae songs,
for instance in The Mighty Diamond's 'Them Never Love Poor
Marcus' [25], this betrayal is sung about with such feeling that it seems

as if it had happened only the previous week. In Michael Thelwell's novel *The Harder They Come*, an attempt is made to demonstrate that an Afrocentric black consciousness in rural and urban ghetto Jamaica predates the 1970s and must have been a basic part of the peasant black consciousness throughout slavery and after. Thelwell introduces two characters, Ivan's grandmother, Miss Mando, and her long time friend, Maas' Nattie, who are both aging Garveyites who have never lost sight of the dignity and strength of Africans. Victor Reid in his Maroon narratives also tries to establish this same theme by showing the connectedness of these characters to an African memory. Burning Spear emerges out of that rural tradition, a tradition that grows increasingly militant in the urban context and within the apocalyptic language and culture of Rastafarianism.

It was the conflation of the poetics of the dread ('preacher preaching on the burning shore') and the imperative of Spear's vocation that created the image that I was trying to celebrate in my trickster poem. In part, this discourse is realised by the 'sampling' of reggae songs throughout the poem. By placing Spear in the 'Blood-red streets of Kingston', I invoke the violent realities of the 1970s and beyond, and these streets become the iconic location for the reggae cauldron. Here Marley walks along 'First, Second, and Third Streets' as the 'Natty Dread'[26], and Peter Tosh is the 'stepping razor' who defines himself as 'tougher than tough'[27]. From this space, my Burning Spear is intended to invoke notions of journey that allude to the travelling motifs that operate in Kamau Brathwaite's *The Arrivants*[28]:

> to sing travelling, travelling, we still travelling
> despite the amassed dead and the fire.[29]

In this space, travelling represents not escape, but a recognition of the history of nomadic existence, of constant movement that is the condition of the New World African, an ambivalent recognition of both a state of continuing homelessness, but also of a dynamic movement in history which is still open to change. I allude, too, to Anthony McNeill's eloquent poem 'A Wreath for the Suicide Heart' and the line 'Love is Earth's mission/ despite the massed dead'[30] – an apocalyptic image of slaughter which I also drew on in another poem written for Don Drummond ('It is the Cause (Belleview Ska')[31] in *Prophets*.

The prophet, then, tries to invoke a sense of black people's history of survival, of travelling hopefully in the face of tragedy, couched in the beautiful lyricism of the reggae song and the sweet seduction of the music. McNeill is a fitting allusion because of his position as maverick outsider in Jamaican literary society. His genius has never been questioned, but his enigmatic dance with madness and his failure to soar into success in the manner of a few Caribbean writers offers a fascinating pattern that I saw repeated in West Indian literature and West Indian society in general. In *Prophets*, it is this pattern that I am drawn to in sequences of poems that examine, sometimes obliquely, the journeys of several Jamaican artists who can be described as tragic prophet figures. Among them are John Hearne ('Equinox'[32]), Roger Mais ('Road to Emmaus'[33]), Don Drummond ('It is the Cause (Belleview Ska)'), and McNeill ('Requiem for the Harrowed Poet'[34]). In each of these sequences, the spirits of these men possess Thalbot, a protagonist in the narrative, a prophet unable and unwilling to speak to the sin that he sees before him; a prophet who wanders around trying to escape his destiny. Thalbot finds an affinity with these spirits because in them he recognises a pattern of failure, but also a pattern of creative genius that rails against this failure – a sense of alienation and distance from the society to which they burn to speak. I saw these prophets of Jamaican writing as tragic because they struggled to find the language and aesthetic that could give meaning to their visions and that would have allowed them to speak to the 'masses'. In Burning Spear, on the other hand, I saw a stability and a clarity of vision that allowed him to make his way through the canker of the city and still speak with dignity. In Spear, too, I saw an archetype that transcends the parochial and enters the space of the international, the trans-cultural. His name, of course, contains the powerful evocation of the original 'Burning Spear' or 'Flaming Spear', Jomo Kenyatta, the Kenyan leader who captured the imagination of blacks all over the world for his resistance to British colonial power.

In the poetic figure of 'Burning Spear', I was also trying to redress the image of the Rastafarian that I kept seeing in the literature that emerged in the 1950s and 1960s. In Roger Mais' *Brother Man*, which is still one of the more important and forward-thinking novels by a Jamaican, I saw only a partial recognition of the creative cultural archetype. It is partial because Mais disarms the Rastafarian as a political entity and focuses only on his spiritual element, his position as a Christ figure. The image of the Rastafarian in the work of Orlando Patterson (*An Absence of Ruins* and *The Children of Sisyphus*[35]) is even less sympathetic, for here the Rastafarian is a misguided charlatan or an abject fool who has bought into a myth that has no redeeming value. Our first extensive vision of the Rastafarian as potential spiritual and social revolutionary appears in Brathwaite's 'Wings of A Dove'[36]. In this the Rasta is a prophet who is willing to speak of revolution against the social system that has oppressed black people in Jamaica. As Gordon Rohlehr recognises of Brathwaite's representation:

> The Rastafarian is in many ways a reincarnation of the spirit of the militant Puritan millenarianism. The new avenging army of the righteous are 'de poor dem', and the Apocalypse will be the real destruction of a real city of merchants and oppressors.[37]

Rohlehr is right that the Rastafarian echoes the revolutionary puritan movements of groups such as the Levellers and Diggers with their egalitarian ideologies and apocalyptic visions of the inversion of the current social order by social action and/or divine intervention. It is an apt comparison because historically those groups (and those who are part of their tradition such as William Blake) represent the last expressions in Western culture of an undivided sensibility. Within some Rastafarian groups and some of the puritan antinomians of the 17th century there are parallel symbolic rejections of conventional social boundaries. The Ranters, for instance, made great play with swearing and cursing (even in their churches)[38]. The non-evangelical posture of Rastafarians suggests, though, a different ethos; and the quest for a spiritual home and cultural dignity in Africa, with all its socio-political implications, makes Rastafarianism unique. However, like the radical Puritans, Rastafarianism does not simply represent a call for a spiritual reckoning, but also a socio-political reckoning that positions the outsider, the rejected and exiled African as the avenger for wrongs – social, political, and spiritual wrongs – inflicted by an oppressive white/brown class. Brathwaite's 'Wings of a Dove' is one of the first reggae poems to invoke this aspect of the Rasta creed, incorporating an iconography that is also central to the reggae lyric:

> And I
> Rastafar-I
> in Babylon's boom
> town, crazed by the moon
> and the peace of this chalice, I
> prophet and singer, scourge
> of the gutter, guardian

> Trench Town, the Dungle and Young's
> Town, rise and walk through the now silent
> streets of affliction, hawk's eyes
> hard with fear, with
> affection, and hear my people
> cry, my people
> shout:
>
> Down down
> white
> man, con
> man, brown
> man, down... (pp. 42-43)

The image of the Rasta walking through Kingston has an eerie link to Marley's 'Natty Dread' or the song 'Trench Town'[40] both of which present the picture of the dread walking through the familiar streets of Kingston like a prophet, owning them and yet feeling the pain of the place. This motif is one that we see in renderings of the Rastafarian persona in poems by Mervyn Morris, Dennis Scott, Kendel Hippolyte and Lorna Goodison[41]. In all these works, the dread is a streetwalker who spends his time skanking through Babylon, speaking, declaring, prophesying. More often than not, the image is linked directly to the notion of the Rasta as a prototype for the poet, for the artist in society – at once a part of the society and at the same time in a constant state of exile.

In my poem to Burning Spear in the 'Trickster' sequence, I was trying to continue the imaging of the Rastafarian as a socio-spiritual prophetic voice by alluding to Brathwaite's Brother Man, who is an updating of Mais' seemingly apolitical Brother Man in the novel of that name. Spear becomes the new prophet, the lichens in his head a sign of his aging, and the fact that he contains within him the wisdom of time. The lichens are no longer a sign of the filth of self-neglect, as they are in Brathwaite's poem:

> Brother Man the Rasta
> man, hair full of lichens
> head hot as ice
> watched the mice
> walk into his poor
> hole, reached for his peace
> and the pipe of his ganja... [42]

Instead, my 'Brother Man' is John the Baptist, a desert-walker by choice and one whose dignified presence signifies the weight of his words:

> Yes, if we have a true prophet,
> sallow and enigmatic with grandaddy charm,   .
>
> like John the Baptist with his head full of lichens,
> mouth full of locusts and wildest honey...[43]

This prophet, who situates his hope in Africa, is a poet inscribed in a distinctive cosmology that he can claim as his own. It is in this that I found in Winston Rodney one of the archetypes that form the complex figure of Jacko Jacobus. Jacko, in my poem, is not a Rastafarian, but he lives in a landscape that has been renamed by the Rastafarian and all the voices that have sought to reclaim the Jamaican landscape as an extension of African space. It is pertinent to note here that besides Rastafarianism there are other Afro-Jamaican religious movements that have shaped the Jamaican psyche and which have been, indeed, critical to shaping the very nature and character of Rastafarianism itself. In many ways, for instance, the Rastafarian is not as directly connected to African spirituality as are the Pocomania adherents, but the Rastafarians have established an Africanist rhetoric in their music and in their cosmology that has had a greater impact on the Jamaican and Caribbean psyche than can be imagined.

In the last passage of the poem, then, I try to place the singer, Burning Spear, in a context that suggests that reggae has moved into another realm of meaning, an aesthetic space that allows it to have relevance and meaning outside the confines of Jamaican society:

> we still travelling – it is you, reggae elderman,
> spear flaming through the cankered landscapes:
>
> in the steaming clubs of Halifax,
> the kerosene jazz dens of Soweto,
>
> the red-lit drug dens of Amsterdam,
> the gritty damp of London's Soho... (p. 69)

At the beginning of the recording of 'Estimated Prophet', the grainy tones of Burning Spear's voice declare, 'You should believe me!' – the call of the prophet to the people who are within earshot. At the

end of my poem, I acknowledge belief in the prophet and in the
validity of the reggae sound as a vehicle for a certain spiritual and
political truth, recognising that it is the music that allows us to make
the journeys of memory and the journeys of return to another, more
hopeful and more grounded memory of origin. In invoking the Blue
Nile – the seat of Brathwaite's first journeys in *The Arrivants* – I
was also drawing on 'Dreamland' by Bunny Wailer[44], (a song covered
masterfully by Third World and Marcia Griffiths):

> There's a land that I have heard about
> So far across the sea
> There's a land that I have heard about
> So far across the sea
>
> To be together on my dreamland
> Would be like heaven to me
> To be together on my dreamland
> Would be like heaven to me

The utopian 'heaven' of Rasta mythology is Ethiopia or the land
that spreads across the entire continent of Africa. It is the place
that Brathwaite describes in the language of glass shards and sparkling
light, an image that brings him back to the beaches of Barbados
and the sparkle blue of the Caribbean sea:

> Dust glass grit
> the pebbles of the desert:
> sands shift
> across the scorched
> world water ceases
> to flow [45]

For Brathwaite, the pebbles will become the 'pebbles' of the islands
('Islands'), the archipelago that skips across the glinting Caribbean
sea, the cracked egg that will birth a new way of seeing the world.
Drawn by Brathwaite's sense of creation as an interaction of hardness
and light working in and around water, I conflate the sea and desert
images into an idyllic image of the Nile, a quintessential reggae
image of mythic splendour and mythic improvisation:

> We believe in the words of the prophet,
> transported as we are by the regal one-drop

to a time when the sea shells glinted
on the splendid Nile, blue and sparkling white. (p. 69)

The 'one-drop' is the signature beat of 1970's reggae music; a pattern that is founded on the notion of the off-beat, the overturning of the steady and predictable beat of western music.

In my construction of the 'Trickster', then, I am moving away from the notion of the 'trickster' as rogue or unscrupulous individual and seeking, instead, to appropriate the erstwhile rogue as a survivor, a heroic construct. There is nothing especially unusual here in terms of diasporic African culture, but in the context of the colonial framings of Jamaican culture, this figure of the rebel outsider is a significant postcolonial break in the way the society defines and begins to understand itself. In a figure like Burning Spear (at least the mythic figure I have constructed in the poem), there is a movement from outsider to leader and to 'estimated prophet' that represents a kind of sleight-of-hand for the which the backdrop is reggae music. In other words, through the medium of reggae, within the very heart of a Jamaican society which retained in substantial ways its colonial race and class structure, people such as Winston Rodney, or Marley in his earliest rude bwoy manifestation, suddenly metamorphosed from the position of being outsiders whom official society regarded with hostility and contempt into being the voices who defined Jamaican culture. By sleight-of-hand I mean the kind of protean, shape-shifting cunning which enables the trickster to achieve a position of dignity and stature without the old ruling order really noticing what has happened. This prophet figure of dignity is but one manifestation of the trickster stance. There are others provided by the reggae subculture, and in the 'Home Melodies' interlude I explore these through other figures: Lee 'Scratch' Perry, who is discussed in a later chapter, and a more recent incarnation, 'Sister Patra', the dancehall queen of the 1990s. In the case of Patra, her sexuality and her audacious feminine strength combine to create a new vision of gender in Caribbean society that is at once controversial and liberating.

My attraction to the Burning Spear figure has its parallel in the work of other poets. Rohan Preston, for instance, uses Spear as an archetypal, defining voice in his brilliant poem 'Music'. In Preston's work there are similar recognitions of the complexities of reggae music as a means for framing his poetic utterance, as an aesthetic grounding that allows him to explore a wide range of themes and ideas. As an introduction to his work, Preston offers a generic, and deeply non-western articulation of reggae's importance:

> Music is our first literature and culture... The drum as music banishes our ills and spiteful thoughts, our hang-ups and downpression. It speaks to our endemic divinity, riddling our souls with spirit-releasing sounds, so that we may properly be strengthened and purified and at peace with our polychromatic, synaesthetic selves. We can then do whatever needs to be done. We can see, feel smell and taste the drum, and it informs us on levels that we cannot name. But we know that music makes us closer to being whole. Much of our quest throughout oral, and written and painted history has been to loosen the rings around our souls. And the drum is the ultimate shaker, the penultimate rattler of those bells... [46]

He goes on to describe Spear and then, to demonstrate the validity of his assertion, to see Spear, the reggae prophet, becoming the poet's channel, his opening to a world of memory, history and, ultimately, a sense of an aesthetic which gives him his grounding as a writer.

> Burning Spear wails with a hole, a hollow, in his voice
> a strained strain, taut from squeezing out the sound, de sound
> de soun': *Marcus Garvey words come to pass.*
> Tired of the echoes, Mau-Mau bawling from Mount Kenya,
> tired of the waiting and politicians, shegries and lies:
> *See the hypocrite them a galong deh.* [47]

In this single moment, Preston condenses a range of allusions that are complex in their multiple intertwinings and that speak to the allusive force of reggae. He reveals his groundedness in the language and discourse of reggae through sampling actual reggae songs, and by the careful use of the language continuum in Jamaican speech. The squeezed out, pained sound of Spear's voice is transformed into a reference to a dub poem by Mutabaruka, 'Every time I hear de soun, de soun...' [48], which was one of the first popular successes of dub poetry. The sound, then, is the force that carries the poet into history via the reference to the Spear song, 'Marcus Garvey', and Spear's name opens Preston to another history of anti-colonial revolution and possibility: the history of the Mau Mau and Kenyatta. But the sound also expresses anger at the contemporary Jamaican political system that 'downpresses' the sufferer. Preston samples another classic reggae track, this time 'Hypocrites' [49], a song recorded by the Wailers in the late 1960s. The refrain 'see the hypocrites dem a galong deh' takes us back to the isolated prophet pointing an accusing finger at the society in which he must live and speak. Preston, like some other Jamaican poets, is able to find his most articulate expressions of political anger in the language and music of reggae. He describes this source, this place of possibility, as a 'space' somewhere in the voice of Burning Spear, which invokes a history that is long and involved, a history that locates the black person, the African, in the context of the New World.

> Burning Spear has a chasm in his voice –
> not an abyss, mind you – but a big gap nonetheless
> through which Nanny and Sam Sharpe, Harriet, Frederick,
> Toussaint and Eric Williams – the long train of Maroons
> stream up; where Paul Bogle tells the colonial tribunal
> (for him never did have any sort of fair hearing, you know)
> tell today's jury, how them hang him for asking:
> *Am I not...* But him couldn't go no further
> 'Black' and 'Man' no fit too well in the same sentence
> *(You favor flying pattoo, you favor...)*
> For that was the sentence, the missionary terms
> for a Cain, canine (p. 161)

These lines are layered with echoes and sounds that seek to connect the complexity of the African experience across several worlds through language and music. Preston is recovering in the voice of Spear the capacity to speak of a wide range of experience that only the rhetoric of the poetic imagination is able to contain in one articulation. Through Spear, he finds Nanny, for she appears in Spear's song 'Queen of the Mountain'[50], an account of the magical folk heroine whose use of African arts to defeat the attacks of the British during her days as a Maroon are legendary and mythic in the Jamaican imagination. Preston embraces that memory, and by so doing he embraces the magic of her power. It is an embrace that brings to mind Lorna Goodison's anthem, 'Nanny' [51], a poem that posits the theory that Nanny did not arrive in the Caribbean by accident, but was sent there, fully prepared, by those in Africa who had watched their people being taken away to a strange and uncertain land. Preston goes on to see Spear's voice puncturing a more comfortable kind of myth:

> You see these little Caribbean islands sailing away,
> sculpted like beautiful tourist postcards,

> these little irregular punctuations in the sea
> connected by vast amounts of salt and water
> nutritious from the bones of the Middle Passage
>
> *Do you remember the days of slavery*
>
> these little lands created by blowing bubbles
> no make them fool you – them too small
> to contain the voices, too small to hold the history
> think of the water instead
>
> Burning Spear has a hollow in his voice
> the spirits much too big for the media, cracking
> spilling the ancestors onto digital
> harvest moon and jukwunu
> exploding guts, tar, feather, cat-o-nine tails (p. 161)

Preston has Spear's question deny the image of the islands as images of tourist recreation. In his image of the archipelago, he echoes Walcott and Brathwaite, as he does in sending the reader to the image of the sea as the vast repository of memories of the numberless victims of the Middle Passage. In his long poem, *Turner* (1994)[52], David Dabydeen also uses this image of the sea as a place of creative amnesia, a place of landlessness where it is possible to construct a new memory. Preston then goes directly to the idiom of the reggae song (and further samples) for two stanzas of poetic clarity and prophetic assurance:

> *When the rain stops falling down*
> *And they ain't got no water*
> *They're gonna bow down to the ground*
> *Wishing that they were under*
>
> *When the stars start falling off*
> *And the fire is burning (red hot)*
> *There will be a weeping and gnashing of teeth*
> *At four in the morning.* (p. 161)

This prophecy is couched in the language and spirit of the New Testament *Revelation* and the prophecies of Jesus in the Gospels. But it also echoes a range of reggae tracks by Marley, Bunny Wailer, The Mighty Diamonds, Lee Scratch Perry and dozens of others, for the images of fire, of weeping and wailing and gnashing of teeth are elemental to the prophetic meaning of Rastafarianism.[53] Babylon will burn. In the rest of the poem we note that the reggae ethos has taken him beyond the confines of Jamaica or the Caribbean and allowed him to see possibility and revolutionary hope in South Africa. There is, too, a quite deliberate updating of the reggae references beyond the roots reggae of the 1970s to the dancehall and ragga culture of the 1980s and 1990s, where a revisioning of reggae's revolutionary/spiritual force can still be found:

> Hear the names of the dancehall deejays
> Colonel Mite and Lieutenant Stitchie sewing up the wounds
> Ninja Man and Daddy Lizard at Cross Roads
> Shelley Thunder with the (small) double ax of Shango

The fire and aggression of the dancehall is rejuvenating and restorative and the interdependence of history and the present continue to be felt. Cross Roads is a spot in Kingston, Jamaica, but it is also the place of spiritual meeting in West African and Afro-Caribbean belief systems. Shelley Thunder[54] and her powerful lyric force carries the authority of the god Shango. The power is in the word, and the path towards this place is through the voice of Burning Spear. Preston is involved in an act of layering, of discovering connections while still working that steady drum and bass theme of Burning Spear's music. In this space, he is able to allude to Marley's 'Babylon System' even as he describes the suffering of the South African blacks: 'their feet trodding on grapes and vineyards'. It is impossible not to hear Marley's call from the above song, 'We've been trodding on the wine press, much too long./ Rebel! Rebel!/ We've been taken for granted much too long/ Rebel! Rebel!' in the midst of this.

From South Africa, he then turns to the United States, and he allows the spirit of Spear to address another kind of oppression:

> P.E. penultimate – all the voices coming out
> squirming like worms, squeezed through telephone
> and PA system: *Public Enemy Number One*
> through the steel pipes of Rikers and Compton,
> Spofford and Alcatraz – bloody ass, Babylon
> the pimp, the warden smiles widely
> there's weed growing among his teeth
> may look like it, but the ancestor has not returned. (p. 162)

Indeed, the ancestor's return will presage the rebellion that is needed. The poem is not able to transform the world – Mikey Smith made that very clear – but the poem, like this one, is able to articulate the spirit and vision of the political reality. To do this, Preston employs reggae as a vehicle to carry him into a world of images and allusions. Burning Spear is his gateway and his licence. He assumes the prophetic posture of Burning Spear to speak as he does. Like Marley, Burning Spear has devoted many of his compositions to the world of black experience outside of the Caribbean and this serves as a model for Preston to embark on his own 'musical' musing into the refrain, 'Do you remember the days of slavery...'

Spear, then, for both Preston and myself, has become not simply a source of lyrical motifs and philosophical ideas for our poetry, but a veritable icon for the importance of reggae in our quest to negotiate our sense of the present and our understanding of the past. This prophetic figure offers our work a mythological grounding that is especially dynamic for its immediacy and relevance. Other reggae figures have come to assume that same place in the work of other Caribbean poets.

CHAPTER NINE

'JAH MUSIC'

MARLEY AND SOME 'REGGAE' POETS

(MCNEILL,SCOTT AND GOODISON)

SOME TENTATIVE DEFINITIONS IX

'Aaaieee! Dis rebel music!'

this reggae music undulates
like a sheet caught up
by wind

woman
stands silhouetted
by the white of the sheet

the movement of wind
in softer waves
sounds

like dub
crawling across
the belly of the city

poem-making folk like me
seek metaphors
to draw

soundcharts
of the pattern of this
water music, flowing, flowing

but words can only imitate,
and everything barely
catches

the way
reggae sounds on Sunday,
lifting the body to softer places

At the core of my thesis in this book is the argument that reggae has provided the Jamaican writer with an aesthetic which offers a way to close an historic divide. This is the gulf between the largely middle-class, formally educated writer and the world of the working-class and peasant majority, a division marked by profound differences of language and culture. I have also argued that while an earlier generation of Jamaican writers frequently pursued a radical nationalist agenda, they did so within an aesthetic which privileged elite colonial forms. Reggae, I argued, provides an aesthetic which is thoroughly postcolonial and which derives from the majority of the Jamaican people.

It is, of course, not quite as simple as that. The phenomenon of the middle-class writer adopting the accents of the poor has come under scathing observation by Mutabaruka amongst others. His critique of writers who go 'slumming' in search of revolutionary subjects is one that should remain in the mind of any writer who is involved in expressing the suffering of others in a class-defined space. His anger is specifically directed against acts of pretence or impersonation, but his accusation inevitably touches on the position of all middle-class writers who are drawn to deal with the position of the poor in the Caribbean, and this is a theme that has inevitably preoccupied many writers. It is a tragic puzzle, a fascination with the capacity for hope and resilience even in the midst of poverty and hardship. At its worst the stance can replicate a certain kind of naïve middle-class curiosity ('How do they manage to be so friendly?'), and for any writer not of the working-class it is a theme fraught with problems of voice, with the dangers of being, as Mutaburuka accuses, a scavenger-poet who is exploiting the hardships of the people. Mutabaruka's poem declares:

> revolutionary poets
> 'ave become entertainers
> babblin out angry words
> about
>   ghetto yout'
> bein shot down
> guns an' bombs

                              yes
            revolutionary words bein
            digested with
                              bubble gums
                              popcorn an
                              ice cream
            in tall inter conti nental
                              buildins

            revolutionary poets
            'ave become entertainers
            oppressors recitin about oppressors
            oppressin the oppressor
                              where are the oppressed?[1]

I recognise Mutabaruka as asking writers like myself whether
the very notion of Natural Mysticism does not amount to another
instance of the artist contriving an aesthetic on the backs of other
people's suffering. My response to this is that the integrity of the
engagement with this aesthetic depends upon the manner in which
the artist recovers an individual sensibility within it, upon the degree
of the writer's self and social awareness and the degree to which
this is transmuted into realised art through both vision (what I have
called Natural Mysticism) and a seriousness about artistic form.
This might appear to suggest that I see the writer bringing a kind
of middle-class, sophisticated self-reflexiveness and artistic formalism
to reggae, to write **over** it in the way that Paul Simon might be seen
to do in *Graceland*.[2] This is, of course, possible, but it overlooks the
fact that self-reflexiveness, the foregrounding of an individual sensibility
and a concern with artistic form are all part of the vocabulary and
capacity of reggae itself, something that can be seen in the lyrics of
singers from Marley to Buju Banton. If the poems by Anthony McNeill,
Dennis Scott and Lorna Goodison, which I discuss later in the chapter,
achieve this kind of integrity of individualised response within a reggae
framework, they are only following Marley's example in doing so.
    Marley's song 'Running Away' (*Kaya*) dramatises the tensions
of this kind of self-awareness. The song ends with a very revealing,
unusually vulnerable and self-reflexive confession:

            You must have done something wrong
            Why you can't find the place where you belong

(*Talking*)
I'm not running away,
Don't say that
Don't say that,
cause I'm not running away
I've got to protect my life
And I don't want to live with no strife
It is better to live on the house top
Than to live in a house full of confusion
So, I made my decision and I left you
Now you coming to tell me
That I'm running away
But it's not true
I'm not running[3]

The brilliance of this lyric is contained in irony, in its trick of pronoun construction. Marley begins in the typical posture of the prophet/preacher denouncing an unmentioned 'you':

You must have done
Something wrong
Said you must have done
Something wrong
Why you can't find the place where you belong

Yuh running and yuh running
and yuh running away
But yuh can't run away from yourself.

The suggestion is that he is addressing someone else, offering, in true Marleyesque fashion, certain salient truths about living, about humanity and the foibles of the human character. Then he introduces a rather mysterious proverbial aside, mysterious because it appears incongruous within the clearer march of admonition that is taking place:

Every man t'inketh his burden is the heavies'
Every man t'inketh his burden is the heavies'
But who feels it knows it, Lord
Who feels it knows it, Lord...

What becomes clear is that Marley's laconic musings amount to a sophisticated dialogue with the self. On the one hand, he is assuming the voice of those who are accusing him of betraying his sense of loyalty to home and to 'things-Jamaican', and in another voice, he attempts to respond. The 'trick' lies in the use of the accusative second person singular voice, which is a naturally ambiguous pattern of speech because it allows the speaker to use that voice as a distancing mechanism in first person speech. Marley, during the period of *Kaya*, had spent some time in exile after an attempt on his life by political thugs. At the same time, the street talk was that Marley was abandoning the ways of Rasta and becoming far too deeply involved in the Babylonian system of the rock and roll world, leaving his roots, his identity and himself behind. Much of this flowed out of speculations about the inclusion of Americans in his band, the BMW, the visible affluence, all of which suggested a betrayal of his principles and values as a 'grounds' rootsman. It did not help that Marley was enjoying a relationship with Miss World, Cindy Breakspeare, a light-skinned society woman who hardly fitted the profile of a rasta queen. Marley's song, 'Running Away' is a defence of his credentials as a prophet, as a man, as a Rastaman, and as a Jamaican. Thus his statements shift from voice to voice, creating a dialogue that would look something like this:

> **People:** Yuh running and yuh running... etc...
> **Marley:** But yuh can't run away from yourself...
> **People:** Yuh must have done
>   Something wrong
>   Why you can't find the place
>   Where you belong.

In his defence Marley asserts that he cannot run from himself, from his identity. He throws up the 'su-su' (gossip) of the street in a subtle but clear act of confrontation: 'This is what you say, but here is the truth. I know what you are saying about me...' Then, as the song begins to fade away, the heart of the song is spoken. The 'message', which is perhaps one of Marley's most overtly personal articulations, is contained in typical reggae fashion, at the end of the song, as if it is an out-take, a ramble that could be easily cut out from the body of the song, something that only appears because the microphone is, unbeknown to the singer, still 'hot'. But this apparent casualness is in reality a brilliant rhetorical stroke, absolutely integral to the song, as the verse form, the use of rhyme, makes clear. He explains, alluding to the violence and turmoil that marked his life at the time, that he is really in exile as an act of escape, as a way of getting away from the threats on his life. He then addresses the full brunt of the accusation against his integrity contained in the body of the song, by stating, 'But it's not true/ I'm not running...' At this point it becomes clear that the refrain, sweetly harmonized by the I-Threes, is bitterly ironic and is in essence a taunting cry. Suddenly, the extremely dry and pained quality of Marley's rendering, the almost 'old man's' tone his voice takes on, begins to make sense. The argument he has with himself is rooted fully in his perception of his role. As a prophet, with a responsibility to the community, he must address his own as much as his people's accusation that he is selling-out, that he is abandoning the battlefield at a time when there is upheaval in the nation and many are dying.

Alongside this complexity of voice, Marley had no less a sense of the aesthetic power of the form he used and the redemptive power of realised art. Marley it was who sang, 'One good thing about music/ when it hits you feel no pain',[4] and it is of course, from Marley's work that the very idea of Natural Mysticism derives. In his songs one can see, again and again, the spiritual dimension of healing and possibility expressed within a painful realism concerning the social context from which the music emerges. It is this dimension that is lacking in, for instance, Orlando Patterson's pre-reggae novel *Children of Sisyphus*.[5] For while Patterson is able to construct a convincing image of the squalor and pain of the people of the Dungle, his existential pessimism, grafted from Camus and Sartre, prevents him from discovering the mysticism that allows the society to keep recreating itself, to keep surviving in the midst of the squalor. The Dungle that Patterson describes in *Sisyphus* does not appear to be a fertile ground for the creation of anything, particularly something as unique and powerful as reggae music; but that world was, in reality, the space out of which this remarkable creative force emerged. This is not a romanticisation of reality, but an awareness of the spiritual at the heart of the 'natural'. It is only from a dialectic of this kind that a lyric such as 'No Woman No Cry'[6], could emerge, a lyric that is at once tragic, and yet, at the same time, triumphant and believably so:

> I remember when we used to sit
> In a Government yard in Trench Town
> And then Georgie would make the fire
> As it was logwood burning through the night
> Then we'd cook cornmeal porridge

'Alf which I share wid you
You see my feet is my only carriage
So I've got to push on through
And when I'm gone
Everything's gonna be all right...

By its very existence, the song transforms bitter realities into a source of creativity. Music, then, is the restorative force that presents the mystical in the midst of the natural business of living.

We are not speaking of a tension between irreconcilables here – although exploring the tensions within this construct is something that many artists have capitalised upon to great effect. There is something altogether more organic about this relationship, and it emerges in songs and poems and novels that are not uncomfortable with a vision which is multifaceted, that expresses a degree of apparent contradiction. We see this in Lorna Goodison's capacity to speak in a strongly feminist voice in a poem such as 'Judges'[7] and still be able to celebrate a woman's fortitude in staying in a relationship that is clearly abusive as in 'For My Mother (May I Inherit Half Her Strength)'[8]. The same exploration of apparent contradictions and the sweetly realised dance between the sacred and the profane is also to be found in the work of Anthony McNeill and Dennis Scott.

McNeill's 'Saint Ras'[9], for instance, in the very title of the poem, articulates that walking contradiction of circumstances that characterises the reggae condition. 'Ras' is, of course, a shortened form of the word Rastafarian and has come to be a common title for Rastafarians: Ras Michael, Ras Joe, Ras Tony, etc. Ras, then, becomes a term of entitlement that labels the individual a dread, a man of the faith. But 'ras' is also a pun on the expletive 'raas' which differs only by the context of its expression and by a lengthening of the vowel sound. 'Raas' as a variation on 'arse', is used as a shortening of the swear phrases 'rass clart' or 'blood clart', respectively 'arse cloth used to clean excrement from the anus', or 'sanitary towel'. Thus, 'Saint Ras' is at once a dignified acolyte of the Rastafarian faith and a walking abomination – the sacred and profane in lock-step movement. The poem extends this contradictory impulse and, as in Scott's 'No Sufferer' poem, discussed later in this chapter, is centred around the incongruity between the rasta's faith and hope and the struggle and pain of his life.

In McNeill's case, through the very honest personal dimension displayed in his encounter with the rasta/prophet figure, McNeill comes up with something that is an answer to Mutabaruka's probing and important accusation. McNeill is discovering a sensibility and a creative reality within this working-class revolutionary figure that allows him to understand his own alienation and his own struggle to come to grips with the suffering that he witnesses. McNeill, with some humility, wants to be guided along the path of empathy and creativity, to establish a bridge across class and economic distance, a bridge, which if it is to have truth, must be rooted, as I believe McNeill's is, in the integrity of the art. McNeill creates a persona who is in search of the 'true island of Ras', the true island of peace and hope. The Rastaman is an alien in the urban landscape, for he must live in exile from the capitalistic system that dominates this space.

> One step from that intersection
> could, maybe, start peace. But he dread-
> fully missed, could never proceed
> with the rest when the white signal
>
> flashed safe journey. Bruised, elbowed-in,
> his spirit stopped at each crossing,
> seeking the lights for the one sign
> indicated to take him across
>
> to the true island of Ras. (p. 135)

This dream of a place of peace is clearly not going to be realised because the city, the world of Babylon, is a space that is antagonistic even to the dreams of the dread, an exile in his own land:

> But outside his city of dreams
> was no right-of-passage, it seemed.
> Still-anchored by faith, he idled
>
> inside his hurt harbour and even
> his innocent queen posed red
> before his poised, inchoate bed. (p. 135)

McNeill very explicitly rejects the dualism of inner spirituality and outward suffering in the material world. There is no escape from that even in the dread's personal space. It is only in the harsh temporal streets that the possibility of the dream can begin to exist. And, though his divinity is undermined, his alienation continually reinforced by exposure to the real world, it is there that the dread must, and can find possibility. It is again the striking contradiction of the natural and mystic:

> Now exiled more, or less
>
> he retracts his turgid divinity,
> returns to harsh temporal streets
> whose uncertain crossings reflect
> his true country. Both doubt and light. (p. 135)

McNeill's encounter with Rastafarianism is filled with this kind of ambivalence, a strained consciousness that reflects his own anxieties and profound questioning of the world of mysticism and faith in an unjust world that demands a secular reckoning. It speaks also to the tensions between his utter commitment to art and the inevitable uncertainties about its relevance in a society where so many lack for their basic needs. He discovers in Rastafarianism and reggae, a capacity to speak of these contradictions without having to deny either.

There are other poets who have found in the Rasta/reggae praxis an idiom that has seeped subtly into their poetry, informing, in the process, the ideological context within which their work must be read and understood. Dennis Scott, in the early 1970s, was clearly discovering, along with people such as Kamau Brathwaite, the potential of the idioms of Rasta-talk to provide an appropriate enriching of the language of scribal poetry. Scott is less concerned with using the rhythms of the reggae lyric or making overt references to the music. What he does do is declare a confidence in the poetic potential of the language of reggae music by making use of its language registers. At the same time, Scott has, like Goodison, found in the reggae prophet figure a prototype for the poet. The confluence of the mystical, which is couched in the biblical language of the apocalypse, and the natural, which is described in the world of poverty, political disease and social anxiety, is clearly represented in his collection *Uncle Time*[10]. The 'Black Mass' sequence, for example, constitutes a study in the apocalyptic language of the book of Revelation which parallels the discourse of James Baldwin's *The Fire Next Time*[11], and the stark realities of Southern racism. In 'For the Last Time, Fire', Scott is in the world of his play, *Dog*[12], a world of class conflict in the urban Jamaican setting, where the tension between the wealthy, privileged classes and the working classes is being played out in Manichean terms. Tellingly, in *Dog*, the rebels, the revolutionaries – the dogs – who threaten the anxious and beleaguered middle class are associated with reggae, with the music of Bob Marley. The same oppositions are at work in 'For the Last Time, Fire':

> She came to the house like an old cat, wanting
> a different kind of labor.
> But the Banker was busy, feeding his dogs, who were nervous.
> Perhaps she looked dangerous.
> The child threshed in her belly
> when she fell. The womb cracked, slack-lipped,
> leaving a slight trace of blood on the lawn. Delicately,
> the phoenix placed the last straw on its nest.
>
> Mrs. So-and-so the Banker's wife beat time
> in her withdrawing room. Walked her moods
> among the fluted teacups, toying with crusted foods.
> The house hummed Bach, arithmetic at rest.
> The phoenix sang along with the record,
> and sat.
> But the villagers counted heads, and got up. [13]

In the play *Dog*, a pregnant bitch arrives at the home of a wealthy family. She has the pup/child in the yard. This begins a complicated narrative about a war between dogs and people. The allegory is quite blatant, and Scott's play constructs a far less sophisticated class struggle than in this poem (which appears to be a distillation of the dramatic piece). But this revolutionary quest is very important in Scott's work, and he finds in the reggae/Rasta ethos a language that is local and not borrowed from outside, one that enables him to speak to questions of race, identity and political transformation. Thus, in 'No Sufferer', which ends the *Uncle Time* collection, the Rasta figure, the brotherman of Kingston's streets, connects with the Natty Dread persona of Marley's album of that name, who sings in the jazz-inflected strains of 'Revolution'[14] a powerfully political song which is wholly indigenous in its expression. As in Marley's songs, the political and spiritual come together in a compelling prophetic-political assertion in 'No Sufferer'[15]. In this poem, Scott seeks to excavate the magic of possibility and pride contained within the 'sufferer' so that the 'sufferer' is not simply a statistic, a cipher of an abject existence, but an individual capable of voice. The poem begins with an evocation of the ghetto's suffering, the sense of hopelessness and invokes Zion as the place of solace and peace, and also as the literal 'heaven' of Rasta ideology– Africa:

> but in
> the sweating gutter of my bone
> Zion seems far
> also. I have my version.

Scott's tendency to employ motifs that create a current of resonance throughout the entire body of his writing is revealed in the word 'bone' which has come to represent the entire self of the person – his core, his marrow (as in *Roots to the Bone*, the punning title of an album by the trombonist Rico Rodriguez[16]). The allusion is also to Scott's play, *An Echo In the Bone*[17], which traces the journey of Africans from the continent into slavery across the middle passage through a ceremony of remembrance and possession. The 'gutter' of his 'bone' represents his abject condition, but it is also his place of deepest meaning, the place where memory and current reality converse. In this place, Zion, the place remembered by the 'Rivers of Babylon', seems far away. The 'version' that will emerge is the new voice that the sufferer is able to speak in. The version is, of course, a reggae allusion, a reference to an instrumental version of a song, often sold as the flip side of the hit 45 rpm disc. The version frequently amounts to a stripping down of the recording of all vocal elements and a complex re-mixing of the instrumentation that allows the drum and bass to dominate. The 'version', therefore, suggests a transformative and creative construct which becomes the medium on which the 'dub organizer' can experiment, improvise, and shape a varied and deeply complex 'dub' track. This has always been Lee 'Scratch' Perry's (and King Tubby's) forte, and it is an approach to the reggae arrangement that has also come to be a part of the recording of vocal tracks. Thus, in some of the live recordings made by Burning Spear, there are long sequences in which the instrumentation is stripped down to the drum and bass and a series of percussive and improvisational interplays between the vocal, guitar and piano sections[18]. These are complicated by the dynamic use of reverbs, echoes, distortions and so on. Thus the 'version' that Scott is alluding to is not merely a stripping of voice – indeed voice often appears on the version track, albeit in a distorted and truncated form, but the version is a fragmented space within which the creative impulse is most perfectly realised.

The version is also the bedtrack (or 'rhythm'), the track whose bass and rhythm components have served as the basis for many other songs. To this day, Jamaican deejays and record producers still make use of certain bedtrack rhythms that are over thirty years old. The creativity rests in the artist's ability to shape something distinctive and powerful on the basis of these standard tracks. The version is therefore not a singular variant on a theme, but a multiplicity of variations. It is this principle that draws Thelwell in *The Harder They Come* to use the 'vershan' as a motif in the titling of his chapters. He attempts, in that novel, to create a pattern of varied tracks that vamp on the same theme but that contain the distinctive qualities of the characters who are the focus of each section. Reggae offers the artist a way to conceive of the novel form, a way to construct his narrative in a manner that links with the culture he is describing in the work.

The version of Scott's persona in 'No Sufferer', is a version linked to the 'drum', and this drum harks back to Rasta drumming, to the drumming of the African retentions in the Caribbean, and even further, to the drumming of Africa. Again, the theme of echoes is caught in the very quality and nature of the sound of the drum. For the sufferer there is comfort, healing, and the finding of self in the music that courses through his veins:

> the blood's drum is
> insistent, comforting.
> Keeps me alive.   Like you.
> And there are kinds of poverty we share,
> when the self eats up love
> and the heart smokes
> like the fires behind your fences, when my wit
> ratchets, roaming the hungry streets
> of this small flesh, my city [19]

There is threat too in this figure roaming the streets of the city. The ratchet is a complex image of action and mounting tension and a literal allusion to a knife used by the 'rude boys' in Jamaica's reggae subculture. The threat is akin to Marley's assertion: 'Don't try to show off/ And mek yuh fren dem laugh/ For I will cut you up? And I will take the last laugh…'[20] or Peter Tosh's 'I'm stepping razor/ Don't you watch my style/ I'm dangerous, I'm dangerous.'[21] But in the midst of this, there is hope and the possibility of healing. Here, the word 'dread' becomes a loaded one, for the dread is a multiplicity of things in the reggae/Rastafarian language scheme. The Rastafarian herself or himself is a dread, with her or his dreadlocks, someone who can evoke dread and a sense of danger in the observer. But the phrase, 'it dread' is also a statement of hardship, of pain, of struggle, a word associated with other coinages like 'sufferation' and 'botheration'. Thus the world in which the Rasta must survive is a dread one, a dreadful one. There is also the biblical resonance within the word, of an apocalyptic order in which God intervenes on the side of his chosen ones and puts to sword the ungodly. And so, the 'dread time' that Scott speaks of is at once negative and positive. The times are dread and painful, but these are the times of the dread when the dread comes into his or her own. 'Guess Who's Coming to Dinner', as Black Uhuru sang, or as Marley prophesied:

> Natty dread rides again
> Through the mystics of tomorrow
> Natty dread rides again
> Have no fear have no sorrow [22]

The vulnerable humanity of the dread persona in Scott's poem is a critical feature – it represents the naturalness, the mortal reality ('while whatever may be human chains me/ away from the surfeit of light') that stands in opposition to the mysticism of Mabrak – the black lightning of possibility in Rastafarian discourse. The sublime, the place of spiritual uplift is the place of hope in the midst of suffering. This dialectic fascinates Scott, and it offers him a way of understanding the meaning of art in the context of the Third World where it is important that the artist find the capacity to be at once politically honest and true to the pain of existence and, at the same time, to be able to transcend this pain and find beauty in the creative process and in this process discover a deeper sense of the mystical in life. This reggae characteristic allows Scott to end the poem on an assertion which is deeply spiritual and yet earthly and pragmatic:

> Mabrak
> and the safe land of my longing,
> acknowledge I. [23]

The 'I' that must be acknowledged is first the individual who demands recognition. But the 'I' in Rasta discourse is also the collective

'I and I' which refers to the people who are connected to this 'I'. Thus there is a sense of community in this call for recognition that embraces both the ego 'I' and the communal 'I', but it is also a reference to the Rastafarian God, Selassie 'I', as Rastafarians do not speak of Selassie as Haile Selassie 'the first', but intone the letter 'I' as a kind of mantra. Indeed, 'I' is talismanic for rastas, being used to transform standard Jamaican English into the enigmas of Rasta talk. Thus peppers become 'i-pers', and calalloo, becomes 'ilaloo' and 'vital' becomes 'ital' which comes to mean a range of things that are equivalent to the term 'kosher' in Jewish speech. 'Ites', 'Irie', 'Iyah', are all words that have become a part of urban Jamaican speech, all of which have their source in the mystical 'I'. We hear Marley transforming words like 'hour' into 'i-wa', thus imbuing the moment, the prophetic moment, with the weight of spiritual significance. Thus 'acknowledge I' which ends Scott's poem, carries the weight of a highly condensed range of reference, and reveals that Scott is discovering in reggae and Rasta speech a complexity of mythic possibilities that are immensely useful to him as a poet writing in Jamaica and seeking to find an aesthetic home in the Jamaican environment.

However, of all the 'scribal' poets involved with reggae, it is Lorna Goodison who has, I believe, gone furthest in exploring (and acknowledging) the reggae aesthetic. It is not that she contains everything she writes within the framework of reggae or that she necessarily has an agenda for creating a reggae aesthetic. She is clearly going back beyond reggae to some of its sources, writing into verse the folk culture, the salvaged memory of herbs, of folk idioms, and of the power of Jamaica's folk memory, and using sources which are only just becoming less marginal to reggae: the history and culture of women. She has made a synthesis, whose 'joins' are almost imperceptible, of various aesthetics – the jazz/blues/soul praxis of America, the classical/colonial/British influence of her colonial education, and the African/Jamaican world of the 1970s and beyond. All these come together in varied kinds of poems that nevertheless share a singular quality that is grounded in the Jamaican language, a Jamaican sensibility and most tellingly, a compelling prophetic posture.

Thus, though Lorna Goodison has established herself primarily as a poet committed to the business of making books, it is very evident that in her poetry, reggae music and reggae culture have been translated into an aesthetic that feeds the literary instinct, that her work is shaped by reggae in a way which extends beyond the lexicon she

uses or the rhythms she employs and enters into the realm of ethos
– a posture and relationship to the Jamaican psyche and the Jamaican
landscape that is connected to the reggae instinct. Her poem 'Jah
Music', dedicated to Third World band member, Michael 'Ibo' Cooper,
shows this very clearly:

> The sound bubbled up
> through the cistern one night
> and piped its way into
> the atmosphere
> and decent people wanted
> to know
> 'What kind of ole nayga music is that
> playing on the Government's radio?' [24]

Critics such as Ted Chamberlin have recognised in Goodison's
poetry a commitment to the use of dialect as a way of expressing a
cultural or national identity.[25] In readings such as this, reggae is
seen primarily as a linguistic force in the literature that is influenced
by it, and there is no doubt that in terms of language – in the use of
syntactical and lexical variations – reggae has had a significant
impact on Caribbean poetry. Goodison's poetry demands that we
examine the connection at a far deeper level. What I see in her
work is a way of understanding the world around her that has reggae
music at its centre. Reggae offers Goodison the role of prophetess,
the moral authority to walk the streets of Kingston and warn of the
consequences of its destruction and decay. The language does not
always appear to be particularly reggae-derived, but the ethos is.
When she speaks of 'my people', or 'my children', she is rooted in
the Biblical construct of the children of Israel contending with
themselves and with the calamities of being in exile in Egypt, a
metaphor which is central to many prophetic reggae lyrics. Marley
repeatedly sings of 'my people' or 'my children' and Burning Spear
has, as I argued in the previous chapter, taken on, convincingly,
the position of an elder standing before his people, for whom he
sees himself as being responsible. This prophetic posture is adopted
by Goodison in several of her poems. In her poem 'Jamaica 1980',
in examining the canker of political violence and self-destruction,
her tone is that of the discouraged prophet:

> For over all this edenism
> hangs the smell of necromancy

and each man eat his brother's flesh
Lord, so much of the cannibal left
in the jungle on my people's tongues.

We've sacrificed babies
and burnt our mothers
as payment to some viridian-eyed God dread
who works in cocaine under hungry men's heads.[26]

The appeal to the Lord, the reference to Eden, point to the poem's biblical framework, but the more important indicator is the use of the first person plural, the collective, prophetic voice. She is as much interested in what the prophet must say as she is in what the prophet feels; she utters her own lament but must speak to a nation in which she must survive:

And mine the task of writing it down
as I ride in shame round this blood-stained town.
And when the poem refuses to believe
and slimes to aloes in my hands
mine is the task of burying the dead
I the late madonna of barren lands.

She is both inside and outside of the circumstances, conscious of the earnestness she must adopt to carry out her spiritual role, a role which she addresses not with irony but tension and uncertainty. In 'The Prophet Jeremiah Speaks' she explores this tension in the quandary of a prophet who is reluctant to speak. The prophet is a biblical figure, but the landscape is a modern one. She constructs a mythic narrative, at once Biblical and contemporary, which places the prophet figure as the 'go-between' between the mystic, or 'Godness', and the natural, the people. The role of the poet is to bridge that gap:

Today I will not speak.
I shall take these warnings
born to me as loud visions
and I shall cover them
till they do not breathe.

For they hate the sight
of me, these people.
When I appear in the marketplace

> they see indigo rays stream
> from my mouth, they hear
>
> high-pitched prophecy
> shatter their careful illusions.
> But still God bids me show them
> the poor. (I saw a man last
> Thursday fight another human
>
> for the right to eat, from a bag
> of garbage outside a health
> food shop. Did nobody else
> see anything unusual in that?) [27]

The poet/prophet is caught in a terribly difficult situation, wanting to settle into a normal life, a life void of the pressures of griot-like responsibility, but acutely aware that the role is something that invades the consciousness, compelling her to speak with the fire of conviction. The tension is important and integral to the reggae ethos as the earlier discussion of Marley's 'Running Away' set out to show. Goodison's work, then, not only has an affinity with the multiple dimensions of Marley's vision and his position as an artist, but in her poem dedicated to Marley, 'Calling One Sweet Psalmist' she is explicit about her indebtedness:

> On the outskirts of Addis
> this is a rider
> guide to the line
> of Kings passing
> he is waiting to take me
> I rise and go with him.
>
> The journey is one
> of seven days and seven nights
> we pass through landscapes
> of sheer drops
> the wind in this part
> of the country is spiced [28]

In the metaphor of the journey towards the mecca-space of Rastafarian mythology, Ethiopia, Goodison acknowledges Marley as the prophet whose psalms guide her on a journey within to the womb space of the poet:

Nourish me then
when all death
has been drawn from me
with liquid amber
and wild bees' honey.
You I leave to marvel,

you to create burial spectacle
the whole me is moving
to another height
(calling one sweet psalmist)
I've been promised a play
of David's harp.

(Come in now one sweet psalmist)
new songs are being released
in me, I chant now
celestially, I am become
what I was born to be
I am, I am sweet psalmist. [29]

The poet sees in Marley a model for her role, one that will allow
her to assume the role of maker of beauty in art and spiritual song-
maker, even as she must engage in the painful activities of writing
down the horrors of a society in disarray, of burying the dead, of
responding to the fire that calls for speech ('At least until the high
fire/ within forces these hot/ scorching warnings out'). This brings
us back to Goodison's definition of the reggae sound as an aesthetic
base for her work. 'Jah Music' is rooted in a history where we encounter
the class and racial demarcations of Jamaica. The 'decent people'
regard the music as belonging to low-class people, a class defined
by its race: 'What kind of ole nayga music is that...?' This music is
not simply defiling the air but, by appearing on the Government
radio station, is threatening the socio-political structure. Goodison
makes it clear that this working-class music has survived as an
underground force despite its repression. When it emerges with the
'bubbling' sound of the reggae organ, Goodison is both using the
political metaphor of the water spring and drawing attention to the
sound of the music in the Marley allusion: 'We bubbling on the
top one hundred/ Just like a mighty dread.'[30] She both acknowledges
reggae's tremendous social and political importance and makes this
a metaphoric manifesto for the poetry she is creating. Both reggae's

mission and hers is to offer light and healing. Emerging from a ghetto space, in the colours of Rastafarianism (red, gold and green), it blossoms into a magical force that will heal, a musical essence whose power to transform exceeds the assumed paraphernalia of the genre (ganja, rum, etc.):

> But this red and yellow and dark green
> sound
> stained from travelling underground
> smelling of poor people's dinners
> from a yard dense as Belgium
> has the healing.
> more than weed and white rum healing.
> more than bush tea and fever grass cooling [31]

Goodison makes it clear that this new music emerges with its own aesthetic distinctions, its own artistic values which unseat the largely class-defined principles of 'good art' that have operated in colonial society and beyond independence in the persistence of neo-colonial cultural structures. Here the music shapes a new classical construct: the usurping of the 'symphony conductor' by the 'dub organiser', the reggae genius, the Lee 'Scratch' Perry who sits at the mixing board and gives aesthetic form to the music in such a way that it can offer psychic healing as well as addressing the socio-political ills that have both caused the pain and shaped the music. The music, then, adopts both a revolutionary (or at least an aggressive) posture **and** creates beauty which can heal the soul. In speaking of reggae in these terms, Goodison is expressing her own aesthetic inclinations in the language of the reggae artist.

These three poets, then, reveal the potential range and complexity possible in a poetry that draws on the aesthetics of reggae. The effect is not predictable verse caught in the polemics of political advocacy, but verse that allows the poet to discover a sense of self through an aesthetic that is at once liberating and challenging. Reading these poets through the principles of the reggae aesthetic, and through the poetics of Bob Marley, reveals much about the poems that would not otherwise have been as apparent. Therein lies the potential of the reggae aesthetic as a source for critical discourse. In the next chapter, through a discussion of the work of Lee 'Scratch' Perry, I suggest the potential inherent in reggae as a model for formal innovation in other artistic forms.

CHAPTER TEN

LEE 'SCRATCH' PERRY:

MADMAN/PROPHET/ARTIST

TRICKSTER II

2

Legend puts the Scratch man in trees,
comfortable in this lofty nest, where airwaves

have a clearer path to the sampling antennae
of his dangerous, bright mind.

A few were baptised to the strange
syncopations of unsteady sycophants,

but all looked to see the boy
with a sweet falsetto grained with desert grit

singing the father's songs, just as
the Scratch man prophesied would happen.

CT: '...if you could be a bird or a fish or any kind of animal, what would you be?'
LSP: 'I am a bird right now, and a fish in one. A birdfish in a tree. [stands up] These two limbs, they are my roots. When I stretch my arms I am a bird. And these are my two feet, they are tree leaf walking with the tree of life. I am also a flying fish. All I have to do is identify I-self and I am he that I am. [sings] 'I am he who cannot die, I rebuild the sky, I am he who cannot die, and I refuse to cry...'[1]

Lee 'Scratch' Perry is arguably the most innovative reggae composer ever produced by Jamaica. His genius has always been characterised by a strange eccentricity that has granted him a distinctive, legendary status among Jamaican musicians. 'Scratch' is the quintessential 'dub organiser', for his strength has always rested squarely on his capacity to create music out of the simplest and most rudimentary of materials. In this, 'Scratch' is a living incarnation of reggae music. His sources are broad-ranging, and his capacity for improvisation daring. On the jacket art of one of his more recent works, *From the Secret Laboratory* (1990)[2], a recording of quirky compositions whose mixing is complex and multilayered, Perry is wearing a regal scarlet crown, trimmed with gold. In the background – as part of his dominion – are the Alps, snowcapped and all. In the compositions for this album, Perry explores the conceit that his recording studio is a laboratory and that he himself is a mad scientist. (The title track is subtitled 'Scientific Dancehall'). In this space, he is able to conjure music that is playful, insanely earnest, iconoclastic, twisted, and both profoundly Jamaican and universal. The backdrop of the Alps is no accident. After the destruction of his Black Ark recording studios in Kingston in 1980, Perry eventually moved to settle in Switzerland. He made it clear in various interviews that the conditions of political gang warfare in Kingston and the constant crowd of hangers-on at Black Ark had made it impossible for him to continue working there:

'So I leave and let them know what dem gwine do with it. Right? Who take sick in Jamaica did have to take sick. Who get blind in Jamaica did have to get blind and who get dead in Jamaica did have to get dead. Because the Ark of the Covenant was the brain. The Ark of the Covenant wouldn't take their strain anymore and their roughness and their toughness and their dreadness, and their badness and their gunmen who come by night, ask you who are you, 'Get up bwoy, who are you?' When prisoner love tief artist so, 'Where is all them tape deh all them ting?' Rude boy dress like soldiers. And them want no mercy, no more mercy. Blood? No.' [3]

His relationship to Jamaican society, to the Jamaican music industry, and to the local reggae audience has never been straightforward. There was undoubtedly a period in the 1970s when the Black Ark[4] sound was a genuine and highly innovative force in Jamaican music, but it is also the case that Perry's reputation has mostly been higher outside Jamaica than within it. At one level, Perry's persona and his highly individual 'auteuristic' recordings appear to fit more closely into the Western romantic archetype of the isolated, alienated artist than the archetype of the community-based reggae artist, and this no doubt contributes to his appeal to serious (mainly white) reggae enthusiasts outside Jamaica. However, a listen to the 'African Hitchhiker' track on *From the Secret Laboratory* and a closer look at both his music and his persona reveal Perry as a wholly and distinctively Jamaican self-creation. The song is worth quoting at some length:

> I am an alien from outer space
> And I got no home and I'm living in my briefcase
> I am a, I am a, I am a hitchhiker
> I'm hitching and hiking straight from Africa.
> I am the word professor, I am the word processor,
> I am the green monitor.
> My name is Father Christmas, Marcus,
> And I am a mus'....
> ....
> While others were chasing riches
> I was chasing witches, agents of demons and hosts of vampires
> There's a cross of fire there on my heart
> To prove I am the living torch.
>
> I am a, I am a, I am a hitchhiker
> I'm hitching and hiking straight from Africa.
> I am a magician, I am a musician
> I love magic, yes, music for me is magic in the ear...
> ....

> Clearing the way for the Lord,
> Clearing the way for the God,
> Clearing the way for the King,
> Clearing the way for the t'ing
> I am an alien from outer space
> Come to warn the human race...
>
> I am an elephant from outer space
> I am the elephant from outer space
> Living in my briefcase...
>
> What is good I accept,
> What is not good I reject
> Eh, music is like a kid, yes, music is like a baby
> I am an alien I say, I am an alien from outer space
> You want to know what's in my briefcase?...

Here is Perry, taking one leap from the hold of the slave ship to define the world in the image of the travelling New World African. Here is Perry, the trickster medicine man bearing his gifts, with the most serious of wars to win, with a memory as deep as Burning Spear's, but hidden under the guise of the manic legerdemain.

For me, Perry is the enigmatic master of the strangeness of the reggae dub form, and he, like no other artist, has managed to reveal its limitless capacity, both for stunning simplicity and for the kind of complex multilayering of sound which makes *Super Ape*[5] such a profound musical experience. It is in Perry that I find the most meaningful example of the creativity of the trickster, and it is through his genius that I have come to understand the potential for genius inherent in reggae music and its aesthetic.

Besides some inspired self-compositions, Perry's greatest accomplishments reside in the manner in which his engineering and producing feats have transformed and elevated the work of other reggae artists. I am convinced that there would not have been the Bob Marley we know without Lee 'Scratch' Perry. Some of the most innovative work done by the Wailers in the early 1970s – work that includes strangely haunting tracks like 'Mr. Brown', 'Satisfy My Soul', 'Kaya', and 'Sun is Shining' [6]– was done with Perry at the helm, evidently probing, pushing, and seducing the Wailers into very dub-based, loose, and quirky musical arrangements. The Wailers began as a ska band, and ska is nothing if not tightly organised and neatly structured. The music sprints along with energy and buoyancy, but the arrangements owe their structure and predictability to the jazz bandstand: the big band sensibility in which a wide array of horns, a stand-up double bass, steady piano, unobtrusive guitar, pounding drummer, and vocalist who had to ride over all this were standard expectations. Once ska had slowed to rock steady and then to reggae, there was more space, and this space was filled by the innovations of the recording mixing board. Where ska tended to be recorded in a live setting – pretty much in the manner of the old jazz recordings of the pre-1960s – reggae was relying more and more on the mixing board (just as at about the same time the Beatles were bringing their own kind of mixing innovations into the studio). Lee 'Scratch' Perry was one of the truest innovators in that sense. His material was naturally limited. He was working with very little in terms of recording equipment. He used a simple four-track recording board and would spend his time mixing tracks into the sound that he thought would work best.

The tracks he produced during that period with the Wailers were not the best recordings in terms of production values, but they were daring and represented a stretching of style and form into something very distinctive. When the Wailers eventually produced *Catch a Fire* and *Burning* for Chris Blackwell, the tracks were cleaned up and the sound was tidied (and on *Catch a Fire* given a rock ambiance), but the hard work of stretching the potential of reggae had already been done. Perry worked with the confidence that reggae had its own internal values that would stand up to and not be compromised by radical experimentation. When asked about his favourite reggae musicians – those who had done sessions with him – Perry, in the interview in *Straight No Chaser* quoted above, offered one of the most brilliantly articulated expositions on the validity of the reggae aesthetic. He names Ernest Ranglin, a remarkable 'jazz' guitarist who, like Don Drummond, became a part of the laboratory of innovation which was trying to construct an indigenous musical form. Perry's response is vintage 'Scratch', complete with trickery, mysticism, and sheer wit. Perry connects the creative energy of music with the street politics of Kingston, constantly aware that a nationalist agenda operates in the evolution of reggae:

Ernest Ranglin had a thing going, I really take in his portion of the gift he put into a ting they call reggae to build it up. The energy was thinking bout a guitarist to make music look international, me a go think about the best guitarist. Me could call it jazz reggae, me no have

to call it reggae punky party, it could be anything. Cos is part of the
music me was using, pop, jazz, rap, every fuckin' ting. Blues, everything,
rhythm and blues, and *mix it up to build a country*. It wasn't to build a
politician dem or coke-ist dem. They fight against ganja with coke, to
support gun and politician call game. [7] [my italics]

In this passage, Perry demonstrates that reggae was a distinctive
form which absorbed anything which came its way. On top of the
basic backbeat, Perry would bring the various instruments in and
out of the mix on the board, the effect being a *tour de force* of engineering,
giving texture and dimension to the reggae tunes performed by these
artists. This dimension of Perry's work, the role of 'dub-organiser',
offers a crucial and as yet little explored model and encouragement
to writers working within the reggae aesthetic to engage with issues
of structural experimentation that can carry Caribbean literature
away from its dominant naturalism or conventional realism towards
a more radical aesthetic which nevertheless remains accessible.

I was also fascinated by Perry's persona because of the reputation
he always had. I knew of Perry as a mad man when I lived in Jamaica.
One of the stories I heard on the streets was that Perry had a tree
in his yard on which he hung records – forty-fives. It was his record
tree. I was also told that Perry lived in a tree, and that he had bouts
of madness. Two years ago, in an interview I conducted with Linton
Kwesi Johnson, I was told many more 'Perry tales'. The soul of the
stories, I recall, rested in the Shakespearean notion of a man with
'method in his madness'. Johnson concluded laughing that he never
felt that Perry was mad. Perry, he was convinced, understood that
the artist needed space and that kind of space was hard to come by
in the congested and almost anarchic world of the Jamaican recording
studio. To ensure that he was left alone, Perry would 'go mad'. Left
to his own devices, he could produce his music without being interrupted
by the untalented, the boorish and the visionless.

When Marley was making the album *Kaya*, he drew on the spirit
of 'Scratch'. It is no accident, then, that *Kaya* is perhaps one of the
most enigmatic of Marley's recordings; and of course, the earliest
recording of the eponymous track 'Kaya' was with Perry on *Soul
Revolution*.[8] Some felt that Marley had left behind the predictable
tones and themes of his previous work, had left the rockers stylings
of reggae and gone to something more ephemeral, something that
was too much driven by the guitar. Some felt that Marley was being
far too introspective, far too personal in this album. But it is in all

these things that we can begin to understand the genius of Marley
and the importance of Lee 'Scratch' Perry's contribution to the work.
What happened with *Kaya* is something that I think is undervalued.
For Marley to write and perform, so effectively, diverse songs of philosophical weight and mystery, of emotional and romantic splendour,
of personal anxiety and self-doubt, songs rich with lyricism, all within
the reggae genre, represented a great moment. What Marley managed
in *Kaya* was to show the range possible in reggae. It makes sense,
then, that Marley also collaborated with Perry to produce the track
'Punky Reggae Party'[9], one of Marley's important crossover experiments
that was influenced by the punk movement in the United Kingdom.
Perry's genius lay not just in the fact that he knew other musical
styles, but in the fact that he understood the place of other styles
of music within reggae. He understood the strength of the reggae
sound and had little doubts about the music's capacity to be stretched
and tested. I find in Perry, for this reason, the perfect archetype of
the 'trickster' innovator in the reggae world. I have always regarded
the Perry-influenced *Kaya* as perhaps one of the most important
'literary' influences for me.

In 'Trickster II' in the 'Home Melodies' interlude in *Jacko Jacobus*,
therefore, I tried to evoke poetically the way in which the reggae
aesthetic has been shaped by the innovations of people such as Perry,
to whom 'Trickster II' is dedicated. From within reggae culture, Perry's
example gave me release from the narrative's tyranny for order and
linear chronology to shift to a more surreal poetic mode. This is a
mode that seems at odds with the stereotypical view of reggae as a
genre dominated by political realism, that is purely declarative and
never introspective, reflective, or surreal. *Kaya* argues against that
stereotype and, as an imaginative reconstruction of my indebtedness
to *Kaya* and Lee 'Scratch' Perry, I wrote a poem that set out to challenge
archetypes and stereotypes, a poem that rests its meaning in the
language and iconography of reggae and Rasta, and yet subverts
those notions, intentionally eluding easy meaning. My intention was
to question madness, the madness of trickery, the very madness of
the musical genius. The reggae of this poem, then, lies in its own
attempt to stretch the genre, and yet to remain completely inscribed
within it. This poem could not exist without reggae, for it is a poem
about reggae, even as it is a poem about the Jamaican ethos which
is filled with mystery, with natural mysticism.

I begin with the allusion that ended the first poem of the movement.
John the Baptist is the prototype for Burning Spear, but the John

that we meet with as Burning Spear in 'Trickster I' is the living, constantly defiant voice of prophecy. The voice of the John the Baptist in 'Trickster II' is going to contend with his 'fixed' narrative history, to seek a magical way out of his fate at Salome's hands. For it is through such acts of trickery that the prophet is able to function in the context of Jamaican society. Perry's 'madness', his capacity to invoke a range of western television icons in his work, gave me the license to drag in a range of allusions, each with an appropriate connection with this business of trickery, deception, and survival:

> A voice cried out in the wilderness.
> We all came to hear the voice
>
> in the Cockpit valleys, to hear
> the man with a skull in his hands.
>
> He was mad.
> It was all quite obvious.
>
> We listened but saw no revelations,
> just a sweet madness of new rhythms.
>
> Afterwards, we drank mannish water,
> ate curried goat, and slept peacefully. [10]

Like the Children of Israel of Jesus' day, the people come to the Cockpit Country in search of a sign – something that would suggest that there is an other-worldly moment occurring there. The people are unwitting witnesses of genius, of magic, but they lack the capacity to recognise the genius in their midst – it appears far too 'normal', too much part of their existence. The man before them appears obviously mad, and this is not the source of shock and uncertainty – public madness is part of the Jamaican landscape. But this madman, the trickster, is very much aware of his accomplishments. The skull-in-hand posture is an allusion to *Hamlet* and that other trickster, Yorick, but there is an element of macabre prophecy in this skull-carrier, for he is foreshadowing the posture of his fate, a head on a platter, chattering away. Mortality, then, is a part of his consciousness. In many ways, then, this poem is a duppy story, a story about a strange apparition or ghost, a theme that is dealt with in 'Mr Brown' one of the Perry/Marley produced tunes of the early 1970s, on *Soul Revolution*:

> Mr Brown is a clown who rides through town in a coffin
> In a coffin where there's three crows on top and two is laughing
> What a confusion
> What a botheration
>
> From Mandeville to Sligoville
> Coffin running around
> Upsetting, upsetting, upsetting the town
> Asking for Mr. Brown

The capacity to speak of these creatures, these images of rural fear, rests in the spiritual audacity of the Wailers, who declare on that same album, 'I'm a duppy conqueror'[11]. The declaration in this latter song is directed at those people who spend their time laughing at a man who has been arrested and spent time in jail. He has just been released, and he is praising God for his ability to survive in prison. But there is an element of dangerous threat in the song, mixed with its blues lament:

> The bars could not hold me
> Four walls could not control me, now
> They try to keep me down
> But God keep me around
>
> Yes I've been accused
> But wrongly accused now
> But through the power of the Most High
> Them have to turn me loose
>
> Don't try to cold me up on this bridge, now
> I've got to reach Mount Zion, highest region
> But if you are a bull-bucker
> I'm a duppy conqueror, conqueror [12]

The lyric then utilises a bridge metaphor in its own 'bridge' verse to create the threat, the danger that is contained in this individual. This narrative about being released from prison is a reality (as it was for Bunny Wailer and Peter Tosh in their lifetimes), which is transformed into a spiritual odyssey, an allegory for spiritual growth and success. Mount Zion, the place of greatest spiritual achievement, is what the singer is reaching for, but he makes it clear that anyone who seeks to deter him from his path will be dealt with seriously:

> Don't try to show-off
> And mek yuh fren dem laugh (what a la-la)
> For I'll cut you up
> And I will take the las' laugh
> I'm crying. [13]

My own Perry figure, in 'Trickster II', has a similar capacity to be at once rooted in the temporal world, yet be situated in a transcendent and visionary realm. He can see eternity in the mundane. This capacity is part of what gives shape to this poem, in particular, and to the larger narrative of *Jacko Jacobus*. But those of us who arrive to see the 'Scratch' man as 'madman' are too often unable to see the magic in the music he has created. We fail to see the sign because we are looking for the wrong thing. This failure to see the magic, the mysticism in the rhythms of reggae, is typical of some of those of us who have been working as writers and artists in the Jamaican context.

The pattern of prophecy and revelation functions as a basic motif in the reggae ethos. In 'Trickster II', the connection is made between the music of 'Scratch', with all its attendant madness, and the music of Bob Marley, the 'boy/ with a sweet falsetto grained with desert grit'. In the third movement, I begin to outline the basic qualities of the reggae generated by this magic-maker. The music in *Kaya* is my entry into the place of metaphor, symbolism, and images born out of the Jamaican landscape in reggae music. These are the elements that give credence to the possibility that I write about in my poetry. The world of creativity, in which something brilliantly fresh and painful is created again and again, amounts to a moment of struggle and survival, of death and resurrection:

> There would be nothing of the crucifixion,
> no resurrection repeated each time another
>
> reggae operator is born, again, again,
> no revelation without this locust-eating prophet. [14]

In the fourth movement, a surreal image is connected to the image of Perry on the cover of *From the Secret Laboratory*. Here it is that the prophet/poet defies the fate meted out to John the Baptist. This Perry/prophet is dogged in his instinct as a seer and a speaker. His voice continues despite the grotesquery of his execution. He even outlives, in this state, his executioner, Salome, as the platter upon

which the head of the prophet was placed becomes the shiny compact
disc from which, even after his sacrificial death, the music still
emerges.

> All that is left is his bodiless head
> chatting, chatting, tongue like a flapping bell,
>
> tongue among the teeth. Salome too is dead,
> but the head still creates this twisted
>
> sound here on Switzerland's slopes.
> Rastaman defies the chill and prophecies,
>
> his head on a compact disc like a platter
> spinning, spinning, spinning, new sounds.

As in Marley's 'Duppy Conqueror' this reggae-like convergence
of the spiritually mystic, the disturbing and the mundane becomes
a way of understanding the complexity of Jamaican existence. This
quality appeals to me greatly because of my own preoccupation with
a spiritual dimension for the poetic instinct.

Yet while the prophetic/madman/trickster figure has long been
recognised as critical to the Jamaican psyche, I feel that there has
been a failure to grasp its true centre, in the same way as there has
been a failure within Jamaica to recognise the true genius of Lee
Perry.

In Jamaican literature, the prophet figure has been explored largely
as a political entity by a number of novelists, mindful of the powerfully
seductive influence of the charismatic Jamaican leader on the society.
This figure is by no means limited to Jamaica. Indeed, throughout
Caribbean literature, the image of the Christ-like leader of the masses
recurs. Almost always, this figure is shown to be thwarted, an often
comic charlatan whose gullible followers are drawn into a mutually
destructive pact. It is part of the archetype that the followers will,
suddenly, without warning, turn on the leader and destroy him. In
Mais's *Brother Man*, while the narrative is not intended to be funny,
the community's evaluation of the prophet is heavily cynical,
characterised by a distinct assumption that the prophet/messiah is
a ginal, a trickster. It is, in that sense, bleakly comic when Brother
Man is beaten near to death by a mob that once allowed him to
heal them and be their leader. The Christ connection is hardly veiled
in Mais's work, and he is very careful to construct a mythology around

Brother Man that will allow his predictable resurrection at the end of the work.

There are other more sardonic portrayals of the failed leader in West Indian literature, of the man who wins a large religious following. He eventually announces that he is now ready to die for them, to be crucified so he can be resurrected and save them. He has his body tied to a cross and hoisted and then demands that his followers stone him. In most versions he changes his mind when it is clear that the people are in earnest. Sometimes he is disgraced; at other times he is sent to an insane asylum where he languishes certified as a madman. Naipaul, in *Miguel Street*[15] presents such a character in the person of Man-Man. In Jan Carew's *The Wild Coast*,[16] we encounter the same story, this time set in rural Guyana. The story appears again in Earl Lovelace's *The Dragon Can't Dance*,[17] Lawrence Scott's *Witchbroom* [18] and in less comic incarnations in Andrew Salkey's *A Quality of Violence*[19], Orlando Patterson's *The Children of Sisyphus*[20] and Ismith Khan's *The Crucifixion*[21]. This narrative parallels the actual story of Bedward, an itinerant Jamaican preacher who promised to ascend to heaven on a given day and to take the rest of the disenfranchised Jamaicans with him. The people gather for the ascension which is never accomplished. Bedward is arrested and put in an insane asylum where he dies. In novels by Dawes[22], Hearne[23], Lamming[24], and Sylvia Wynter[25], we get further versions of this same narrative. In these texts, this figure is also used to point out the fickleness of the people and their preoccupation with the business of making heroes only to destroy them as soon as they tire of them. In these versions, the prophet is rarely seen as a figure whose voice is not only necessary to the society, but emerging from the soul of the community. On the contrary, these figures are almost always imposing their egos on their followers, their manic delusions of grandeur inflicting harm on the community. In its turn, the community is seduced and then comes to its senses. I am not arguing against the truth contained in such satirical portrayals. There have been too many political figures who have assumed the roles of saviours of the people, feeding off the community, while maintaining a strong allegiance to the ruling elite. But I feel that the way this prophet archetype has been treated has come to obscure something far more potent within it.

While there are significant differences in tone, particularly between the Jamaican and the Trinidadian tellings of the prophet-myth, between, say, Naipaul's Man-Man and Mais's Brother Man, it is not until the more reggae-inscribed work of Kamau Brathwaite [26] and marina ama omowale maxwell[27] that we find the deeper resonances of the sacrificial prophet figure being addressed in Caribbean writing. In reggae, the fickleness and unreliability of the 'people' is acknowledged, but, for the most part, the prophet figure is not subjected to ridicule. Indeed the prophet figure becomes endemic to the reggae ethos, for in the midst of apocalyptic times the prophet represents a serious presence and voice.

> How long shall they kill our prophets
> While you stand aside and look... [28]

Both Brathwaite and maxwell relate to this reggae ethos in poems addressed to the memory of the murdered dub poet, Mikey Smith. Here there is no trace of the twisted humour that we note in the calypso retellings. The narrative is earnest; the prophetic figure is wholly tragic, murdered by a people who have been shaped by the political disorder of the society. In omowale maxwell's poem, Smith is presented as the prophet of the community:

> Warrior/Houngan we salute you
> Frail body
> Towering Spirit
> It is a savagery/that you have known.
>
> Our Revolutions *must* be different.
>
> Limping lizard
> Prophet of the tribe
> It is a brutality/visited upon you.
>
> Our revolutions *must* be different.
>
> 'It is not
> It is not
> It is not enough'–
> to make a change
> To make blood
> To make slaughter
>
> Our Revolutions *must* be different

> Our poets cannot be eaten
> Our shepherds cannot be stoned
> *We* rip out the logos of our beginnings
> *We* trample the heaven-heart of our growth[29]

Maxwell's 'sampling' of Kamau Brathwaite's 'Negus' [30] ('It is not/ It is not/ It is not enough') points to the existence of at least some community (even if just of writers) which shares an abhorrence of the tragedy of Smith's stoning; but what is more telling is the manner in which the popular dub poet becomes a fitting symbol for the Jamaican artist who must walk the streets of the city, speaking prophecy and truth. This posture is not simply an appropriation of the Christian or Judaeo-Christian sensibility, but a conception of the Jamaican and Caribbean artist seriously given to the notion of prophecy, or to the role of the griot in direct dialogue with society.

I am not arguing that reggae-inspired artists should be engaged in didactic propaganda. This would be contradictory, even impossible in an aesthetic that is as much about the individual's capacity to be creative, to engage in sensual play, and to be distinct in her or his encounter with society, as it is about speaking prophetically about the ills of society or its moral confusions. Ultimately, however, the reggae artist is often involved in a situation that pits the individual version against the communal version. When these versions are in conflict, the reggae artist arrives at a position of risk, of being ahead of popular taste, or being ignored when fashions and tastes move on – the creative death of being condemned to recycle increasingly similar songs to an ever decreasing audience. There is, indeed, the real risk of being killed, as was Mikey Smith, though this may have little to do with the practice of art. The attempt on Marley's life, though, was almost certainly politically motivated, as may well have been the murder of Peter Tosh. The list of other murdered reggae musicians includes, among others, King Tubby, Nitty Gritty, Hugh Mundell, Prince Fari, Major Worries, General Echo, Dirtsman and Pan Head. It is within this context or space of risk that one can see both the 'antic disposition' of the Perry persona and the John the Baptist figure in my 'Trickster' poem. Perry is serious about bringing about a cultural, postcolonial revolution in the face of the political establishment and the coke-dealers who conspire to hold back this revolution. But who among those malign forces could take seriously the ravings of such an obviously mad man? This is indeed an important dimension of the trickster/ prophet persona, and one which, as I am arguing, we fail to read correctly.

The secularist agnosticism and materialism of Jamaican fiction of the 1940s, 1950s and 1960s, situated as it was in modernist ideologies and Marxist discourse, was understandably or predictably hostile to the prophet figure, grounded in spirituality. Ironically, this absence of the spiritual in much of the fiction is at odds with the intense and sincere spirituality of Jamaican society. The cynicism in these novels, then, represents a telling demonstration of the class and ideological gap between the artists of that time and the community. Roger Mais is perhaps the only exception in *Brother Man*. But Salkey, Patterson and Wynter all stand distant from the spirituality that they observe in their characters and, from that position of distance, take cynical pot-shots at the belief systems of the working-class community. It is a chasm that was only bridged when reggae began to offer a language which could speak simultaneously of spiritual and political notions without embarrassment. The reggae aesthetic, then, allows the prophet to have some validity, some efficacy, and enables the creative arts to speak in spiritual terms without having to undermine such spirituality through an existentialist mistrust. The door is opened, then, for magic, for firmly held myth, for the prophetic voice. It is this voice that emerges in Lovelace's *The Wine of Astonishment*,[31] Erna Brodber's *Myal*[32] and in all of Goodison's poetry. It is a theme that I explore in some depth in my long poem *Prophets*, in which I seek to suggest that the prophetic role is not merely a symbolic one – a kind of allegory for the political arena – but is in fact a deeply ingrained part of the spiritual dimension of the Caribbean psyche.

In reggae we observe the artist assuming a relationship with the audience that is not distant or void of responsibility. The artist is trying to speak to and for that community. The head spinning on the platter chatters because it has something to say to the people. It is not an isolated ego, free of any connection to the community, and it is this quality that stands out in the role of the artist in the reggae aesthetic. The connectedness to the community does not, however, preclude introspection and the articulation of a singular vision. The artist is positioned in such a way that she/he is able to speak to the community even as she/he is speaking to herself/himself. It is also a connectedness which requires a variety of creative trickster strategems, not least because connectedness itself involves real risk.

I have sought to reflect this quality in my own poetry. While involved in the business of exploring the complexities of politics and social order, this quality also involves a lyrical journey into my own singular vision. These discourses converge in the concept of the griot / prophet as they have converged, with differing inflections, in the music of Lee 'Scratch' Perry, Winston Rodney and Bob Marley.

In a sense, I am speaking here about the manner in which postcolonialism encounters and embraces postmodernism. Superficially, the politicised framing of literary analysis from a largely non-western nation attempting to free itself from the colonial past and the self-reflexivity and individualised self-indulgence of postmodernism would seem to operate in mutually incomprehensible spheres. My argument is that in reggae they have already met. They transformed each other as they did so, but their emerging character is both coherent and observable.

Perry's version of postcolonialism is defined in the movement towards making a 'country', which he describes as equivalent to making reggae music. This is, indeed, a postcolonial act, the shaping of a new and distinct identity out of the raw materials of popular and folk culture. Perry's descriptions of the making of reggae position him as a creator deity, a mythological trickster figure who uses the mixing board as his weapon of postcolonial reconstruction. The music is not simply directed at Jamaican society but practically asserts the importance of the nation as an entity established in relationship to an international world order. This is a world order, we need to remind ourselves, that by its willingness or unwillingness to recognise a society can undermine all new national efforts. It is by the revolutionary act of self-assertion – for instance, by the audacious unwillingness to compromise language and cultural distinctiveness – that such a national identity is achieved. At the same time, music like Perry's and Marley's is directed against neocolonialism, attacking the complicity of those local politicians and dominant economic classes who sustain neocolonial hegemony in Jamaican society. The creation of the music, 'mix up to build a country' (or as Junior Byles sang, 'Skanking for justice'[33]) is seen by Perry as defying the efforts of politicians and drug lords in Jamaica to undermine all efforts at creating a national sensibility.

At the same time, Perry has been establishing the complex internal anatomy of reggae as a music that draws upon a diverse range of styles and influences to create an aesthetic that is also clearly in his head. His manner, his posture and the enigmatic mystique of his alchemy of sound – individualised, idiosyncratic and realised – all serve to create a mythic framework for reggae. His reiterated statement that his recording studio represented the ark of the covenant, a place of mystical protection, though offered in literal terms (of a magical-realist kind), contained an unquestionable metaphorical truth. The reggae studio is presented as a place of creativity, but also as a shrine of spiritual devotion. Music, then, is granted the status of deep spiritual significance, of pure reverence, dread and apocalyptic, even as it was also, as Scratch's recordings often were, deeply irreverent, playful, joyously silly and earthily erotic. The ark was the place of safety where this nation within a nation, this nation of music, that prefigured the Jamaica which ought to exist, could survive. Departure from the ark was tantamount to exile into Babylon. This was an argument that Perry used to explain the tragic fate of people such as Bob Marley and Peter Tosh. They had abandoned the ark in the first place by parting company from his studio and by becoming too involved in the world of Babylon. But even that articulation constituted a trickster posture, for Perry himself burnt his ark and abandoned Jamaica in frustration[34]. Perry therefore offers himself as a prophet in exile, a Jonah caught in a place of uncertainty where on the one hand he wants to speak to his society and on the other is wary of returning to Jamaica. Perhaps the suitcase of 'African Hitchhiker', carried through the years of Lee Perry's wanderings in the desert, is what survives of the ark.

In Lee Perry's posture of eccentric individualism, the boundary-crossing of his sense of place and above all the hybridity of his music, we see then not only a postcolonial but a postmodernist sensibility. In this postmodern space, the speaker is constantly aware of the construction of the enigma that he is enacting. The music of Perry is markedly self-reflexive and self-referential, as are his cryptic comments in interviews. That Perry's vision of Jamaica (and of himself) is characterised by displacement, disjunction, and uncertainty places it at the heart of postmodern realities. This vision clearly offers Perry a certain creative freedom, the capacity to explore non-realist and non-linear constructions while still being thoroughly inscribed in the reggae sensibility. When he is asked about being any creature he would want to be, Perry declares himself to be a bird, a quintessential postmodern moment as the artist moves from metaphor to metonym, transmuting the individual into whatever he wants to be. As a trickster, Perry has been able to expand and allow for a new complexity in the patterns of discourse in reggae. Quite simply, Lee 'Scratch' Perry, as prophet and madman, could not function, could not exist within an environment that is not at once postmodern and postcolonial.

Nor, for that matter, could Bob Marley or Burning Spear or Peter Tosh. And, I should add, nor can the poet Kwame Dawes, the novelist Colin Channer, the poets Rohan Preston and Geoffrey Philp, or the host of contemporary West Indian writers who are creating a new space in West Indian aesthetics.

Natural Mysticism, I contend, offers a way for these seemingly disparate entities to converge.

CONCLUSION

HAUL AN' PULL UP

SOME TENTATIVE DEFINITIONS XIV

'one good thing about music...'
Bob Marley, 'Trenchtown Rock'

When this slash of a blade,
this blunt object mauling,
this gut grumbling
of subterranean tremors,
causes the body to tremble,
the links of the spine to snap,
when the wash of lyrics
is like an anaesthetic
numbing you to the pain,
what else to do but dance.

There is a memory in the chant
of the lyrics man, conjuring up
that land we have all heard about
and want to see across the sea;
the whip, the gun, the blood
that hurts to hold in the heart,
but this music cools the scorching,
and we are taken by the mystery:
light like a feather, heavy as lead,
so ain't nothing left to do, but dance.

This book is offered as part of a dialogue that I hope will continue and as an encouragement to others to explore in depth and expansiveness what could only be outlined here. I offer it because I think that what is new in recent Caribbean writing has not been treated to the kind of analysis that it deserves. I base this on my conviction that exploring literary connections with reggae is one of the most important ways towards understanding the work of many contemporary writers working in the Caribbean or from a Caribbean context. The dub poetry movements in the Caribbean, Canada and Britain are giving way to more varied and complex forms of poetry which are concerned with both performance and the page, but still largely influenced and shaped by the elements of the reggae aesthetic that I have tried to define above. Writers who are working outside the Caribbean, but from a distinctly Caribbean base, have been able to find their own 'folk' grounding in reggae culture, the most forceful and defining creative grounding to come out of our region. Reggae, I believe, offers the closest thing to the kind of sensibility that T.S. Eliot saw in the metaphysical poets of the seventeenth century, a sensibility that engages in a dialectic of body and spirit, reason and emotion, a sensibility not yet divided by the dualism of western scientific rationalism. Earlier generations of Caribbean writers grew up in a Eurocentric colonial environment which privileged those dualistic modes of thought. As a result there was no literary reflection of cosmologies derived from Africa or India and transformed by Caribbean experience. These were cosmologies which erected no barriers between conceptions of secularity and sacredness; which were the products of sensibilities that treated human experience in an holistic way, and which constructed a mythic view of the relationship between humanity and an environment that was both physical and spiritual. As an art form which existed in a secular world, reggae reintroduced the principles of spiritual awareness and the need for this dimension to be regarded as elemental to the human condition. This was not, in the vast majority of instances, a specifically Christian dynamic of salvation or damnation, but an expression of the fact that Caribbean peoples possess a profoundly spiritualised sensibility that allows sexuality, political discourse, self-reflection, and social commentary to be expressed in the context of an open cosmological structure. Reggae provided a model for this kind of discourse, a model that has given strength and dimension to the work of writers such as Lorna Goodison, Kendel Hippolyte and Robert Lee, to name just a few.

I am not arguing that reggae represents the only means to this poetic position. George Lamming's call for an encounter with the folk sensibility back in the early 1950s is clearly a precursor to what I am exploring here. However, whereas that encounter had distinctly anthropological overtones, with writers becoming interpreters of a submerged culture, the encounter with reggae has been one in which one artist has observed another artist constructing something distinctive and unique. There are many ways that West Indian writers can be read, and recognising the validity of a reggae aesthetic represents only one such path to the effective reading of their work. I have, though, interviewed a number of contemporary Caribbean writers who told me that they did not see themselves as having been influenced or shaped by reggae, but who, after a closer consideration of their work, expressed their recognition that reggae had indeed played some part in the construction of their own aesthetics – their sense of grounding as artists and their trust in the authenticity of the West Indian voice.

There are other writers who have explicitly located their poetic instincts in reggae. They include dub-poets such as Mutabaruka, Oku Onuora, Lillian Allen, Benjamin Zephaniah, Jean Binta Breeze and Linton Kwesi Johnson; but the list also includes playwrights such as Ginger Knight, Barbara Gloudon, and Trevor Rhone. Beyond that, an emerging cadre of writers based inside and outside of the Caribbean is revealing a strong reggae grounding in their works, writers such as Geoffery Philp, Opal Palmer Adisa, Rohan Preston, Lorna Goodison, and Colin Channer to name just a few. Again, Jean Breeze and Linton Kwesi Johnson, in their recent work, show a movement beyond 'traditional' dub poetry, but one which remains deeply inscribed in the reggae aesthetic. At the same time, established voices such as Kamau Brathwaite and John Agard have written work which reflects a strong awareness of the dynamics of reggae music as an aesthetic influence. In short, I think it is possible to argue that the patterns revealed and crystallized in reggae music serve as useful tools to explore the work of writers who are working in a postcolonial space in which the construction of a distinctive voice is crucial to the realisation of an autonomous Caribbean literary tradition. I hope other critics will take on the task of tracing reggae influences in the works of other writers; my task has been to suggest that such readings can be remarkably rewarding.

I write this now because I fear that the further we move away from the genesis of reggae, the less we will grasp the nature and force of its influence on the writing emerging from the Caribbean. I also write this now because I suspect that while many artists from the Caribbean have come to love and appreciate reggae as a musical form, we have not yet begun to tap into the range of creative possibilities inherent in the form, in the aesthetic that it draws upon. I am convinced that as writers really begin to hear the dynamics that shape this music, they will begin to create works of art that manage to capture the dimensions of this music, work that will have reggae's uniquely compelling qualities. By this I mean, in particular, work which possesses reggae's postmodernist innovative vitality and its capacity to tap deep into our folk heritage as New World Africans; its capacity to speak to and for the broad mass of Caribbean peoples while at the same time prizing the distinctiveness of the individual artist's voice; its capacity for social relevance and concern for realised art.

There is much more work to be done. The pioneering work of Carolyn Cooper on gender dynamics and the construction of the female in reggae demands further attention. There can be no feminist or womanist discourse about Caribbean writing without an examination of the position of women in reggae culture and the way in which its often explicit misogyny relates to the very 'democratic' construction of the music. As well, there has been very little critical work done on the theatre and dramatic writing and its relationship to the reggae aesthetic in Caribbean society. In truth, there has been very little critical work available on the last twenty or so years of Caribbean theatre. This is a significant absence because much of what has been most powerfully contemporary and compelling in Caribbean writing has taken place on the stage. I would argue, too, that detailed work on the individual lyrical and musical artistry of seminal musicians such as Bob Marley, Burning Spear, Lee 'Scratch' Perry is long overdue. Such books would prove incredibly rewarding in deepening our appreciation of the individual artist's particular genius as well as revealing the range and diversity within reggae. Finally, there is a great deal of potentially rewarding work to be done on the influence of reggae iconography in Caribbean art.

Reggae music is in constant flux, constantly reinventing itself and the fact that it continues to reflect and engage in dialogue with changes that are taking place around the world (Sly and Robbie and bangara rhythms) speaks to its dynamism as a musical form and as an aesthetic. I have tried to make it clear that the aesthetic I am exploring in this book is one that I have chiefly related to roots reggae, a musical style that is quite dated. Since the early 1980s, the dominant force in reggae has been the dancehall and the deejay. The musical style has also changed significantly, moving away from the easy pace of the 1970's roots sound, to a more frenetic and rapid style of ragga. There is change, but there is also continuity. As Rohan Preston has pointed out to me in our discussions of this development, the new music is a product of a shift of sensibility. Roots reggae was an urban music, but an urban music which was frequently the product of artists whose origins were still in the country. Preston reminded me that the artists that we have come to regard as the vanguard of the roots period were all men and women with a rural upbringing: Bob Marley, Toots Hibbert, Jimmy Cliff, Winston Rodney, Joseph Hill, and Bunny Wailer all had rural beginnings. Roots reggae privileged the roots figure who was connected to the language, idioms and ideologies of rural Jamaican society even as she/he tried to survive within the context of the urban setting. The urban-born deejay emerged in a Kingston that has become far more urbanised than it ever was in the 1960s and the 1970s. The music that has appeared since the early 1980s has spoken directly to those violent and unsettling times and has appeared to shed all connections with rural Jamaica in its deployment of a highly urbanised digital electronic technology. And yet there is continuity. What lies behind the rapid digital beat of ragga but the rhythms of poco and kette drumming? What is that one hears in recent CDs by Buju Banton and Anthony B but reworkings of ska and a very conscious possession of a reggae's musical heritage? What is that one hears in theirs and Sizzla's, Capleton's, and Morgan Heritage's recent recordings but the need to speak of the spiritual within the secular world, to sing praise songs to Jah and to sing of the delights of sexual energy?

There is clearly a great deal of work that needs to be done on how this evolution of reggae forms has affected the shape of the aesthetic I have described. However, I am convinced that the fact of reggae's evolution since the days of roots reggae does not mean that the aesthetic I have derived from it is irrelevant and dated. There has been a significant and perhaps inevitable time lag between the emergence of particular reggae styles and the emergence of writing influenced by that reggae idiom, and the writers whose work I explore (which has still to be properly absorbed into our reconstruction of what constitutes Caribbean literary culture) have all been grounded in the roots reggae idiom in some way or the other. But the defence of my thesis can be far more basic than that. As in the blues, there is a history of the evolution and the passing of particular forms as current musical idioms. But while there has been a decline in blues music performance and the appropriation of blues stylings by artists working in other musical forms, there remain some fundamental qualities, which are as true of more recent offshoots of the blues as of blues in its earliest incarnations, that offer the opportunity for writers such as Albert Murray and Kalamu ya Salaam to speak convincingly of a blues aesthetic. I would argue that this principle holds true for the reggae aesthetic.

Readers of this book will realise that it is not just my construction of a reggae aesthetic that is founded upon the reggae music that emerged in the 1970s. Some will recognise that my sense of Jamaica is shaped by this period. The image, in one sense, is a dated one. It has been ten years since I have lived continuously in Jamaica. Consequently, I am always aware of the seduction of nostalgia in everything I write. Caribbean writing has been profoundly shaped by the effects of exile, often, it seems, writing about the period before the current one. It is an effect I cannot escape. Because I have been away from Jamaica, it is poetry that has completely dominated my writing over the last seven years. It is difficult for me to write plays without having Jamaica in my head all the time, without something which is more than a memory, even a comprehensive and consuming memory, as my central source. I have turned to poetry not only because of the absence of a need for collaboration in its production, but also because the poetic instinct is about reflecting an aesthetic, about principles of meaning that feed into my efforts to rationalise this business of living as an artist, about principles whose essence persists through time, though particular forms of expression may be more transitory. Yet while I live with this absence from the landscapes of Jamaica – physical, political, and social – I think my position as a writer outside Jamaica is quite different from that of the generation of writers who left the region in the 1950s and 1960s. And the difference is reggae, which gives me the sense of being part of some global, electronic Caribbean community, from whose sounds and lyrical concerns I can still get some sense of 'home', and its changing sensibilities.

I have, indeed, written much about my constant quest for home, for a place of cultural comfort. It is a quite practical issue at times. With family so far away it is difficult to get a loan from a brother or sister to get a piece of furniture or to find a relative to take the children for a little. It becomes harder and harder to sustain images, those collective images of family, to sustain those instincts passed on from generation to generation in the constancy of the village or the home town. My travelling and the travelling of my family has made it imperative for us to make decisions about how we define home. As a poet, a weaver of words, a scholar of literature, I understand that it is only in the mastering of the particular and the parochial that a sophisticated universalism can be achieved. The person who is able to make that journey from the particular to the universal is, I am sure, better equipped to handle the pressures of exile and migration. I am quite certain now that my sense of home is rooted largely in Jamaica because that is where my immediate family lives. But I am also highly conscious of the Middle Passage as an historical prototype for my own journey through time and space from Ghana to the Caribbean. As a Ghanaian-Jamaican I am profoundly grateful for reggae which, free of the twisted prejudices of class and race and anti-Africanism that operated in Jamaica when I first arrived there, has traversed my multiple worlds in powerful ways.

I have now lived in the United States for seven years; slowly making sense of the complex differences between my memories of home and this taste of Dixie. The South is a powerful place because of its intensely experienced history of race and nationalism. Where I live in Columbia, reggae is not a big thing. There is no reggae radio station, and while reggae records are sold in the malls, there are few concerts and even fewer reggae bands. And yet I have found in the poetics of the reggae aesthetic a means of exploring South Carolina's strangely familiar dance between the profane and the sacred, the historical and the contemporary, its poverty and its wealth: the very 'third world' complications of its existence. It is this linking of experience that led to the writing of *Jacko Jacobus*, a poem that places a Jamaican in these two landscapes, these two cultures. In writing this long narrative poem I found connections that made the pulse of reggae quite at home in the swamplands of South Carolina.

I share Lee 'Scratch' Perry's desire to make a 'country' and his conviction that reggae, with its open capacity for formal experimentation, has given him unrestricted access to multiple voices and multiple experiences. I am convinced of the transportability of the reggae aesthetic, that it provides an effective foundation for artistic expression and interpretation. When I write, I am always trying to discover ways to capture the anatomy of the reggae song in words. This dance between music and literature is a challenging and sometimes trying one. How does one replicate, for instance, the anticipatory and precursive space of the version? Reggae is there in the staccato pulse of Brathwaite's 'Negus', in the chant of Linton Kwesi Johnson's 'Sonny's Lettah', in the improvisational play of Lorna Goodison's poetry, and the dancehall audacity of Jean Binta Breeze's verse. All this is true. The connections between reggae as a musical form and the soundscapes of poetic language are compelling. But reggae extends beyond that, and this is what I hope this book has managed to convey.

FOOTNOTES

Preface

1. *Waiting in Vain*, New York, Ballantine, 1997.

Introduction

1. *The Last Enchantment*, London, MacGibbon and Kee, 1960; and *Interim*, Kingston, Institute of Jamaica, 1978.
2. See for instance, for Claude McKay, *Banjo: A Story without a Plot*, New York, Harper and Brothers, 1929; *Gingertown*, New York, Harper and Brothers, 1932; *Banana Bottom*, New York, Harper and Brothers, 1933. For Tom Redcam, see *Becka's Buckra Baby*, Kingston, Jamaica Times Printery, 1903; *One Brown Girl and –*, Kingston, Jamaica Times Printery, 1909. For H.G. De Lisser, see *Jane's Career: a Story of Jamaica*, London, Methuen, 1914; *Susan Proudleigh*, London, Methuen, 1915; *Triumphant Squalitone: a tropical extravaganza*, Kingston, Jamaica, The Gleaner Co., 1917. For A.H. Mendes, see *Pitch Lake*, London, Duckworth, 1934; *Black Fauns*, London, Duckworth, 1935. For A.R.F. Webber, see *Those That Be in Bondage*, Georgetown, Daily Chronicle, 1917.
3. See David Boxer, *Edna Manley Sculptor*, Kingston, The National Gallery of Jamaica and The Edna Manley Foundation, 1990; and David Boxer, 'Edna Manley: Sculptor', *Jamaica Journal*, 18:1, 1985, pp. 25-40; and Gloria Escoffery, 'The Hon Edna Manley OM 1900-1987', *Jamaica Journal*, 20:1, 1987, p. 60.
4. George Campbell, *First Poems*, Kingston, City Printery, 1945.
5. Louise Bennett, *Verses in Jamaican Dialect*, Kingston, 1942; *Jamaican Humour in Dialect*, Kingston, 1943; *Jamaican Dialect Poems*, Kingston, 1948; *Mis' Lulu Sez: A Collection of Dialect Poems*, Kingston, 1949; *Lulu Says: Dialect Verses with Glossary*, Kingston, 1952; *Laugh with Louise: A Pot-Pourrie of Jamaican Folklore, Stories, Songs and Verses*, Kingston, 1961. Her work became more widely known with *Jamaica Labrish: Jamaica Dialect Poems*, Kingston, Sangsters, 1966.
6. Walter Jeckyll, *Jamaican Song and Story*, 1907; Dover reprint, 1966.
7. Martha Beckwith, *Black Roadways*, original pub., 1929; reprint Negro University Press.
8. *In a Green Night*, London, Cape, 1962, p. 18.
9. 'The Day the First Snow Fell', Bim, 18, 1953, p. 99; reprinted in *Other Exiles*, London, Oxford University Press, 1975, p. 7.
10. See *The Hills Were Joyful Together*, London, Cape, 1953; *Brother Man*, London, Cape, 1954; *Black Lightning*, London, Cape, 1955.

11. See Claude McKay, *Selected Poems*, New York, Bookman Associates, 1953.

12. The first applications of the Prospero/Caliban relationship to the Caribbean language situation are to be found in Aime Césaire's play *Le Tempêt*, and George Lamming's *The Pleasures of Exile*, London, M. Joseph, 1960.

13. See Rex Nettleford, 'Jamaica's National Dance Company', *Jamaica Journal*, 2/3, 1958, pp. 31-37; and Kamau Brathwaite, 'Chronicles of Unchaos: Rex Nettleford's Dance Jamaica', *Jamaica Journal*, 18/4, 1986, pp. 46-51.

14. See Cary D. Wintz, ed., *Remembering the Harlem Renaissance*, New York, Garland, 1996; David Levering Lewis, *When Harlem Was Vogue*, New York, Knopf, 1981; and Nathan Irvin Huggins, ed., *Voices from the Harlem Renaissance*, New York, OUP, 1976.

15. I am thinking in particular of Harris's *The Palace of the Peacock*, London, Faber, 1961; *The Far Journey of Oudin*, London, Faber, 1962; *The Whole Armour*, London, Faber, 1962; *The Secret Ladder*, London, Faber, 1963; and of Brathwaite's *Rights of Passage*, London, OUP, 1967; *Masks*, London, OUP, 1968 and *Islands*, London, OUP, 1969; all these were collected in *The Arrivants: A New World Trilogy*, London, OUP, 1973.

16. See Sebastian Clarke, *Jah Music, The Evolution of the Popular Jamaican Song*, London, Heinemann Educational, 1980; Howard MacGowan's articles were published in *The Gleaner* during the 1970s and 1980s; Pamela O'Gorman, 'An Approach to the Study of Jamaican Popular Music', *Jamaica Journal*, 6/4, 1972, pp 50-54 and Steve Barrow and Peter Dalton, *Reggae: The Rough Guide*, London, The Rough Guides, 1997.

Chapter One

1. Ujamaa produced one CD, *Chokota*, UJ1, Frederickton, 1991.

2. Lillian Allen, in an interview with Kwame Dawes, '360 Degrees Black: A Conversation with Lillian Allen, *West Coast*, no. 22, Spring/Summer, 1997, pp. 78-91.

3. Hear, for instance, 'Rockers Dub' on *Original Rockers*, Greensleeves, 1979, 1987.

4. Freddie McKay, on the LP *Picture on the Wall*, Studio One, 1971.

5. Sung by Johnny Nash with the Wailers c. 1972, on *The Best of Johnny Nash*, Columbia, 1996.

6. Hear Alton Ellis, *Cry Tough*, Heartbeat, 1993, and *Sunday Coming*, Studio One 1966/Heartbeat, 1995; Ken Boothe, *A Man and His Hits*, Studio One, 1970; and *Mr Rocksteady*, Studio One, 1968; Marcia Griffiths, *The Original (At Studio One)*, Studio One, 1973, 1997.

7. Sung by Phyllis Dillon, on *One Life To Live*, Treasure Isle/Studio One, 1972.

8. On *Kaya*, Tuff Gong/Island, 1978.

9. See Ngugi wa Thiong'o, *Decolonising the Mind: The Politics of Language in African Literature*, Harare, 1987.

10. I am thinking of Shabba's 'Wicked Inna Bed' on *As Raw As Ever*, Epic, 1991; Yellowman's 'Government Boots', Patra's 'Workerman' on *Queen of the Pack*, Epic, 1993; Michigan and Smiley, 'Nice Up the Dance' on *Rub A Dub Style*, Studio One/Heartbeat, 1980; and Ninjaman's 'A So' We Stay' on *Out Pon Bail*, Exterminator, 1990.

11. Hear Toots and the Maytals, 'Sweet and Dandy', Beverley's, 1969, included on the Island Jamaica anthology, *Time Tough*, 1996; Culture's 'See Them A Come' on *Two Sevens Clash*, Lightning, 1977; and Stanley and the Turbines 'Balm Yard' on *Big Bamboo*, Jamaican Gold, 1993.

12. Hear The Wailers' 'Trench Town Rock' on *African Herbsman*, Trojan, 1974; Black Uhuru's 'Mondays/Killer Tuesday' from *Chill Out* and 'Party in Session', on *Liberation: The Island Anthology*, 1993; and Sly and Robbie's work with Ini Kamoze (*Here Comes the Hotstepper*, Sony, 1995); and their own compilation *Taxi Fare*, 1987.

13. Hear the Fugees, 'No Woman, No Cry' on *The Score*, Columbia, 1996; and the recent recordings of Capleton, 'Original Man' on *I Testament*, Def Jam Music, 1998 and Bounty Killer's 'Hip Hopera (with the Fugees) on *My Xperience*, TVT/VD Records, 1996.

14. See Gordon Rohlehr, *Calypso and Society in Pre-Independence Trinidad*, Port of Spain, 1990.

15. *Contradictory Omens: Cultural Diversity and Integration in the Caribbean*, Kingston, Savacou Publications, 1974.

16. See Jeremy Poynting, 'From Shipwreck to Odyssey: One Hundred Years of Indo-Caribbean Writing', *Wasafiri*, No. 21, Spring, 1995 and *The Second Shipwreck*, Peepal Tree, forthcoming; and Sasenarine Persaud, 'Kevat: Waiting on Yogic Realism', *Critical Practice*, New Delhi, v. 6/2, 1998.

17. Denis Williams, *Image and Idea in the Arts of Guyana*, Georgetown, Ministry of Information, 1969.

18. Wilson Harris, *History, Fable and Myth in the Caribbean and Guianas*, Georgetown, 1970; and *Tradition, the Writer and Society*, London, New Beacon, 1967 and *Selected Essays of Wilson Harris*, ed. A. Bundy, Routledge, 1999.

19. See in particular Langston Hughes, *The Big Sea*, New York, Hill and Wang, 1940; *Simple Speaks His Mind*, New York, Hill and Wang, 1950; and 'On Being a Black Poet' in *The Langston Hughes Reader*, New York, Braziller, 1958; and Robert Marquez and David Murray in the Introduction to *Man-Making Words: Selected Poems of Nicolas Guillen*, Habana, Editorial de Arte y Literatura, 1973.

20. Jamaica 21 Anthology Series, Institute of Jamaica Publications, 1987.

21. c. 1963; reissued on Peter Tosh, *The Toughest*, Heartbeat, 1996.

Chapter Two

1. *Uncle Time*, University of Pittsburg Press, 1973, pp. 6-7.

2. From *Marcus Garvey*, Mango/Island, 1975.

3. 'What the Twilight Says: An Overture', introduction to *Dream on Monkey Mountain and Other Plays*, London, Cape, 1972, pp. 3-40.

4. From 'Jouvert', *Islands*, p. 11.

5. For the starkest versions of this vision of the Caribbean see V.S. Naipaul's 'nothing was created in the West Indies', *The Middle Passage*, London, Deutch, 1962, p. 29; Derek Walcott's 'these disjecta membra' in 'Ruins of a Great House', *In a Green Night*, 1962, p. 20; and Orlando Patterson's novel *An Absence of Ruins*, London, Hutchinson, 1967.

6. *Natural Mystic*, unpublished novel.

7. For instance, Mais's *The Hills Were Joyful Together*, *Brother Man* and *Black Lightning*; Vic Reid's *New Day*, Neville Dawes's, *The Last Enchantment* and *Interim*, John Hearne's *Voices Under the Window*, *Stranger at the Gate*, *The Faces of Love*, *The Autumn Equinox* and *The Land of the Living*; Sylvia Wynter's *The Hills of Hebron* and Orlando Patterson's *The Children of Sisyphus* and *An Absence of Ruins*.

8. 'Do It Twice', *Songs of Freedom*, Island, 1992.

9. From *Two Sevens Clash*, Lightning, 1977; available on CD from Shanachie.

10. From the album, *War Ina Babylon*, Island, 1976, prod. by Lee Perry.

11. *Uncle Time*, pp xiii-xv.

12. Barbara Lalla, *Defining Jamaican Fiction: Maroonage and the Discourse of Survival*, Tuscaloosa, University of Alabama Press, 1996.

13. See *Witchbroom*, London, Heinemann, Caribbean Writers Series, 1992.

14. Stephen Grey, 'A Sense of Place in New Literatures in English, Particularly South Africa', quoted in Rita Barnard, 'Dream Topographies: J.M. Coetzee and the South African Pastoral', in *The Writings of J.M. Coetzee*, ed. Michael V. Moses, *South Atlantic Quarterly*, 93:1, Winter 1994, pp 36-38.

15. Jean D'Costa, *Sprat Morrison*, Jamaica, Ministry of Education, 1972.

16. See *Hurricane*, London, OUP, 1964; *Earthquake*, OUP, 1965 *Drought*, OUP, 1966; *Riot*, OUP, 1967; and *Jonah Simpson*, London, Bogle L'Ouverture.

17. Both are to be found in *The Sun's Eye*, ed. Anne Walmsley, Longman Caribbean, 1968, a popular reader in the schools at that time.

18. See in particular the Kaywana trilogy, *Children of Kaywana*, London, Secker, 1952; *The Harrowing of Hubertus*, London, Secker, 1954 (also issued as *Kaywana Stock*, 1959) and *Kaywana Blood*, London, Secker, 1958.

19. E. Townsend, J. Carnegie and Herb McKenley, *Herb McKenley: Olympic Star*, Kingston, Institute of Jamaica, 1974; and Noel White and George Headley, *George 'Atlas' Headley*, Institute of Jamaica, 1974.
20. *Miguel Street*, London, Deutch, 1959.
21. V.S. Reid, *The Young Warriors*, 1967, and *Nanny Town*, Kingston, Jamaica Publishing House, 1983.
22. Two of the texts which brought this knowledge to us were F.R. Augier, S.C. Gordon, D.G. Hall and M. Reckord, *The Making of the West Indies*, Longmans, 1960; and Alma Norman, *The People Who Came*, Longman, 1968.
23. 'Misty Morning', *Kaya*, 1978.
24. 'Catch A Fire', *Catch A Fire*, Tuff Gong/Island, 1973.
25. Kamau Brathwaite, 'Jazz in the West Indian Novel, *Bim*, 44, pp 275-284 and *Bim* 46, pp115-126; and 'The Love Axe/l: Developing a Caribbean Aesthetic, 1962-1974', *Bim*, 16:61 (1977) pp 53-65; 16:62, pp 100-106; 16:63, pp. 181-192; a revised, updated and enlarged version is to be published by Peepal Tree Press in 1999.
26. Examples of Fela's work can be found on Fela Ransome-Kuti and The Africa 70's *Afrodisiac*, Regal Zonophone, 1972 and *Gentleman*, Creole, 1979.
27. Hear Alpha Blondy's *The Best of Alpha Blondy*, EMI; Majek Fashek's *Prisoner of Conscience*, Mango, 1990; and Lucky Dube's *Victims* and *Taxman* both on Shanachie, 1993 and 1997 respectively.
28. See the photographs of Garvey as an European emperor, and see Veerle Poupeye-Rammalaere, 'Garveyism and Garvey Iconography in the Visual Arts of Jamaica', *Jamaica Journal*, 24/1, 1991, pp. 9-21, where Garvey is quoted as saying, 'We must train the young Rubens, the young Rosetti, the young Reynolds... of the Negro Race', p. 11.
29. 'Redemption Song', *Uprising*, Tuff Gong/Island, 1980.

Chapter Three

1. Albert Murray, *The Hero and the Blues*, Columbia, University of Missouri Press, 1973, pp. 87-88.
2. Grace Nichols, Introduction to *Sunris*, London, Virago, 1996, pp. 2-3.
3. 'Jazz in the West Indian Novel', *Bim*, 44, pp 275-284 and *Bim* 46, pp. 115-126.
4. See *History of the Voice: The Development of Nation Language in Anglophone Caribbean Poetry*, London, New Beacon, 1984.
5. See 'Blues: Basie, Klook, Miles, Trane, So long, Charlie Parker and Bass' in *Other Exiles*, pp. 12-17.
6. *What Is Life?*, Chicago, Third World Press, 1994, p.10.
7. 'Serious Reggae Business' on *Trinity*, Tabu Records, 1995.

8. *More Poco*, VP Records, 1990; *Digital B Presents Kette Drum*, DBLP (Bobby Digital Productions), 1995.

9. *Ska Boogie - Jamaican R & B, the Dawn of Ska*, Sequel Records, 1993; and *Foundation Ska: Studio One Presents the Skatalites*, Heartbeat, 1997.

10. Hear the Heptones *On Top*, Studio One, 1968; and *Sea of Love*, Studio One/Heartbeat, 1997; and the Mighty Diamonds on *Go Seek Your Rights*, Virgin Front Line, 1990; and *The Best of the Mighty Diamonds*, Hitbound, Channel One Records, 1997.

11. On *The Best of Johnny Nash*, Columbia, 1996.

12. Hear for instance Buju Banton's *Til Shiloh*, Loose Cannon, 1995, and *Inna Heights* Jet Star 1997; Capleton's *Prophecy*, 1995, and *I Testament* 1998, both Def Jam/African Star; Sizzla's *African Woman*, Greensleeves, 1997 and *Sizzla*, Jetstar Reggae Max, 1998; and Anthony B's *Universal Struggle*,Charm, 1998.

13. Hear 'Chances Are', *The Complete Wailers 1967-72*, Part 1, JAD/EMI.; 'One Cup of Coffee', 'It Hurts to be Alone' from *Songs of Freedom* and 'I'm Still Waiting', from *Wailing Wailers at Studio One*, Heartbeat.

14. 'Get Up Stand Up', *Burnin'*, Tuff Gong/Island, 1973.

15. 'Equal Rights' on *Equal Rights*, Virgin, 1977.

16. 'Revolution' *Natty Dread*, Tuff Gong/Island 1974.

17. 'This Time', *Two Sevens Clash*.

18. Culture, *Nuff Crisis*, Shanachie, 1988.

19. See Sheila Barrett, 'Notes on Contemporary Dance-Theatre in Jamaica 1930-1982', *Jamaica Journal*, 46, 1982, pp. 80-93.

20. *Song of Solomon*, New York, Knopff, 1977.

21. *The Hero and the Blues*, Columbia, University of Missouri Press, 1973.

22. See Gordon Rohlehr, *Calypso and Society in Pre-Independence Trinidad*, Port of Spain, 1990.

23. See John Thieme, *The Web of Tradition: Uses of Allusion in V.S.Naipaul's Fiction*, London, Hansib, 1988.

24. *Salt*, London, Faber, 1997.

25. *Witchbroom*, London, Heinemann Caribbean Writers Series, 1992.

26. *Chopstix in Mauby*, Leeds, Peepal Tree Press, 1996.

27. 'Spoilers Return', *The Fortunate Traveller*, London, Faber & Faber, 1982. pp. 53-60.

28. *The Lonely Londoners*, London, Wingate, 1956.

29. Selvon in general tried to avoid making any comments on his own writing if he could help it. He has, though, some interesting things to say about the necessary discovery of a creole narrative voice when he was writing the *Lonely Londoners* in an interview with Daryl Dance in *New World Adams: Conversations with Contemporary West Indian Writers*, Leeds, Peepal Tree, 1992, pp 236-237.

30. *The Sure Salvation*, London, Faber, 1981.

31. *The Harder They Come*, London, Pluto Press, 1980.

32. See for instance a collection of essays on Caribbean literature such as *The Islands In Between*, London, Three Crowns, 1968, ed. L. James, which mostly ignores the relationship of Caribbean popular culture to literature.

33. I am thinking in particular of Oku Onuora (Orlando Wong), Mutabaruka and Mikey Smith. More details of their work is given below.

34. Publishing details of these works are as follows: Lorna Goodison, *Tamarind Season*, Kingston, Institute of Jamaica, 1980; Linton Kwesi Johnson, *Voices of the Living and the Dead*, London TRJ Publication, 1974; *Dread, Beat and Blood*, London, Bogle L'Ouverture, 1975; and *Inglan Is A Bitch*, London, Race Today Publications, 1980; Anthony McNeill, *Hello Ungod*, Baltimore, 1971; *Reel from 'The Real Life Movie'*, Kingston, Savacou Publications, 1972; and *Credences at the Altar of Cloud*, Kingston, Institute of Jamaica, 1979; Mervyn Morris, *The Pond*, London, New Beacon Books, 1973; *On Holy Week*, Kingston, Sangsters Book Stores, 1976; and *Shadow Boxing*, London, New Beacon Books, 1979; Mutabaruka, *Outcry*, Kingston, self published, 1973 and *First Poems, 1970-1979*, Kingston, Paul Issa, 1980; Oku Onuora, (as Orlando Wong), *Echo*, Kingston, Sangsters, 1977; Andrew Salkey, *Jamaica*, London, Hutchinson, 1973; *In the Hills Where Her Dreams Live*, Habana, Casa de las Americas, 1979; and *Away*, London, Allison and Busby, 1980; Dennis Scott, *Uncle Time*, Pittsburg, University of Pittsburg Press, 1973. There was also Kamau Brathwaite's *Black + Blues*, Habana, Premio Casa de las Americas, 1976; *Days and Nights*, Kingston, Caldwell Press, 1975. Outside this period there was Michael Smith, *It A Come*, ed. Mervyn Morris, London, Race Today Publications, 1987; and Jean Binta Breeze, *Riddym Ravings*, London, Race Today Publications, 1988.

35. Ras Dizzy's publications (see also *A Prince Who Is A Pauper*, 1973) were all published as mimeographs in Kingston. *One Love*, ed. Audvil King, London, Bogle L'Ouverture, 1971; Roy Taylor, *Ras Fari*, Jamaica, Author, Prototype, 1976.

36. Publishing details of the novels mentioned in the text are as follows: Erna Brodber, *Jane and Louisa Will Soon Come Home*, London, New Beacon, 1980; Hazel Campbell, *The Rag Doll and Other Stories*, Kingston, Savacou Publications, 1978; James Carnegie, *Wages Paid*, Habana, Premio Casa de las Americas, 1976; Neville Dawes, *Interim*, Kingston, Institute of Jamaica, 1978; Hall Anthony Ellis, *The Silence of Barabomo*, Kingston, author, 1979; Neville Farki, *Countryman Karl Black*, London, Bogle L'Ouverture, 1981; John Hearne, *The Sure Salvation*, London, Faber, 1981; Perry Henzel, *Power Game*, Kingston, Ten-A Publications, 1982; John Morris, *Fever Grass*, London, Wm. Collins, 1969, and

The Candywine Development, London, Wm. Collins, 1970; Ivor Osbourne, *The Mango Season*, London, Rex Collings Ltd., 1979; Orlando Patterson, *Die The Long Day*, St. Albans, Herts., Mayflower Books, 1972; Victor Reid, *The Jamaicans*, Kingston, Institute of Jamaica, 1978; Michael Thelwell, *The Harder They Come*, London, Pluto Press, 1980; N.D. Williams, *Ikael Torass*, Habana, Casa de las Americas, 1976.

37. *Myal*, London, New Beacon Books, 1988.
38. *Uncle Obadiah and the Alien*, Leeds, Peepal Tree Press, 1996.
39. *Prash and Ras*, Leeds, Peepal Tree Press, 1997.
40. *Singerman*, Leeds, Peepal Tree Press, 1992.
41. *Anancy's Score*, London, Bogle L'Ouverture Publications, 1973.
42. 'Mr Brown', on *Soul Revolution*, Trojan Records, 1969/1988.
43. Sistren, ed. Honor Ford-Smith, *Lionheart Gal: Life Stories of Jamaican Women*, London, The Women's Press, 1986. And see Honor Ford-Smith, 'Sistren: Exploring Women's Problems through Drama', *Jamaica Journal*, 19:1, 1986, pp. 2-12.
44. Both in Trevor Rhone, *Old Story Time and Other Plays*, London, Longman, 1981; the screen play for *The Harder They Come* is unpublished.
45. *An Echo in the Bone* is included in *Plays for Today*, ed. Errol Hill, Longman Caribbean, 1986. *Live and Direct from Babylon* and *Dog* are both unpublished.
46. See Rex Nettleford, 'Pocomania in Dance-Theatre', *Jamaica Journal*, 3:2, 1968, pp. 21-24; and Shirley Maynier Burke, 'Islands': Interview with Rex Nettleford, *Jamaica Journal*, 19:3, 1986, pp. 13-20.
47. On Osmond Watson see Gloria Escoffery, 'Osmond Watson's Masquerades', *Jamaica Journal*, 16:1, 1983, pp 40-43, and Alex Gradussov, 'Osmond Watson talks to Alex Gradussov', *Jamaica Journal*, 3:3, 1969, pp. 47-53; on Kapo (Mallica Reynolds) see Alex Gradussov, 'Kapo: Cult Leader, Sculptor, Painter', *Jamaica Journal*, 3:2, 1969, pp. 46-51; on Everald Brown see Veerle Poupeye-Rammelaere, 'The Rainbow Valley: The Life and Work of Brother Everald Brown', *Jamaica Journal*, 21:2, 1988, pp. 2-8; on Milton George see Gloria Escoffery, 'The Intimate World of Milton George', *Jamaica Journal*, 19:2, 1986, pp. 28-37.
48. Hear Desmond Dekker and the Aces, 'Rude Boy Train' c. 1967, and The Clarendonians, 'Rudie Bam Bam', (c. 1967), both on *Rudies All Around*, Trojan Records, 1993.
49. Hear Count Ossie, 'So Long, Rastafari Calling', on *Grounation*, 1973, CD reissued on VP records.
50. Hear Lee 'Scratch' Perry's albums *Black Board Jungle Dub*, (c. 1973) Orchid, 1996, and *Super Ape*, Island, 1976/1997.
51. Hear Prince Allah, 'Lot's Wife', on *Only Love Can Conquer* (1976-79), Blood and Fire, 1997.
52. Hear Ras Michael and the Sons of Negus, 'Birds in the Tree Top', on *Rastafari*, 1975, reissued on CD on VP Records.

53. Hear Third World's '96 Degrees in the Shade' on *96 Degrees in the Shade*, Island, 1977.

54. See 'Love Axe/l', *Bim*, op. cit., and Peepal Tree forthcoming.

55. Writers associated with the Focus group included George Campbell, Gloria Escoffery, M.G. Smith, Basil McFarlane, Philip Sherlock, A.L. Hendricks, John Figueroa, Roger Mais and H.D. Carberry.

56. 'Florida Bound', *Florida Bound*, Leeds, Peepal Tree, p. 61.

57. For an example of this unhelpful polarisation see Patricia Ismond, 'Walcott vs, Brathwaite', *Caribbean Quarterly*, 17, 1971, pp. 54-71.

58. Lecture delivered by Kamau Brathwaite, at the University of South Carolina, Columbia, Fall, 1997.

59. See Derek Walcott, 'The Muse of History', in *Carifesta Forum*, ed. John Hearne, Kingston, 1976.

60. See *From Our Yard, Jamaican Poetry Since Independence*, Kingston, Institute of Jamaica, 1987, pp xxii-xxiii.

61. 'Reggae Fi Dadda' in *Tings an' Times: Selected Poems*, Bloodaxe, 1991.

62. See Mervyn Morris, quoted in *From Our Yard*, p. xxii.

63. 'Trailor Load' is on *As Raw as Ever*, Epic, 1991.

64. Hear Supercat's 'Mud Up' on *Don Dada*, Columbia, 1992.

65. Gordon Rohlehr, Introduction to *Voiceprint*, Longman, 1989, p. 18

66. See much of the verse in *Dub Poetry: 19 Poets from England and Jamaica*, ed. Christian Habekost, Neustadt, Germany, Michael Schwinn, 1986, which collectively reinforces a sense of the form as narrowly declarative and rigid in rhythms.

Chapter Four

1. See Lorna Goodison's 'Upon a Quarter Million', *Heartease*, New Beacon, 1989, for a celebration of such buses.

2. We were listening to albums such as Third World's *96 Degrees in the Shade* (1977); Aswad's eponymous *Aswad* Mango/Island, 1975; Jacob Miller's 45, 'Tenement Yard collected on *Inner Circle: Reggae Greats*, Island; and Steel Pulse, *Handsworth Revolution*, Island, 1978.

3. Hear for instance 'Rub A Dub Soldier', on *Rough* (LP only).

4. Leroy Smart's 'Ballistic Affair' was a huge hit. An accessible compilation is *Let Everyman Survive*, Jamaican Gold, 1993.

5. Ken Boothe's classic was 'Everything I Own' and his smoothest hits are included on *Everything I Own*, Trojan Records, 1997.

6. This was Cedric Im Brooks with his group The Light of Saba. Currently all that seems available is his *United Africa*, Water Lily, 1978. There is an important interview with Cedric Brooks by Shirley Maynier Burke in *Jamaica Journal*, 11:1, 1977, pp 14-15.

7. Kamau Brathwaite in an published interview with the author, 1997.

8. Quoted in the introduction to *New Poets from Jamaica*, ed. Kamau Brathwaite, *Savacou 14:15*, 1978.

9. From the late 1960s Clement Dodd's Studio One at Brentford Road, Duke Reid's Treasure Island at Bond Street, Joe Gibbs Amalgamated and Jogibs Records at Duhaney Park fuelled a wholly Jamaican owned and controlled cultural industry.

10. *New Day*, New York, Knopf, 1949.

11. See Claude McKay, *Constab Ballads*, London, Watts & Co., 1912; Una Marson, The Moth and the Star, Kingston, 1937; and, of course, Louise Bennett, *Jamaica Labrish*, Kingston, Sangsters, 1966, for the most interesting attempts to use Jamaican nation language with some seriousness in poetry.

12. See Velma Pollard, *Dread Talk: The Language of Rastafari*, Kingston, Canoe Press, 1994.

13. For a discussion of Rastafarian philosophy see Joseph Owens, *Dread, The Rastafarians of Jamaica*, Kingston, Sangsters, 1976, and Leonard Barrett, *The Rastafarians: A Study in Messianic Cultism in Jamaica*, Puerto Rico, Institute of Caribbean Studies, 1969; Verena Reckord, 'Reggae, Rastafarianism and Cultural Identity', *Jamaica Journal*, no 46, 1982, pp. 70-79; and Pamela O'Gorman, 'On Reggae and Rastafarianism – and a Garvey Prophecy', *Jamaica Journal*, 20:3, 1987, pp. 85-88.

14. See Verena Reckord, 'Rastafarian Music: An Introductory Study', *Jamaica Journal*, 11:1, 1977, pp. 2-13; and Garth White, 'Master Drummer', *Jamaica Journal*, 11:1, 1977, pp. 16-17.

15. See Barrett, op. cit. and Roy Augier, Rex Nettleford and M.G. Smith, 'The Rastafari Movement in Kingston, Jamaica', *Caribbean Quarterly*, vol 13, no. 3, pp 3-30, and vol 13, no. 4, pp. 3-15, 1960.

16. Reissued on the CD *The Original Golden Oldies, vol 2*, Prince Buster Records Shack, 1998.

17. Reissued on the compilation CD *The Upsetter Compact Set*, Trojan Records, 1988.

18. *Rastafari* was reissued on CD by VP ; *Kibir Am Lak* is on Greensleeves.

19. *Grounation* was reissued on CD by VP Records; *Tales of Mozambique* by Dynamic Sounds Recording Co., Kingston, Jamaica.

20. On *The Complete Wailers 1967-72*, Vol 1, JAD/EMI, 1998.

21. Hear *Yabby You: Jesus Dread 1972-1977*, Blood and Fire, 1997. Records such as these, while produced in small numbers and rarely given radio time, could be heard on the tapes played on the buses.

22. The artists who had this kind of status included Marley, Peter Tosh, Gregory Isaacs and Burning Spear (Winston Rodney) and more recently Shabba Ranks and Buju Banton.

23. I am thinking of such artists as Papa Michigan and General Smiley (*Rub A Dub Style*, Studio One, 1980), Pluto Shervington ('Ram Goat

Liver'), Lovindeer and Ranking Trevor.

24. See Carolyn Cooper, 'Slackness Hiding from Culture: Erotic Play in the Dancehall', *Jamaica Journal*, 23:1, 1990, pp. 44-51.

25. Hear the occasionally vanishing bassline on Sly and Robbie's production of Black Uhuru's 'Guess Who's Coming to Dinner' (12 inch version) on *Liberation*, Island Records.

26. Hear King Tubby's mixes of Augustus Pablo tracks on *King Tubbys Meets Rockers Uptown*, Rockers International, 1976; and hear Lee 'Scratch' Perry's *Super Ape*, Island, 1976.

27. There are of course many thousands of covers of songs not remotely connected to reggae; deliberate 'cross-overs' such as Marley and Perry's 'Punky Reggae Party'; novelty insertions into reggae such as Eek-A-Mouse's Chinese styles, on, for instance, *Wa Do Dem*, Greensleeves, and the introduction of new rhythms, such as Sly and Robbie's experiments with bangara (Bhangra) rhythms on Chaka Demus and Pliers 'Murder She Wrote' on *Tease Me*, Mango, 1991.

28. Hear 'Small Axe' featuring King Stitt and '54/46' featuring Toots Hibbert on Buju Banton's *Inna Heights*, Germain Records, 1997; and 'Marley Memories' on Anthony B.'s *Universal Struggle*, Star Trail Productions.

29. Any number of artists or tracks could be listed, but hear what was then the highly innovative mobile bass-line of Leroy Sibbles on the Heptones compilation *Sea of Love*, Studio One/Heartbeat.

30. On Justin Hinds and the Dominoes, *Ska Uprising*, Trojan Records.

31. 'Green Island' is collected on *Don Drummond Memorial*, Treasure Island/Esoldun, 'Schooling the Duke' is on *The Best of Don Drummond*, Studio One, and 'Addis Ababa' is on *Foundation Ska*, Studio One/ Heartbeat.

32. 'The Anfinished Revalueshan' is on *Tings An' Times*, LKJ, 1990.

33. 'Eastern Standard Time' is on *The Best of Don Drummond*, Studio One.

34. On the album *Trinity*, Shanachie, 1996.

35. The early work of Toots and the Maytals provides the supreme example here. Hear 'Broadway Jungle' and 'It's You' on the compilation anthology *Time Tough*, Island.

36. 'Mr Brown' is easily available on the compilation, *The Cool Ruler Rides Again 1978-83*, Music Club International, 1997.

37. For instance: Burning Spear, 'Marcus Garvey', on *Marcus Garvey*, Island, 1975; Sylford Walker, 'Lambs Bread', on *Lambs Bread*, Greensleeves, 1979/1990.

38. For instance: Marley's 'Jump Nyabingi' on *Confrontation*, Tuff Gong/ Island, 1983, and 'Crazy Baldhead', on *Rastaman Vibration*; Max Romeo's 'Chase the Devil' on *War Ina Babylon*, Island, 1976.

39. For instance, Glen Brown's 'Away with the Bad' and 'Save our Nation' on *Boat to Progress*, Greensleeves/Shanachie; The Heptones, 'Mr.

President' on Lee 'Scratch' Perry's *Arkology*, Island; Black Uhuru's 'Solidarity' from *Anthem*, Island, and, of course, Marley's 'Get Up, Stand Up' from *Burnin'*.

40. For instance: Wailing Souls, 'Bredda Gravilicious' on *Wild Suspense*, Mango; Mighty Diamonds, 'One Brother Short' on *Deeper Roots*, (included on *Go Seek Your Rights*, Virgin Frontline); Peter Tosh, 'Downpressor' on *The Toughest*, Heartbeat; Linton Kwesi Johnson, 'New Crass Massahkah' on *LJK A Capella Live*, LKJ, 1996; and Junior Byles, 'Curley Locks' on *Beat Down Babylon (The Upsetter Years)*, Trojan Records; Junior Reid, 'Higgler Move' and Half Pint, 'Landlord' both on *King Jammy: A Man And His Music*, vol 3, Ras.

41. For instance: Prince Buster, 'Black Head Chineman' on *The Original Golden Oldies*, vol 1, Prince Buster Record Shack; Peter Tosh, 'Brand New Second Hand' on *Legalize It*, Virgin; Lee Scratch Perry, 'White Belly Rat', on *The Upsetters with Lee Perry and Friends, Build the Ark*, Trojan Records.

42. For instance: Peter Tosh, 'I am the Toughest' on *The Toughest*, Heartbeat; Spragga Benz, 'Born Good Looking' on *Jack It Up*, VP, 1995; Bob Marley's 'Small Axe' on *Burnin'*; and Shabba Ranks' 'Wicked Ina Bed' on *Just Reality*, Vine Yard, 1990; or 'Mr. Loverman'.

43. For instance: Mighty Diamonds, 'Go Seek Your Rights', on *Right Time*, 1976; The Wailing Souls, 'Very Well' on *Wild Suspense*, Island, 1979; The Abyssinians, 'African Race' on *Satta Massa Gana*, Heartbeat, 1976/1993 and Freddie McGregor, 'What Difference Does It Make' on *Bobby Bobylon*, Studio One/Heartbeat,1980.

44. For instance: Bob Marley, 'Trench Town Rock', on *African Herbsman*, Trojan, 1974; Nitty Gritty, 'Sweet Reggae Music', on *Trials and Crosses*, VP, c. 1985; The Heptones, 'Get in the Groove' from *Sea of Love*, Heartbeat, 1997; Burning Spear, 'We Build Our City on Reggae Music', on *People of the World*, Slash/ Greensleeves, 1986.

45. For instance: Slim Smith and the Uniques, 'People', on *Best of the Uniques 1967-1969*; Toots and the Maytals, Do the Reggay', on *Time Tough*, Island.

46. For instance: Burning Spear, 'Slavery Days' on *Marcus Garvey*; Bob Marley, 'Buffalo Soldier' on *Confrontation*, Tuff Gong/Island; Junior Delgado, 'Sons of Slaves', (c. 1975) on *Lee Perry and Friends, Open The Gate*, Trojan Records, 1989.

47. For instance, 'Carry Go Bring Come', 'The Higher the Monkey Climbs', 'Botheration', all c. 1966-67,on *Ska Uprising*, Trojan Records, 1993.

48. For instance, The Maytals, 'Six and Seven Books of Moses' on *Time Tough*; Peter Tosh, 'Amen' on *The Toughest*; Bunny Wailer, 'This Train', on *Blackheart Man*, Island, 1976; and The Wailers, 'Put it On' on *Burnin'*.

49. Henry Louis Gates, *The Signifying Monkey: A Theory of Afro-American Literary Criticism*, New York, OUP, 1988.

50. Hear for instance, Cutty Ranks, 'The Bomber', 'The Stopper' on *The Stopper*, Fashion, 1991; and Cobra, 'Bad Boy Talk' on *Badboy Talk*, Penthouse, 1991.

Chapter Five

1. The epigraph to *The Arrivants*, London, OUP, 1973; and see Kamau Brathwaite, 'Kumina – African Survival in Jamaica', *Jamaica Journal*, no. 42, 1978, pp. 44-63.
2. *In A Green Night*, p. 18.
3. From *Handsworth Revolution*, Island, 1978.
4. From *Catch A Fire*, Island, 1973.
5. Lucky Dube, 'Trinity' on *Trinity*, 1996; and Peter Tosh, 'Till Your Well Runs Dry' on *Legalize It*, which has a long country and western type introduction.
6. *Heart of the Congos*, Blood & Fire.
7. Perry's dub mix 'Dreader Locks' on *Junior Byles, Beat Down Babylon*, Trojan Records, where the deejay version over fragments of the vocal track give the poignancy of the song a more threatening edge, without losing the original pathos.
8. Timothy White, *Catch A Fire: The Life of Bob Marley*, UK, Corgi, 1984.
9. Issued as a single, collected on *Songs of Freedom*, Island, 1992.
10. Leroy Pierson, sleeve notes to *Junior Byles: 'Curly Locks'*, Heartbeat Records, 1997.
11. See Kamau Brathwaite, *Wars of Respect*, Jamaica, Agency for Public Information, 1977, and Cary Robinson, *The Fighting Maroons of Jamaica*, Kingston, Sangsters, 1969; and Sylvia Wynter, *Jamaica's National Heroes*, Kingston, Jamaica National Trust Commission, 1971, for further information about Nanny.
12. For further information about Paul Bogle and the Morant Bay rebellion see Jamaica Information Service, *The Morant Bay Rebellion*, Kingston, 1961; H.P. Jacobs, *Sixty Years of Change 1806-1866*, Kingston, Institute of Jamaica; Ansell Hart, *The Life of George William Gordon*, Kingston, Institute of Jamaica, 1972; Bernard Semmel, *The Governor Eyre Controversy*, London, McGibbon and Kee, 1962.
13. For Marcus Garvey see amongst much else, Marcus Garvey, *The Philosophy and Opinions of Marcus Garvey* (1923,1925), London, Frank Cass, 1968; Amy Jaques Garvey, *Garvey and Garveyism*, Kingston, author, 1963; E.D. Cronon, *Black Moses: the Story of Marcus Garvey and the UNIA*, University of Wisconsin, 1955.
14. *The Harder They Come*, Soundtrack, Mango/Island, 1972.
15. On *Burnin'*, Island, 1973.

16. General Echo's (aka Ranking Slackness) 'Arleen' is on *12 Inches of Pleasure*, Greensleeves.

17. Ranking Trevor's 'Love Bump' appears never to have been reissued.

18. Ernie Smith's work can be found on the double CD, *After 30 Years Life is Just For Living*, 1998.

19. Pluto Shervington's 'One More Jamaican Gone Abroad' was released as a single c. 1976; there is a *Best of Pluto Shervington*, vol 1 & 2 on K &K.

20. Doctor Alimantado's 'Best Dressed Chicken in Town' is available on the Greensleeves CD of that name, 1978.

21. Michigan and Smiley's 'Diseases' is on the CD, *Downpression*, Greensleeves, 1982.

Chapter Six

1. Burning Spear, *Live in Paris*, Blue Moon, 1990.

2. Albert Murray, *The Blue Devils of Nada*, p. 203.

3. *Legalize It*, Virgin, 1976.

4. 'One Cup of Coffee', cut for Lesley Kong is on *Songs of Freedom*, Island, 1992.

5. 'No Sympathy' is on Peter Tosh, *The Toughest*, Heartbeat.

6. 'I Made a Mistake', 'Love and Affection' and 'Lonesome Feeling' are on *The Birth of a Legend*, Island, and on *Simmer Down at Studio One*.

7. Alton Ellis's love songs are to be heard to best effect on *Sunday Coming*, Heartbeat.

8. Ken Boothe's early work is on *A Man and His Hits*, Studio One and *Mr. Rocksteady*, Studio One.

9. Some of the Heptones best work is on *On Top*, Studio One, *Fattie, Fattie*, Studio One (both original albums reissued on CD, and the compilation CD, *Sea of Love*, Heartbeat.

10. Dennis Brown's available early 70s, literally juvenile work is on *No Man Is An Island*, Studio One, 1970; and *Just Dennis*, Trojan Records, 1972.

11. A good sampling of Gregory Isaacs early 70s work, which shows the precise point of the emergence of his distinctive style is on *Loving Pauper*, Trojan Records, 1998.

12. Leroy Smart's work can be found on *Vintage Classics*, and *Let Everyman Survive*, Jamaican Gold.

13. Bob Andy, in particular, is seminal to the development of the reggae love song, as a writer whose work has been performed by countless singers. His own classic albums are *Bob Andy's Songbook*, Studio One, 1972; and the brilliant album *The Music Inside Me*, which is unfortunately currently unavailable.

14. Marcia Griffith's 1970s work is on *The Original – At Studio One*, Studio One, 1973; *Naturally*, Shanachie, 1978; and *Steppin'*, Shanachie, 1979.

15. 'Rock It Baby' is on *Catch a Fire*.

16. 'Do the Reggay' is on *Time Tough*, Island.

17. Bunny Wailer's 'Ballroom Floor' is on *Retrospective*, Shanachie.

18. The Heptones 'I Got the Handle' is on *On Top*. Studio One.

19. 'Adam and Eve', on *The Complete Wailers 1967-72*, Part 1.

20. 'Stir It Up' is on *Catch A Fire*.

21. 'Is This Love' is on *Kaya*.

22. Carolyn Cooper, 'Chanting Down Babylon: Bob Marley's Song As Literary Text', *Jamaica Journal*, 19:4, 1986, pp 2-8.

23. Listen, for example, to Garnett Silk's album, *It's Growing*, Blue Mountain/VP, 1992 and songs such as 'You Gonna Leave Love'; Buju Banton's 'Wanna Be Loved' and 'Hush Baby Hush' on *'Til Shiloh*, Loose Cannon, 1995; and Morgan Heritage's 'Down With You' on *One Calling*, Greensleeves, 1997.

24. *Waiting in Vain*, New York, Ballantine, 1997, pp. 144-145.

25. *Ibid.*

25. In *Birthright*, Leeds, Peepal Tree, 1997, pp. 66-67; also in *Wheel and Come Again*, Leeds, Peepal Tree, 1998, pp. 99-100.

26. 'Farewell Wild Women' is in *Selected Poems*, University of Michigan Press, 1992 and *Wheel and Come Again*, p.90.

27. There have always been women in reggae such as Hortense Ellis, Joya Landis, Phyllis Dillon, Marcia Griffiths and in the era of roots, Judy Mowatt. However, it is significant that both Marcia Griffiths and Judy Mowatt, both outstanding artists in their own right, probably earned far more as two-thirds of the I-Threes (along with Rita Marley), Bob Marley's back-up group, who were never as much in the foreground of the music as Bunny Livingston and Peter Tosh in the Wailers. Since the mid 1980s, there has been the emergence of artists such as J.C. Lodge, Twiggy, Chevelle Franklyn, Krystal and Juliet Nelson, though the fact that most of their work is on singles rather than albums reinforces the earlier perception. However, more recently, the position of artists such as Patra, Lady G and the very up-front Lady Saw has very definitely begun to challenge the gender dynamics of reggae in the dancehall.

28. Carolyn Cooper and Paulette McDonald, 'Dancehall Revisited/Kingston November 1992'in *Review: Latin American Literatures and Arts*, No. 50, Spring 1995, pp. 29-31.

Chapter Seven

1. Important collections of The Maytals work includes: *Never Grow Old*, Studio One/Heartbeat, 1966/1997; *Sensational Ska Explosion*, Jamaican Gold, 1993; *Sweet and Dandy*, Beverley's, 1969/1998; and *Bla Bla Bla*, Esoldun. Prince Buster's own sides can be heard on *Fabulous Greatest Hits*, Sequel, 1967/1993; and his productions on *Original Golden Oldies*, vols 1 & 2, Prince Buster Record Shack. 1989. Justin Hinds and the Dominoes work is available on *Ska Uprising*, Trojan Records, 1993; and *Peace and Love*, Trojan Records, 1998.

2. Important collections of Don Drummond's work can be heard on *Don Drummond Memorial*, Treasure Isle/Esoldun, 1992; *The Best of Don Drummond*, Studio One, 1980; *Ska Boo-Da-Ba*, TopDeck/West Side, 1965/1998; *Skatalites and Friends at Randy's*, VP, 1998; and *Foundation Ska*, Studio One/Heartbeat, 1997.

3. 'Addis Ababa' and 'Beardsman Ska' are on *Foundation Ska*; and 'Marcus Junior' is on *Ska Boo-Da-Ba*.

4. The Wailers 'Simmer Down' is on *Foundation Ska*, Heartbeat.

5. The Alpha Boys Academy was an approved school established for working class delinquent youths by the Catholic Church in Kingston. It provided a first class musical education and its graduates included, as well as Don Drummond, Tommy McCook, John 'Dizzy' Moore and Lester Sterling, all who became part of the Skatalites; Joe Harriot, Harold McNair, Rico Rodriguez, Leroy 'Horsemouth' Wallace and Leroy Smart among reggae's and Jamaican jazz's finest musicians. See S. Barrow and P. Dalton, *Reggae: The Rough Guide*, 1997, p. 9.

6. Norman Weinstein, *Orchid Ska*, New York, Mellea Press, 1991, p. 26; also in *Wheel and Come Again*, from which the page references in the text are taken.

7. 'For the Don' in *Reel from 'The Life-Movie'*, Kingston, Savacou Publications, p 41. Also included in *Wheel and Come Again* from which the page references in the text are taken.

8. Mervyn Morris, 'Valley Prince' in *The Pond*, London, New Beacon, 1973, p. 7. Also included in *Wheel and Come Again* from which the page references in the text are taken.

9. *Brother Man*, Cape, 1954.

10. See the discussion in Chapter Ten below, pp. 221-237.

11. See Timothy White's *Catch A Fire*. There is also a legend that Bunny Wailer cursed Lesley Kong, the producer of the Wailers' first album, with whom the Wailers had fallen out. Kong died from a heart attack at the early age of thirty-eight soon after. I allude to this legend in my poem, 'Black Heart' in *Shook Foil*, pp. 66-68.

12. Dermott Hussey's 'Requiem for Don Drummond', which was broadcast on RJR in Jamaica in 1969, included tributes from Tommy McCook, Bongo Jerry and Jimmy Carnegie. All celebrated Drummond's

importance as a black artist. Mervyn Morris read his 'Valley Prince' on this programme. (Recording obtained from Clive Walker, a reggae researcher in Toronto).

12. Lorna Goodison, 'For Don Drummond' in *Tamarind Season*, Kingston, Institute of Jamaica, pp. 79-80. Also included in *Wheel and Come Again* from which the page references in the text are taken.

13. Glen Brown, 'Merry Up' on *Check the Winner*, Shanachie/ Greensleeves.

Chapter Eight

1. Burning Spear, *Mek We Dweet*, Mango 1990.

2. Lee Scratch Perry, *Reggae Greats*, Island/Mango, 1984.

3. See the poem, 'Ananse' in Kamau Brathwaite, *Islands*, OUP, 1969, pp. 6-8; and *The Arrivants*, 1973, p. 165. And see Laura Tanna, 'Anansi – Jamaica's Trickster Hero, *Jamaica Journal*, 16:2, 1983, pp. 21-30.

4. Derek Walcott, *Dream on Monkey Mountain*, London, Cape, 1972.

5. 'Small Axe', *Burnin'*, Tuff Gong/Island, 1973.

6. The big three were Clement (Coxsone) Dodd (Studio One), Lesley Kong (Beverley's), and Joe Gibbs.

7. See the introduction to Rohan Preston's *Dreams of Soy Sauce*, Tia Chucha Press, 1992.

8. From *Uprising*, Tuff Gong/Island, 1980.

9. From *Kaya*, 1978.

10. I am thinking of Wilson Harris's Guyana Quartet, (*Palace of the Peacock*, *The Far Journey of Oudin*, *The Whole Armour*, *The Secret Ladder*.)

11. Released by the Greatful Dead on *Dead Zone*, Arists, 1987. The tribute album, *Deadicated: A Tribute to the Greatful Dead* was released on Arista, 1991. Spear's version is included on the compilation album, *Chant Down Babylon: The Island Anthology*, 1996.

12. From the album *Knocked Out and Loaded*, 1986.

13. From the New International Version of the Bible.

14. 'Africa Unite' is on *Survival*, Tuff Gong/Island, 1979.

15. Jacob Miller's 'A Chapter A Day' does not appear to have been reissued.

16. *Presenting Burning Spear*, Studio One, 1973; reissued on CD as *Burning Spear*, Studio One, 1998.

17. From *Natty Dread*, Tuff Gong/Island, 1974.

18. From *Burnin'*.

19. From *War Ina Babylon*, Island, 1976.

20. Winston Niney Holness and the Observers, 1971. Reissued on the CD, *Niney and Friends 1971-2, Blood and Fire*, Trojan, 1997.

21. *Jacko Jacobus*, Peepal Tree, pp. 87-88.

22. There is 'Don't Mess with Jill' on *Burning Spear*, Studio One; in truth one of Spear's weaker songs.
23. *Marcus Garvey*, Island, 1975.
24. On *Jah Kingdom*, Mango/Island, 1992.
25. From *Right Time*, reissued on *Go Seek Your Rights*, Virgin, 1990.
26. On *Natty Dread*, 1974.
27. 'Stepping Razor is on *Equal Rights*, Virgin, 1977. 'Tougher Than Tough' is on *The Toughest*, Heartbeat, 1996.
28. See for example the poems 'Folkways', 'The Journeys' and 'Didn't He Ramble' from *Rights of Passage*, 1967 (and *The Arrivants*).
29. *Jacko Jacobus*, p. 87; For convenience, page references in the text are from *Wheel and Come Again*.
30. *Chinese Lanterns for the Blue Child*, Leeds, Peepal Tree, 1998, p. 17.
31. *Prophets*, Leeds, Peepal Tree, 1995, pp. 85-90.
32. *Prophets*, pp. 94-98.
33. *Ibid.* pp. 90-93.
34. *Ibid.*, pp. 99-102.
35. *The Children of Sisyphus*, London, New Authors, 1964; *An Absence of Ruins*, London, Hutchinson, 1967.
36. *The Arrivants*, pp. 42-44.
37. Gordon Rohlehr, *Pathfinder: Black Awakening in the Arrivants of Edward Kamau Brathwaite*, Port of Spain, author, 1981, p. 97.
38. See Christopher Hill, *The World Turned Upside Down*, London, 1972, and A.L. Morton, *The Ranters*, London, Lawrence & Wishart, 1970.
39. *The Arrivants*, pp. 42-43.
40. *Survival*, Tuff Gong/Island, 1979.
41. See the poems 'The Road of the Dread' by Lorna Goodison, *Tamarind Season*, pp. 22-23; 'Jah/Son: Another Way', by Kendel Hippolyte, *Birthright*, pp. 101-106 (and *Wheel and Come Again*, pp. 93-98; 'Dreadwalk' by Dennis Scott, in *Dreadwalk*, London, New Beacon, 1982, pp. 39-40 (and *Wheel and Come Again*, p. 174); 'Rasta Reggae', by Mervyn Morris, *The Pond*, London, New Beacon, 1973, p. 18 (and *Wheel and Come Again*, p. 146).
42. *The Arrivants*, p. 44.
43. *Jacko Jacobus*, p. 87 (and *Wheel and Come Again*, pp. 68-69).
44. Bunny Wailer, *Blackheart Man*, Island, 1976; Third World, *96 Degrees in the Shade*, Island, 1977; and Marcia Griffiths, *Naturally*, 1978; reissued Shanachie, 1992.
45. Kamau Brathwaite, 'Prelude', *Masks*, 1968, pp. 3-6.
46. From the introduction to *Dreams in Soy Sauce*, Kichua Press, 1993.
47. *Dreams in Soy Sauce*, and *Wheel and Come Again*, p. 160.
48. Mutabaruka, 'White Sound', in *From Our Yard*, ed. Pamela Mordecai, Institute of Jamaica, 1987, pp. 176-177.
49. 'Hypocrites' on *Songs of Freedom*, 1992.

50. 'Nanny', on *Resistance*, Heartbeat, 1988. There is also a version on the *Live in Paris*, Greensleeves, 1989.
51. Lorna Goodison, *Selected Poems*, University of Michigan, 1992, pp. 69-70.
52. David Dabydeen, *Turner*, London, Cape, 1994.
53. See such songs as Marley's 'Babylon System' on *Survival*, 1974; Bunny Wailer's 'Botha the Mosquito', on *Liberation*, 1989; Mighty Diamonds, 'Right Time' on *Go Seek Your Rights*, Virgin Frontline, 1990; and Lee 'Scratch' Perry, 'Dreadlocks in the Moonlight', on *Arkology*, Island, 1997.
54. Shelley Thunder was on of the first women deejays. She had a big hit with 'Kuff' in 1988. None of her work appears to be currently available.

Chapter Nine

1. *From Our Yard*, p. 177.
2. *Graceland*, Warner Brothers, 1987.
3. *Kaya*, 1978.
4. 'Trench Town Rock', *Rastaman Vibration*, 1976.
5. *The Children of Sisyphus*, see Chapter 12, pp. 110-120 as an example both of the heavy irony and the external detachment with which Patterson describes a Rasta gathering.
6. On *Natty Dread*, 1974.
7. Lorna Goodison, 'Judges', *Tamarind Season*, pp. 54-55.
8. From *I am Becoming My Mother*, London, New Beacon, 1986, pp. 46-48.
9. *Reel from 'The Life Movie'*, Kingston, Savacou Publications, 1972, p. 39. Page references in the text are from *Wheel and Come Again*.
10. *Uncle Time*, pp. 48-51.
11. James Baldwin, *The Fire Next Time*, London, Michael Joseph, 1963.
12. *Dog* is unpublished.
13. 'For the Last Time, Fire', *Uncle Time*, p. 46.
14. *Natty Dread*, 1975.
15. 'No Sufferer,' *Uncle Time*, p. 53.
16. The CD, *Roots to the Bone*, Mango, contains most of the great *Man From Wareika* LP, Island, 1976.
17. *An Echo in the Bone*, in *Plays for Today*, ed. Errol Hill, Longman Caribbean, 1986.
18. See especially Burning Spear, *Live in Paris*, Greensleeves, 1989.
19. *Uncle Time*, p. 53.
20. 'Duppy Conqueror', *African Herbsman*, Trojan, 1974.
21. Peter Tosh, *Equal Rights*.
22. 'Natty Dread Rides Again', *Survival*, 1980.

23. 'No Sufferer,' *Uncle Time*, p. 53.

24. 'Jah Music', *I am Becoming My Mother*, p. 36. Also in *Wheel and Come Again*, p. 86.

25. J. Edward Chamberlin, *Come Back to me My Language: Poetry and the West Indies*, Chicago, University of Illinois Press, 1993, pp. 258-259.

26. 'Jamaica 1980', *I am Becoming my Mother*, p. 10.

27. 'The Prophet Jeremiah Speaks', *To Us All Flowers Are Roses*, University of Illinois Press, 1995, p. 43.

28. In Goodison, *Selected Poems*, p. 53.

29. *Ibid*.

30. Marley, 'Roots Rock Reggae', *Rastaman Vibration*.

31. Goodison, 'Jah Music', *I am Becoming My Mother*, p. 36.

Chapter Ten

1. Interview with Crispin 'Bro Spry' Taylor, 'Lee 'Scratch' Perry: Return to the Ark', *Straight No Chaser* #40, Spring, 1997, p. 47.

2. Mango/Island, 1990.

3. 'Lee 'Scratch' Perry: Return to the Ark', p. 47.

4. The Black Ark studio in Washington Gardens was Perry's own studio following his work with Studio One and Joe Gibbs. It was the source of the most experimental sounds in Jamaican music between 1974 and 1979 when the studio burnt down, possibly by Perry himself who seems to have had a breakdown as the result of the intense level of the past years' work and the unwanted attention of various scroungers and hangers-on. The output of the Black Ark is still only now being properly assessed as the result of reissues such as *Arkology*, Island, 1997. See Barrow and Dalton, *Reggae: The Rough Guide*, pp. 164-169 and the extensive sleeve notes to *Arkology*.

5. *Super Ape*, Mango/Island, 1976.

6. See *African Herbsman*, Trojan, 1974 and *The Complete Wailers 1967-72*, Parts 2 and 3.

7. *Straight No Chaser*, op. cit.

8. *Soul Revolution*, Lee Perry/Trojan Records, 1970-1971, 1988.

9. 'Punky Reggae Party' is on *Babylon By Bus*, Tuff Gong/Island, 1978.

10. 'Trickster II', *Jacko Jacobus*, pp. 89-91; also in *Wheel and Come Again*, p. 69-71.

11. 'Duppy Conqueror', *Soul Revolution*.

12. This is the longer version of the lyric on *Burnin'*.

13. *Ibid*.

14. 'Trickster II', *Jacko Jacobus*, pp. 89.

15. 'Man-Man', *Miguel Street*, London, Deutch, 1959.

16. Jan Carew, *The Wild Coast*, London, Secker and Warburg, 1958.
17. Earl Lovelace, *The Dragon Can't Dance*, London, Deutch, 1979.
18. Lawrence Scott, *Witchbroom*, London, Caribbean Writers Series, 1992.
19. Andrew Salkey, *A Quality of Violence*, London, New Authors, 1959.
20. Orlando Patterson, *The Children of Sisyphus*, 1964.
21. Ismith Khan, *The Crucifixion*, Leeds, Peepal Tree, 1987, pp 130-132.
22. Neville Dawes, *Interim*, Kingston, Institute of Jamaica, 1978.
23. *Voices Under the Window*, London, Faber, 1955.
24. George Lamming, *In the Castle of My Skin*, London, Michael Joseph, 1953.
25. Sylvia Wynter, *The Hills of Hebron*, London, Cape, 1962.
26. 'Negus', *Islands*, *The Arrivants*, pp. 222-224.
27. For instance the portrayal of the Orisha priest Amouga Houngan in marina omowale maxwell's *Chopstix in Mauby*, Leeds, Peepal Tree, 1996.
28. 'Redemption Son', *Uprising*.
29. 'Our Revolutions Must Be Different', in *The Heinemann Book of Caribbean Poetry*, London, Heinemann, 1992, pp. 135-136.
30. 'Negus', *Islands*, op. cit.
31. Earl Lovelace, *The Wine of Astonishment*, London, Deutch, 1982.
32. Erna Brodber, *Myal*, London, New Beacon, 1988.
33. Junior Byles, 'Informer Man', *Curly Locks: The Best of Junior Byles and the Upsetters 1970-76*, Heartbeat, 1997.
34. See the liner notes to *Arkology*.

INDEX

de Bolas, Juan, 49
Bonnie and Clyde, 28
Boothe, Ken, 89, 127, 133-34, 138, 150
Bovell, Dennis, 81
Breakspeare, Cindy, 204
Brand, Dionne, 143
Brathwaite, Doris, 76
Brathwaite, Kamau, 16, 17, 32, 33, 39, 43, 52, 62, 72-73, 76-80, 83, 94, 95, 161, 176, 181, 187, 189-92, 208, 232-33, 242, 247
Breeze, Jean Binta, 73, 82-83, 242, 247
Brer Rabit tales, 46
Brodber, Erna, 73, 78, 234
Brother Man (Mais), 159, 190-191, 230-31, 234
Brown, Dennis, 127, 138, 141
Brown, Everald, 76
Brown, Glen, 167
Burning (Marley) 51, 118, 185, 224
"Burning and Looting" (Marley), 118, 185
Burning Spear, 9, 18, 19, 34, 37-38, 103; as archetype of the griot/prophet, 181-98, 191, 210, 214, 223, 226-27, 237, 242
Byles, Junior, 122, 126, 235

"Calling One Sweet Psalmist" (Goodison), 216
Calypso, 33, 53, 157
Calypso and Literature, 69-71
Campbell, George, 15, 16, 95-96
Campbell, Hazel, 73, 74
Canada, 26
Candywine Development, The (Morris), 73
Capleton, 67, 244
Carberry, H.D., 46
Caribbean, 15, 16, 17, 19, 20
Carifesta, 75
Carew, Jan, 231
Carnival, 70
Carnegie, James, 73-74

Carter, Nick, 75
Catholic Church, 168
Catch a Fire (Marley), 224
"Catch a Fire" (Marley), 117, 124-25
Chamberlin, Ted, 214
Channer, Colin, 7, 40, 75, 93-94, 143-45, 150, 242
"A Chapter a Day" (Jacob Miller), 183
Children of Sisyphus, The (Patterson), 189, 205, 231
Chopstix in Mauby (maxwell), 70
Chokota (Dawes *et al.*), 92
Christianity, 173, 182
Clarke, Sebastian, 18
Class dynamics: relationship of middle-class writers to working class and reggae culture, 201-202
Cleopatra Jones, 28
Cliff, Jimmy, 127-28, 244
Cockpit Country, 227
Colonialism, 14, 15, 19
Columbia (USA), 246
Columbus, Christopher, 45
"Concrete Jungle" (Marley), 107, 119-121
Contradictory Omens (Brathwaite), 32
"Cool and Easy" (Perry), 100
Cooper, Carolyn, 143, 149, 243
Cooper, Michael 'Ibo', 214
Coore, Cat, 106
Count Ossie, 99-100, 155
Countryman Karl Black (Farki), 73
Craig, Karl, 76
Credences at the Altar of Cloud (McNeill), 72
Cripple (dance step), 110
Crucifixion, The (Khan), 231
Cudjoe, 49, 101
Culture, 67, 89
Cunningham, Merce, 16
"Curley Locks" (*Byles*), 122